LEO STRAUSS AND NIETZSCHE

LEO STRAUSS AND NIETZSCHE

Laurence Lampert

THE UNIVERSITY OF CHICAGO PRESS   *Chicago & London*

Laurence Lampert is professor of philosophy at Indiana University-Purdue University, Indianapolis. He is the author of *Nietzsche's Teaching: An Interpretation of Thus Spoke Zarathustra* and *Nietzsche and Modern Times: A Study of Bacon, Descartes, and Nietzsche.*

The University of Chicago Press, Chicago 60637
The University of Chicago Press, Ltd., London
© 1996 by The University of Chicago
All rights reserved. Published 1996
Printed in the United States of America
05 04 03 02 01 00 99 98 97 96   5 4 3 2 1

ISBN (cloth): 0-226-46825-9
ISBN (paper): 0-226-46826-7

Library of Congress Cataloging-in-Publication Data

Lampert, Laurence, 1941–
    Leo Strauss and Nietzsche / Laurence Lampert.
      p.   cm.
    Includes bibliographical references and index.
    ISBN 0-226-46825-9
    1. Strauss, Leo.   2. Nietzsche, Friedrich Wilhelm, 1844–1900.
  I. Title.
    B945.S84L36   1996   95-10467
    181'.06--dc20   CIP

Excerpts from the poetry of Wallace Stevens are reprinted by permission of Alfred A. Knopf Inc.: "Credences of Summer VIII," *Collected Poems*, copyright 1942 by Wallace Stevens and renewed 1970 by Holly Stevens (p. 166); "The Poems of Our Climate," *Collected Poems*, copyright 1954 by Wallace Stevens (p. 181).

To ROBERT AND MARY LOOKER,

friends and benefactors of Nietzsche studies whose generosity made possible the restoration and preservation of Nietzsche's papers in the Nietzsche Archiv

Contents

Abbreviations

Nietzsche

A	*The Antichrist* (1888)
AOM	*Assorted Opinions and Maxims* (1879)
BGE	*Beyond Good and Evil* (1886)
BT	*The Birth of Tragedy* (1872)
CW	*The Case of Wagner* (1888)
D	*Daybreak* (also *Dawn of Morning*) (1881)
EH	*Ecce Homo* (1888)
GM	*On the Genealogy of Morals* (1887)
GS	*The Gay Science* (1882–87)
HH	*Human, All Too Human* (1878)
KGW	*Kritische Gesamtausgabe: Werke*
RWB	*Richard Wagner in Bayreuth* (1876)
TI	*Twilight of the Idols* (1888)
UD	*On the Uses and Disadvantages of History for Life* (1873)
WP	*The Will to Power*
WS	*The Wanderer and His Shadow* (1880)
Z	*Thus Spoke Zarathustra* (1883)

All references to Nietzsche's writings are to the aphorism number; references to *Z*, *EH*, and *TI* include chapter headings; references to *KGW* are to volume, notebook, and section.

Strauss

AAPL	*The Argument and the Action of Plato's* Laws (1975)
CM	*The City and Man* (1964)
HPP	*History of Political Philosophy* (1987)
LAM	*Liberalism Ancient and Modern* (1968)
NRH	*Natural Right and History* (1953)
OT	*On Tyranny* (1991)
PAW	*Persecution and the Art of Writing* (1952)
PL	*Philosophy and Law* (1935)
PPH	*The Political Philosophy of Hobbes* (1935)
RCPR	*The Rebirth of Classical Political Rationalism* (1989)
SA	*Socrates and Aristophanes* (1966)
SCR	*Spinoza's Critique of Religion* (1962)
SPPP	*Studies in Platonic Political Philosophy* (1983)
TM	*Thoughts on Machiavelli* (1958)
WPP	*What Is Political Philosophy?* (1959)
XS	*Xenophon's Socrates* (1972)
XSD	*Xenophon's Socratic Discourse* (1970)

All references to Strauss's writings are to page numbers.

Introduction

"Some men are born posthumously," Nietzsche said, thinking of himself and knowing full well the risk he ran: leaving his rebirth to his readers, he risked resurrection as someone other than himself. As Elisabeth's Nietzsche, say, or Heidegger's, or the Nietzsche of general rumor, of bare words like "superman," "herd," "revenge," and "Do not forget the whip!"—Nietzsches worth burying again.

Nietzsche did what he could to prepare for the resurrection as himself: "Hear me!" he said, toward the end of his work, "For I am this and this and this. Above all do not mistake me for someone else" (*EH* Preface 1). "Hear me," he said again and again, aware that he was writing dangerous books meant for a few special readers but open to everyone, open to plunder.

Leo Strauss was one of those few special readers. Acute, daring, skeptical, a reader schooled like few since Lessing in the history of philosophic rhetoric, Strauss was a reader prepared to slow down, "to read deeply, to look cautiously fore and aft, with reservations, with doors left open, with delicate eyes and fingers . . ." (*D* Preface 5), a reader with a free mind. And in the one little essay Strauss wrote on Nietzsche, seventeen pages with a command for a title, "Note on the Plan of Nietzsche's *Beyond Good and Evil*," Nietzsche is reborn posthumously, reborn as himself.

Leo Strauss's Nietzsche is the best Nietzsche yet, the one nearest to the still almost secret Nietzsche of Nietzsche's great books. I believe that it is not too much to say that Strauss's essay is the most comprehensive and profound study ever published on Nietzsche. It attains this rank because

—it places Nietzsche in the proper, most exalted company, the company of one, the company of Plato;

—it demonstrates that the two essential issues in Nietzsche's thought are the will to power and eternal return, and shows how these two issues are logically related as the fundamental fact and the highest value;

—it shows the place of nature in Nietzsche's teaching, nature understood as historical and including human spiritual history;

—it shows just who the philosopher is in Nietzsche's view and just what role the philosopher has played in our history;

—and it shows how the philosopher Nietzsche plays that role in the present, solving the highest, the most difficult problem bequeathed to us by our past.

All this in seventeen pages? Strenuous and dense, Strauss's little essay is so controlled in its density that every paragraph buds and flowers into profuse abundance when questioned about its implications and consequences. Or so it has seemed to me. To me it seems a paradigm of the art of writing rediscovered by Strauss himself, the art suggested by Plato's Socrates through his warnings on the dangers of writing in the *Phaedrus*.

Still, Strauss's essay has a face only a scholar could love. Its profundity and astringent beauty become visible only as the rewards of toil to which that deceptively plain face beckons the reader. Toil: that "very long, never easy, but always pleasant work" to which "the works of the great writers of the past" call their readers (*PAW* 37). Strauss's writings lack what Nietzsche's writings flaunt: flair, shock, personality, temptation—Nietzsche's writings announce that they are works of the devil. Nietzsche writes as if he's out to maim. Strauss writes as if it were always his greatest responsibility to appear harmless. But behind that harmless, scholarly appearance lurks something dangerous after all. I wonder, could Nietzsche's little joke about the Platonic Socrates—in front Plato in back Plato in the middle Chimera (*BGE* 190)—be applied to Strauss's Nietzsche? In front Strauss in back Strauss in the middle Chimera, a Homeric monster sheltered within an apparently harmless front and back. You have to pay a small price to glimpse the monster, and not just the price of toil: you have to tame your fear of monsters, especially Homeric ones. And if Plato taught us to fear Homeric monsters, perhaps we'll have to follow Nietzsche's lead and take another hard look at Plato's Socrates: Does that composite beast also shelter a Homeric monster? Nietzsche thought so; and so, it seems, did Strauss.

And yet the Strauss who came to understand Nietzsche so deeply seems to say No to Nietzsche. Why is that? Why, having understood Nietzsche as he did, did Strauss hold him at a distance and hold him up to attack? Why was Strauss content to be seen as Nietzsche's enemy, as someone who shared and fed the already existing prejudice against Nietzsche? Why did he allow the growth of a band of followers who, though they come in a variety of stripes, seem almost uniform in their opposition to Nietzsche? Adequate answers to these troubling questions must depend upon concentrated study of the one essay Strauss devoted solely to Nietzsche. Such study, I believe, draws Strauss far closer to Nietzsche than his cultivated public image of opposition would suggest and provides probable explanations for that opposition.

Strauss is so evasive, so bent on not being caught in his own colors, that he always remains partially submerged under his unparalleled commentaries. Such evasion did not preclude adopting a visible position; on the contrary, it depended upon it: Strauss is overtly a partisan of ancient and medieval Platonic political philosophy, the Socratic Great Tradition. That very overtness, however, consists partly of a resolute pointing to the full mysteriousness of that tradition, its esoteric fastness. Strauss could say, as Plato said, "There does not now exist nor will there ever exist a treatise of mine dealing with these subject matters. Those bearing my name make a Socrates beautiful and new." Just who was Leo Strauss anyway? Is there any chance that he will be born posthumously as himself? A different self than he seemed?

Chapter One

Strauss's Study of Nietzsche

READING NIETZSCHE

Furtively. That's the word Strauss chose to describe how he first began reading Nietzsche: a boy read Nietzsche furtively in an Orthodox Jewish house-
hold in Germany during the early part of this century, for Nietzsche was a
forbidden writer for Jews and Germans alike.[1] Furtive reading worked its
spell: Strauss said privately in a letter to Karl Löwith that "Nietzsche so
dominated and charmed me between my 22nd and 30th years that I literally
believed everything I understood of him."[2]

Publicly though, Strauss preferred never ever breathing a word of having once been taken over by Nietzsche. But other furtive readers of Nietzsche might have guessed as much from Nietzsche's subterranean presence in
Philosophy and Law (German original, 1935), a book Strauss published six
years beyond Nietzsche's dominance. Nietzsche appears by name in that
book only in a few footnotes, but he is the massive unnamed presence of the
Introduction; for Nietzsche's arrival in modern philosophy signaled an unprecedented necessity: "probity," "intellectual conscience," Enlightenment
radicalized by a new bravery that scorns any comforts like God—all this
raised the question of the possibility and desirability of a return to an older
form of enlightenment, the pursuit of which led back through Maimonides

---

1. "A Giving of Accounts" 2. Another famous reader, Hans Georg Gadamer, reports violat-
ing a similar early prohibition on reading Nietzsche by furtive reading; see "Das Drama
Zarathustras."

2. "Correspondence of Karl Löwith and Leo Strauss" 183.

to Plato. In this way Nietzsche provided the occasion for the recovery of Plato. In *Philosophy and Law* Strauss makes use of Nietzsche while not making Nietzsche's role explicit; a furtive reader of Nietzsche had become a furtive writer with Nietzsche on his mind but not on his page.

The decisive role Nietzsche played in Strauss's thinking as a young man is further indicated by the autobiographical Preface which Strauss composed in 1962 for the English translation of his first book, *Spinoza's Critique of Religion*, a book completed in 1928. As Strauss reports matters thirty-four years later, Nietzsche was at the core of the dialogue he carried on with "the new thinking,"[3] a dialogue that led Strauss back to Spinoza and then back to premodern rationalism. The penultimate paragraph of Strauss's 1962 essay makes the unnamed Nietzsche the turning point in his intellectual journey, the liberator from contemporary prejudice who opened the vista backward. And the final paragraph contains a typical maneuver in Strauss's mature treatment of Nietzsche: although Nietzsche is very much included within the denunciation of modern philosophy and its outcome or completion, Nietzsche himself is spared the full force of that denunciation. The final paragraph retracts or qualifies the assertion that the basis of the new thinking is simply an act of will "fatal to philosophy," for Strauss acknowledges that Nietzsche's philosophy claims to be based on a fact, the fundamental fact of will to power.

This maneuver, reservations within a context of blame, is typical of Strauss's periodic mentions of Nietzsche in his mature writings. Within the rhetoric encouraging a condemnation of modern philosophy from Machiavelli to Heidegger, Nietzsche characteristically appears under provisos and qualifications; the reader seems to be cautioned against enclosing Nietzsche wholly within that downward spiral of modern thought leading to the oblivion of eternity and the end of philosophy. Nietzsche's appearance in *Natural Right and History* provides a good example of such treatment.

Nietzsche appears in the midst of the discussion of historicism in *Natural Right and History*, at the point where the historicist thesis has become problematic or self-contradictory (25–26): How can historicism consistently exempt itself from its own verdict that all human thought is historical? Nietzsche himself attacked historicism and its presumption of a transhistorical theoretical viewpoint, and his attack had two aspects. First, historicism's theoretical viewpoint endangers human life, because its analysis

---

3. See *SCR* 12, where the relevant considerations are made as Buber's retort to Nietzschean claims.

destroys "the protecting atmosphere within which life or culture or action is alone possible." As Strauss's footnote indicates, this is a reference to Nietzsche's famous account in the *Uses and Disadvantages of History for Life* of views that are "true but deadly," true but destructive of the myths and fictions necessary for healthy human society. Second, the theoretical viewpoint, because it presumes to stand outside of life, is inevitably a misunderstanding of life. Strauss then summarizes the options Nietzsche faced:

> To avert the danger to life, Nietzsche could chose one of two ways: he could insist on the strictly esoteric character of the theoretical analysis of life— that is, restore the Platonic notion of the noble delusion—or else he could deny the possibility of theory proper and so conceive of thought as essentially subservient to, or dependent on, life or fate.

Did Nietzsche restore the Platonic notion of the noble delusion, or did he deny the possibility of philosophy? Strauss leaves this essential question open, stating only what was done by Nietzsche's successors, most notably Heidegger: "If not Nietzsche himself, at any rate his successors adopted the second alternative." Only in his essay on Nietzsche will Strauss be more forthcoming on how Nietzsche resolved the fundamental dilemma posed by philosophy's recognition both of deadly truth and of the essential limitations on human thought.[4]

But Strauss did make one statement about Nietzsche in which he did not suspend judgment, a very prominent statement occurring as it does in the final paragraph of the first and title essay of *What is Political Philosophy?* (1959). In that setting, Nietzsche appears as the penultimate target in a polemic, the target of a patriot's ferocious denunciation. There is little trace of gratitude on Strauss's part for an educator who had once dominated and charmed him. Instead, the Nietzsche who here appears openly on Strauss's stage is a far greater criminal than could probably have been imagined by those whose propriety required that Strauss's first reading of Nietzsche be

4. Other important references to Nietzsche in Strauss's books include the following: Strauss mentioned Nietzsche once in the text of *PPH* (1936), as one of the stations on the way to "the reabsorption of wisdom by courage . . . the view that the ideal is not the object of wisdom, but the hazardous venture of the will" (165, see also 134 n. 4). Nietzsche is present in two footnotes in *TM* and once, unindexed, in the text (78). In *SA*, Nietzsche plays the crucial role in the Introduction (6–7): Nietzsche's "question of the worth of what Socrates stood for" necessitates a return to the origins of "the Great Tradition," a recovery of Socrates that included taking Aristophanes' attack seriously and distinguishing it from Nietzsche's. Strauss took Aristophanes' attack seriously indeed, seeing it as the crucial document in the ancient quarrel between philosophy and poetry written from the side of poetry; Strauss read both Plato's Socrates and Xenophon's Socrates as responses to the wisdom of poetry's attack on philosophy.

furtive. In a very exposed part of his essay—the very end, where characteristically Strauss turns to the edifying—Nietzsche is denounced as a philosophical criminal of the first magnitude.

> Being certain of the tameness of modern western man, [Nietzsche]
> preached the sacred right of "merciless extinction" of large masses of men
> with as little restraint as his great antagonist had done. He used much of
> his unsurpassable and inexhaustible power of passionate and fascinating
> speech for making his readers loathe, not only socialism and communism,
> but conservatism, nationalism and democracy as well. After having taken
> upon himself this great political responsibility, he could not show his
> readers a way to political responsibility. He left them no choice except that
> between irresponsible indifference to politics and irresponsible political
> options. He thus prepared a regime which, as long as it lasted, made dis-
> credited democracy look again like the golden age. He tried to articulate his
> understanding both of the modern situation and of human life as such by
> his doctrine of the will to power. The difficulty inherent in the philosophy
> of the will to power led after Nietzsche to the explicit renunciation of the
> very notion of eternity. Modern thought reaches its culmination, its high-
> est self-consciousness, in the most radical historicism, i.e., in explicitly
> condemning to oblivion the notion of eternity. For oblivion of eternity, or,
> in other words, estrangement from man's deepest desire and therewith
> from the primary issues, is the price which modern man had to pay, from
> the very beginning, for attempting to be absolutely sovereign, to become
> the master and owner of nature, to conquer chance.

This intemperate attack expressed in such a lively and arresting style could
perhaps be tempered somewhat by reflecting on the sentences that introduce
it, for they speak of what Nietzsche "hoped," and they affirm that he desired
"to be questioned" and that he addressed "the best men of the generations
after him." Or it could perhaps be tempered somewhat by noting that the
strongest denunciation falls on Heidegger, on where Nietzsche's thought
"led after Nietzsche."

Nevertheless, Strauss's words have every appearance of an open denunciation. Where, however, do those terrible words in quotation marks—
"merciless extinction"—come from? I for one have not been able to find
them in Nietzsche's writings. This does not mean that they are not there,
but it does mean that they are not *prominently* there, that they are not there
as something "preached." And what about preached as a "sacred right"? The
sacred here can hardly refer to Dionysos, that dancing god to whom alone
Nietzsche would submit as a disciple. It was not Dionysos who sanctified the
merciless extinctions of our history which have made the phrase "merciless
extinction" so potent and true as an adjunct to the phrase "sacred right." If

in fact Dionysos is also a destroyer, as Nietzsche said (*EH* Books *BT* 3), the destructions characteristic of him—of Pentheus, say, or of Thracian Lykurgos, or of the sailors turned into dolphins for refusal to recognize him—the hardness and cruelty characteristic of Dionysos, are not the preached extinctions of whole populations that entered our history as the pious acts of followers of the jealous God. And to allege in the way Strauss does that Nietzsche "prepared a regime" is to force the reader to draw the conclusion that Nietzsche was among those spiritually and intellectually responsible for National Socialism and its crimes of merciless extinction. But it was Nietzsche who warned good Europeans in the 1880s that there was nothing they should fear as much as they should fear nationalism; and in particular that they should fear German nationalism with its basis in German racial hatred; and more particularly still, that they should fear German hatred of Jews and take steps against it (*GS* 377). After he had fallen mad, Nietzsche dreamed of taking the most extreme step himself: "I am having all anti-Semites shot."

Strauss's irresponsible and damaging statement, Strauss's preaching in his final paragraph, serves as an edifying and spirited conclusion to his essay's indictment of the modern. Strauss's concluding paragraph balances the piety of his opening paragraph which had spoken about zeal and sacred soil and promised that he would "not for a moment forget what Jerusalem stands for." Strauss's pious conclusion thus ends an essay typified throughout by piety—for instance, by Strauss's refusal to reveal "the charm and gracefulness" of Machiavelli's blasphemies (41)—but if Strauss preferred on this occasion to keep those blasphemies covered under pious silence, on other occasions he seemed more than happy to forgo that silence and reveal Machiavelli's blasphemies in so pleasing and memorable a way that they mark a peak of high spiritedness in his writings (*SPPP* 223–25; *TM* 48–52). Strauss's denunciation of Nietzsche, his pious conclusion, ends his essay in the way appropriate to rhetoric, namely as a descent to the people with an edifying message or an opinion to be held (*PAW* 91); "it ends like a tract for the times" (*TM* 55); it ends with a pious denunciation of the impious Nietzsche.

Strauss's statement in *What is Political Philosophy?* about what Nietzsche "preached" and what Nietzsche "prepared" provides the basis for what most of Strauss's followers prefer to say about Nietzsche: Nietzsche is a nihilist, a teacher of evil from whom we need to be sheltered, the secret spiritual mentor of what is worst in twentieth-century life. Strauss seems to have encouraged among his readers what Nietzsche himself described as typical of moderns who lack the time and inclination for reflecting on opposing views (including himself among such moderns for reasons of courtesy): "Because there is no time for thinking and no rest in thinking, we no longer weigh divergent views; we're content to hate them" (*HH* 282).

Why would Strauss encourage the hatred of Nietzsche's views? Why would he think it salutary that others hate the teaching which had proved part of his own liberation? When one considers Strauss's single thematic and comprehensive treatment of Nietzsche, it is evident that the answer cannot be that Nietzsche's views are hateful. Strauss's inflammatory statement in *What is Political Philosophy?* needs to be considered in the light of Strauss's measured statement on Nietzsche, his statement for those with the time and inclination to weigh Nietzsche's divergent views. There and only there does Strauss repay with fitting gratitude one of his chief educators, a philosopher who continued to charm him.

TREATING NIETZSCHE RESPONSIBLY

Strauss's Nietzsche essay was one of the last essays he completed, though not the very last. He wrote it out in finished form in a notebook, a Champion Wiremaster spiral notebook now filed with the Strauss papers at the University of Chicago.[5] In that notebook, the Nietzsche essay is followed by two other essays, "Preliminary Observations on the Gods in Thucydides' Work" and "Xenophon's Anabasis." Strauss dated the three essays—Nietzsche: March 18, 1972–February 12, 1973;[6] Thucydides: March 31, 1973–May 31, 1973; Xenophon: June 6, 1973–September 19, 1973. Strauss died one month later, on October 18, 1973. The Nietzsche essay had been prepared for publication in *Interpretation: A Journal of Political Philosophy*, where it appeared in volume 3 (1973) with only minor changes from the handwritten version in the notebook. Strauss left instructions for the placement of the Nietzsche essay in his final book, *Studies in Platonic Political Philosophy.*[7]

As one of his last writings, Strauss's Nietzsche essay comes at the end of a long career of writings, after he had completed the many books that would be the chief bearers of his legacy. Its style presupposes acquaintance with those books: it is so characteristically Strauss's that it seems to be consciously

5. I am grateful to Joseph Cropsey for permission to examine this notebook and other documents in the Strauss archive.

6. From October 6, 1971, to May 24, 1972, Strauss taught a course on *Beyond Good and Evil* at St. John's College, Annapolis, Md.

7. See the Foreword to *SPPP* (vii), by Joseph Cropsey. The two later essays in the notebook, Strauss's final written works, also appeared first in *Interpretation* and then in *SPPP.*

written in such a way as to be helpful only to those already familiar with his writings and sympathetic toward them.

A writer with an unusual style and message who is addressing an audience he himself has already formed can give himself certain liberties, as Strauss made clear in an essay on Alfarabi (*WPP* 134–54): having "established his character," he can be confident that he will be read in character, that he will be read as someone whose views are already known to his readers. He will therefore be freer to speak his mind. Having won that freedom, Strauss could speak on Nietzsche assured that everyone would already know that an essay on Nietzsche by Leo Strauss would be critical of Nietzsche, that it would denounce Nietzsche. As an essay in a book entitled *Studies in Platonic Political Philosophy*, it would, surely, contrast Nietzsche with Plato to Nietzsche's disadvantage. Anything different would scarcely be noticed; as Strauss said when discussing such cases, a "deviation will be thought to be a repetition" (*WPP* 135).

Strauss's Nietzsche study *is* a deviation which has been thought to be a repetition. For Nietzsche is never denounced. Nietzsche is praised, he is even elevated to the highest plane. And when objections do arise, when, twice, objections finally break out in response to the affirmative presentation of Nietzsche, they are just the objections one would have expected from readers schooled by Strauss—they are "Straussian" objections. But Strauss answers the Straussian objections; he defends Nietzsche. From a Straussian perspective, the essay is a scandal.

PLACING NIETZSCHE AT THE CENTER

Strauss never tired of pointing out that artful writers in the past played little centering games, centering the central matters in lists, paragraphs, chapters, and other such structural sequences, the center being "the least exposed part" in comparison to the beginning and the end (*PAW* 13). Strauss abrogated this "rule of forensic rhetoric" for his own faithful readers by constantly calling attention to it: *his* readers are trained to look to the center; the center becomes the most exposed part (*PAW* 185). In the plan he left for his final book, Strauss went out of his way to violate his roughly chronological order of treatment: he placed his Nietzsche study at, or just after, the center. It is not at all farfetched to suppose that in doing so, Strauss centered the central matter. He thus accorded Nietzsche structurally the prominence due him philosophically and historically—and, at last, the prominence due him as a subject of Strauss's own reflections and as one of his own educators.

Matters are not quite so simple as the present arrangement of *Studies in Platonic Political Philosophy* makes them appear, for if the Nietzsche study now occupies the center of the book as the eighth of fifteen studies, Strauss's literary executor reports in the Foreword to *SPPP* that Strauss had intended to write both an Introduction and a study of Plato's *Gorgias* to be placed after the study of Plato's *Euthydemus*. The center shifts. Counting only the *Gorgias* study, the Nietzsche study would begin the second half, or, in another way of looking at this arrangement, would be paired at the center with "Jerusalem and Athens," a reasonable pairing given the great theme of that essay and Nietzsche's place in it as the one whose "super-man is meant to unite in himself Jerusalem and Athens at the highest level" (149).[8] Counting the Introduction as well as the *Gorgias* study, "Jerusalem and Athens" stands alone at the center with Nietzsche opening the second half, perhaps the most pleasing arrangement:[9] opening on the timely, ending on the pious, Strauss's final book centers the central matter of our spiritual history, Athens and Jerusalem, and begins its second half with Nietzsche, the philosopher who "solved the highest, the most difficult problem," the problem presented by our spiritual history.

Is the book mistitled, then, with Nietzsche at or near its center contradicting the promise of studies in *Platonic* political philosophy? No, for in a fascinating way Strauss will show how Nietzsche can be counted among the Platonic political philosophers in the two most basic ways: Nietzsche platonizes; and Nietzsche does not, after all, avoid "a relapse into Platonism."

THE ARTFUL STRAUSS

"Note on the Plan of Nietzsche's *Beyond Good and Evil.*" Other studies in Strauss's book include "Note" in the title, and there the word seems to be used in its customary scholarly sense as a noun denoting a minor item worthy of some scholarly attention. But in the title for the Nietzsche essay "Note" seems to be used as a verb, an imperative, a command to the reader: note that the plan of Nietzsche's book is the proper entrance way into its contents.[10]

8. In his reflections on the structure of *SPPP,* Alan Udoff contrasts the "eighth" with the "sixteenth" essay, "Jerusalem and Athens" with "Introductory Essay for Hermann Cohen, *Religion of Reason out of the Sources of Judaism*"; see "On Leo Strauss: An Introductory Account" 20. Udoff's superb essay is rewarding as a model of how to read Strauss respectfully and skeptically, and how to render audible "the implications that resonate beneath the surface of Strauss's texts" (19). His book as a whole contains a collection of some of the most informative and interesting essays ever written on Strauss.

9. When counting Machiavelli's chapters, however, Strauss says, "The prefaces to Book I and Book II are, of course, not chapters" (*TM* 48).

10. "Notes on Maimonides' *Book of Knowledge*" (*SPPP* 197, 199) includes observations about the plan that are relevant for the Nietzsche essay as well.

As a reader of Nietzsche's *Beyond Good and Evil*, Strauss emphasizes the plan and shows how the overall plan casts light on the particulars. But with respect to those particulars, Strauss lingers over an odd collection of apparently small details: jokes, objections, asides, riddles, even what Nietzsche does *not* say. Strauss's Nietzsche is like Strauss's Machiavelli: "He fascinates his reader by confronting him with riddles" (*TM* 50). Nietzsche also confronts his reader with direct address: Strauss calls attention to many of the little dialogues Nietzsche holds with his readers, dialogues that draw the reader in to Nietzsche's thought as a direct participant in its unfolding. By focusing on many small and neglected moments in Nietzsche's book, Strauss lets them attain their proper gravity within the whole economy of the book, within the plan. He thereby shows that the plan of *Beyond Good and Evil* calls for slow reading, for philology, for what Nietzsche called "chewing the cud" (*GM* Preface 8), a bovine activity not exactly characteristic of Nietzsche himself. But if Nietzsche himself was a writer given to swiftness and pranks and brevity (*GS* 381), this consciously chosen style had the aim of forcing the reader to slow down in order to figure things out (*D* Preface 5).

It is noteworthy that as a reader of Nietzsche, Strauss dispenses with any assistance from other interpreters of Nietzsche (with a single exception: Strauss avows no access to a certain aspect of Nietzsche's religious experience and directs his reader to Karl Reinhardt). Strauss goes it alone; he seeks no help from Nietzsche's prominent interpreters, not even from Heidegger, nor does he turn aside to show how his interpretation conflicts with theirs or how it might be superior to theirs. As becomes evident from the essay itself, Strauss's schooling in reading Nietzsche does not come from Nietzsche's interpreters but from the history of philosophy prior to Nietzsche, from other great thinkers who generated their own appropriate art of communication. Strauss is able to go it alone as a reader of Nietzsche because he is accompanied by the great thinkers of the Platonic tradition whose writings had formed Strauss's understanding of what philosophy is and how it presents itself.

As a writer on Nietzsche's *Beyond Good and Evil*, Strauss employs an especially subdued manner of argument. The interpretive keys to his sentences and paragraphs are most often found in unassuming logical connectives, little words and phrases like *instead, yet, but, thus, the utmost one can say, more precisely, however*. The constant presence of such connectives gives Strauss's essay its own dialogic quality; Strauss is carrying on an argument, less with Nietzsche than with his own readers, and less with his own readers than with himself: Strauss's reasoning as he encounters Nietzsche's thought is made visible to his audience.

As a writer on philosophers, Strauss made himself both famous and notorious as the writer who disclosed their little tricks and devices—blunders, contradictions, centerings, silences, repetitions—devices that served to advance their views among interested readers while turning aside the uninterested. Does Strauss himself, that "addict of esotericism," as Arnaldo Momigliano called him,[11] make use of such devices in his essay on Nietzsche? Does he himself employ what used to be called "the craftie and secrete methode"?[12] I believe that, to a limited degree, he does. Such devices do not form the core of his argument, but they help to lead to the core and help to disclose it. Strauss's "diabolical cleverness"[13] has not deserted him here, and as always it is in the service of his central argument. As Strauss himself said of the device of number and counting, "It is of the essence of devices of this kind that, while they are helpful up to a certain point, they are never sufficient and are never meant to be sufficient: they are merely hints" (*WPP* 166).

Many readers find such techniques deplorable, or tedious, or simply no longer necessary. Except among those instructed by Strauss himself, there is little appreciation left for the view that a writer might usefully hide something he has to say, thinking that the act of discovering what is hidden through a little directed labor would make what is discovered more valuable, more one's own. But even a writer like Descartes, bent on crushing the persecution that made it impossible for him to say openly what he thought, still held that it was useful to hide his conclusions and to hide the way to his conclusions because to do so was a service to his best readers: only by becoming its codiscoverers could his readers make their own what was already Descartes's own.[14] In my view, with a writer like Strauss such little devices are more than forgivable—they're pleasant and useful, part of the sport and part of the pedagogy. Strauss does not disappoint those whom he lures into labor on his writings.

Having said that, I should perhaps say as well that in my account of what Strauss has written I have done my best to dot all the i's. This does not mean that I think I have exhausted every point made by Strauss; it means that I have done my best to be as explicit as possible on all the points that seemed important enough or obscure enough to mention. My reason for this explicitness is that we're entering the Nietzschean Age: public decency

11. Momigliano, *On Pagans, Jews, and Christians* 259.
12. McGowan, *Montaigne's Deceits* 42.
13. Mansfield, *Machiavelli's New Modes and Orders* 11.
14. See Descartes's *Discourse on Method* 6.71.

does not depend upon our hushing it up that God is dead or that philosophy corrupts; that corruption, that twilight of the idols through philosophizing with a hammer, marks the daybreak of the Nietzschean Age. And I'm not a teacher with secret things to whisper to my reader. Don't look for winks and nods in my book.

HOW TO RIVAL PLATO

Die vornehme Natur ersetzt die göttliche Natur. This unitalicized German sentence is the final sentence of Strauss's Nietzsche study—"noble nature replaces divine nature." Just what is this noble nature, and what is the divine nature it replaces? I will argue that Strauss's whole study indicates that noble nature as Nietzsche presents it—no, *embodies* it—replaces divine nature as Plato presents it. But what logographic necessity dictates that such a dramatic thought be put in a foreign language, Nietzsche's own, and that it be put last, where it must remain unexplained? I will argue that Strauss's whole study indicates that it's not necessary, it's not even desirable, to flaunt such matters, to parade them, to shock and unsettle; it's not necessary to present Nietzsche Nietzscheanly.

The adequacy of this interpretation of the final enigmatic sentence can be settled only through a careful study of Strauss's whole essay. What is obvious, however, from even a cursory reading is the patent fact that Strauss' final sentence encapsulates his whole essay in its two main features: Strauss unfolds Nietzsche's thought with constant reference to Plato, and Strauss presents Nietzsche's rivalry with Plato obscurely. The unwavering constant in Strauss's essay is the contrast between Nietzsche and Plato. Whether it be the very opening, where the issue is the peculiar qualities of Nietzsche's books, or the very ending, where the issue is Nietzsche's understanding of the virtues; whether it be Nietzsche's conception of the fundamental alternative or of the fundamental fact or of the role of morals and philosophy, Strauss's unwavering concern is Nietzsche and Plato.

Nietzsche *versus* Plato. This is the great rivalry, the contemporary version of what Nietzsche himself called "the complete, the genuine antagonism," Plato versus Homer (*GM* 3.25). Just as Longinus saw all of Plato as a constant struggle against Homer for supremacy, a rivalry that was in part responsible for Plato's sublime greatness, though perhaps Plato "was too much a lover of contention,"[15] so too Strauss read Nietzsche as contending for the highest against Plato himself. Nietzsche *versus* Plato: Strauss was

---

15. Longinus, *On the Sublime* 13.4–5.

not merely interested in this form of the modern/ancient antagonism; he said that it made our times the best of times: when asked in what age he would most like to have lived, Strauss "answered that he was lucky to have lived in the present period, because the most comprehensive and deepest account of the whole has been given us by Plato, and the most comprehensive criticism of that account has been given us by Nietzsche."[16]

Strauss provides an essential clue to his understanding of this greatest of philosophical rivalries by a small remark in a posthumously published lecture from the 1950s. Discussing the Nietzschean "philosophers of the future," Strauss said, "It is certainly not an overstatement to say that no one has ever spoken so greatly and so nobly of what a philosopher is as Nietzsche." It is hard to imagine higher praise from Strauss. But then he adds a little qualification that in fact somewhat diminishes that praise: "This is not to deny that the philosophers of the future as Nietzsche described them remind one much more than Nietzsche himself seems to have thought of Plato's philosopher. For while Plato had seen the features in question as clearly as Nietzsche, and perhaps more clearly than Nietzsche, he had intimated rather than stated his deepest insights" (*RCPR* 40–41). What Nietzsche *stated*, Plato *thought*—and thought not fit to utter. Nietzsche and Plato shared the same view of what a philosopher is, a most exalted view that Nietzsche paraded and Plato sheltered. With respect to what a philosopher is, Plato chose "brief indication" (*PAW* 35) whereas Nietzsche chose direct statement. And Strauss suggests that Plato's choice shows that Plato had perhaps a clearer understanding of *this* aspect of what a philosopher is, namely, how much to reveal of himself, what to say of himself.

Who is this Plato who shares Nietzsche's view of the philosopher but who always only indicates and intimates? Who is this Plato whose greatest rival is Nietzsche? Strauss found special access to Plato in the writings of the great medieval Islamic philosophers, especially Alfarabi (ca. 870–950), the founder of a fitting stance for philosophy to take toward revealed religion, a stance which Alfarabi derived from Plato and which set the course not only of Islamic philosophy but of Jewish philosophy as well, and, through Averroës, of an important minority stream of Christian philosophy. According to Alfarabi as Strauss presents him, "the way of Plato" arose out of reflection on "the way of Socrates." The way of Socrates had shown itself to

---

16. Grant, *Technology and Justice* 90; cf. Christian, *George Grant* 292–93. The wording and cadence of this statement seem clearly Grant's own; it would be interesting to know the exact words of Strauss's answer to Grant's question.

be a *limited* way because it concerned itself only with "the scientific investigation of justice and the virtues," and it had shown itself to be an *intransigent* way because it chose "non-conformity and death." Plato corrected the way of Socrates—he removed its limitation and tempered its intransigence. The way of Plato aimed "to supply 'the science of the essence of every being' and hence especially the science of the divine and of the natural things" (*PAW* 16). And the way of Plato set aside Socratic intransigence in favor of compromise. Nevertheless, the way of Plato retained the core of the way of Socrates: it too was a way of replacement, of *ersetzen;* it too aimed to replace the common understanding of things with a radically new understanding. But in the way of Plato as distinguished from the way of Socrates,

> the revolutionary quest for the other city ceased to be necessary: Plato substituted for it a more conservative way of action, namely, the gradual replacement of the accepted opinions by the truth or an approximation of the truth. The replacement of the accepted opinions could not be gradual, if it were not accompanied by a provisional acceptance of the accepted opinions: as Farabi elsewhere declares, conformity with the opinions of the religious community in which one is brought up, is a necessary qualification for the future philosopher. The replacement of the accepted opinions could not be gradual if it were not accompanied by the suggestion of opinions which, while pointing toward the truth, do not too flagrantly contradict the accepted opinions. We may say that Farabi's Plato eventually replaces the philosopher-king who rules openly in the virtuous city, by the secret kingship of the philosopher who, being "a perfect man" precisely because he is an "investigator," lives privately as a member of an imperfect society which he tries to humanize within the limits of the possible (*PAW* 16–17).

Particularly important in this characterization of the way of Plato is the fact that the way of Plato aims at a *replacement* of the accepted opinions: it does not simply oppose them or accommodate itself to them; it accommodates itself to them *because* it opposes them, and it accommodates itself to them *in order to* replace them. Plato's ambitions with respect to the accepted opinions necessitated the choice of "allusive, ambiguous, misleading and obscure speech" (*WPP* 136). Through this choice, Plato established a character for himself. Plato became known as a writer who speaks allusively, ambiguously, misleadingly, obscurely. By virtue of having established his character in this way, Plato freed himself to speak his mind, to speak the dangerous truth explicitly and unambiguously, confident that here too he would be heard in character as one who speaks misleadingly and obscurely, as one who speaks ironically, not meaning what he says. In this way, Plato

mastered the diplomatic art described by Roberto Calasso in another connection as "the art of hiding everything on the surface."[17] The way of Plato
is strategic and cunning. It feigns conformity to mask its non-conformity.
More than that, it feigns conformity to mask its revolutionary intentions.
The way of Plato is secretly revolutionary; it revolutionizes by seeming to
support the conventional.

The great aim of Plato's revolutionary enterprise is to "humanize" society "within the limits of the possible." How is this humanizing to be understood? How is this "philanthropy," as Strauss characterized it on other
occasions (*WPP* 29–33), to be understood? One page later, after discussing
the ground or necessity of Plato's strategy, Strauss says the Platonic philosopher defends "the interests of philosophy and of nothing else" (*PAW* 18). If
these look at first like the parochial interests of some narrow specialist,
Strauss immediately corrects that impression: these are "the highest interests of mankind." To humanize society is to attempt to make a place within
society for philosophy, the highest human undertaking but one whose
height or nobility society as such can never fully appreciate.

Strauss's presentation of Alfarabi's view of the way of Plato can be
summarized thus: Platonic philosophy devised a revolutionary strategy for
transforming society with a view to preserving philosophy. The Platonic
philosopher is a well-sheltered indicator; both his shelter and what he indicates take their direction from his being a philanthropist, a lover of humanity who acts on his love. His actions aim at a replacement of opinions,
with opinions dangerous to philosophy gradually being replaced by opinions
more friendly to philosophy in order that the rational investigation of the
whole may continue. Through this replacement, the philosopher comes to
exercise a secret kingship; the philosopher rules in the only way that it is
possible for him to rule, and he rules in the highest interests of humanity.

Is Alfarabi's Plato Strauss's Plato? There can be little doubt that the answer is Yes after one has studied Strauss's Plato. In *Persecution and the Art
of Writing*, Strauss followed Alfarabi in describing the way of Plato as "a
combination of the way of Socrates with the way of Thrasymachus" (*PAW*
16). Years later, in his own study of Plato's *Republic* in *The City and Man*,
Strauss took over Alfarabi's view as his own. Without mentioning Alfarabi,
Strauss concentrated on Thrasymachus's role in the *Republic* in order to
show how Thrasymachus became necessary for Plato's way of reconciling
philosophy and the city. At a key point in his argument, Strauss emphasized

17. Calasso, *The Ruin of Kasch* 6.

that Socrates and Thrasymachus "have just become friends, having not been enemies before either" (*CM* 123). They have just become friends because Socrates has just argued that the art of persuasion is necessary for the philosopher in order to reconcile the multitude to philosophy: Thrasymachus and his art are indispensable for the Platonic defense of philosophy. But Socrates and Thrasymachus have just become friends for an additional reason: Socrates has just surrendered philosophy's pursuit of the young men and has handed over the instruction of the young to the city's persuasive speakers, suspending his "corruption" of them. Thrasymachus becomes Socrates' friend by becoming Socrates' ally with an honorable mission to perform; he puts himself in Socrates' service—he and his art become "ministerial" to philosophy, to use Strauss's word (*CM* 123–24, 133–34, 136). The way of Plato conscripts rhetoric into philosophy's service—Strauss's commentary on the *Republic* leaves no question that he follows Alfarabi on this decisive point.[18]

Additional confirmation of the fact that Alfarabi's Plato is Strauss's Plato can be gained from Strauss's essay "How Farabi Read Plato's *Laws*" (*WPP* 134–54). Strauss repeats at the end of his essay the basic distinction between the way of Socrates and the way of Plato—that is, Plato's correction of the way of Socrates. But Strauss also suggests that Alfarabi corrects the way of Plato or adjusts the way of Plato to his own setting within Islam. Strauss seems to express his admiration for this correction in his final sentence: "We admire the ease with which Farabi invented Platonic speeches" (*WPP* 154). Alfarabi invented Platonic speeches in the spirit of Plato, the inventor of Socratic speeches—for Plato's Socrates invented Egyptian speeches in the *Phaedrus* which paved the way for a whole new art of philosophical writing. Granted permission by Plato's *Phaedrus*, Alfarabi took himself to be free to invent Platonic speeches to fit the needs of his own audience. Strauss's admiration of the ease with which Alfarabi did so could be something more than admiration for a successful literary achievement: it could be the admiration of one who himself aimed to invent Platonic speeches that would fit the needs of his own audience.

The Plato with whom Strauss constantly contrasts Nietzsche, the Plato who measures Nietzsche and is measured by Nietzsche, is Alfarabi's Plato, successful founder of Platonic political philosophy: a thoroughly politic Plato capable of great invention in the service of the highest political task,

18. Strauss's understanding of the role played by Thrasymachus in the way of Plato is crucial for his whole interpretation of Platonic political philosophy. I consider it in greater detail in chapter 4.

the preservation of the interests of reason in a world of unreason. Plato and Nietzsche are rivals because they are kin, kin who serve the interests of philosophy and nothing else, the highest interests of humanity. Philosophy's interests require action on their behalf. Plato and Nietzsche are kin in aspiring to spiritual rule; they are rivals in their manner of exercising that rule or in their response to their times. How fitting that Strauss ends his essay on Nietzsche and Plato with a *German* sentence emphasizing replacement; it is a Platonic speech about a Platonic task.

OBSCURITY

Stylistic caution.—

A: But if *everyone* knew this *most* would be harmed by it. You yourself call these opinions dangerous for those exposed to danger, and yet you express them in public?

B: I write in such a way that neither the mob, nor the *populi*, nor the parties of any kind want to read me. Consequently, these opinions of mine will never become public.

A: But how do you write, then?

B: Neither usefully nor pleasantly—to the trio I have named.

Nietzsche, *WS* 71

Strauss is well known as the rediscover of esotericism, the art of writing once practiced by philosophers to obscure their heterodoxy while communicating it to the like-minded or potentially like-minded. It is less well appreciated that Nietzsche too rediscovered esotericism. But whereas Strauss seemed to think that esotericism had to be perpetuated as an essential component of philosophy, Nietzsche thought that it had to be ended—betrayed, exposed, discredited, and replaced by a new candor willing to run the risk of openness.

Nietzsche discovered the clue to esotericism early, he tells us late, in "a small and basically modest fact, the fact of the 'pious fraud'" (*TI* Improvers 5), the right which "the 'improvers' of humanity" gave themselves to lie morally. "Neither Manu nor Plato nor Confucius nor the Jewish and Christian teachers ever doubted their *right* to lie." Nietzsche provided a fine definition for the general practice of pious fraud when describing one of its particular forms, Jesuitism: "the conscious holding on to illusion and forcibly incorporating that illusion as *the basis of culture*" (*KGW* VII 16 [23]).

Plato, in Nietzsche's view, was a master practitioner of this craft of active fraud. Nietzsche therefore expressed his fundamental stance toward Plato this way: "I'm a complete skeptic about Plato" (*TI* Ancients 2). Strauss too could be said to be a complete skeptic about Plato. Unlike Strauss, however, Nietzsche was completely open about his complete skepticism, as he demonstrated immediately by calling Plato's "idealism" his "higher swindle." Unlike Strauss, Nietzsche chose to throw light on old obscurities, old swindlers. One of Nietzsche's weapons in his rivalry with Plato is exposé: Nietzsche is not above betraying Plato's lying to the strict probity of modern scholars. He states directly, he does not merely indicate, the reasons for his skepticism about Plato: Plato made "a mighty necessary lie" basic to his perfect city (*UD* 10); Plato "wanted to have taught as absolute truth what he himself did not regard as even conditionally true: namely, the separate existence and separate immortality of 'souls'" (*KGW* VIII 14 [116] = *WP* 428); Plato should be consulted on the value of "a real lie, a genuine, resolute, 'honest' lie" (*GM* 3.19). Furthermore, Nietzsche brings Plato into the open as the paragon of "the evil principle." That is, as a philosophic thinker of the highest aspiration, Plato is "the critic of all customs . . . the antithesis of the moral man," for he aims to become the lawgiver of new customs. Plato, Nietzsche says in this aphorism in *Daybreak*, "intended to do for all the Greeks what Mohammed later did for his Arabs: to determine customs in things great and small" (*D* 496; see *KGW* VII 38 [13] = *WP* 972).

As Nietzsche interpreted it, the philosophers' esotericism was a tool of moral manipulation. Pious fraud enabled philosophers to lie a moral interpretation into the things themselves and subject humanity to the guilt and responsibility intrinsic to the moral view: fear of punishment and hope of reward were seen as a useful and perhaps necessary means to make a population civil and decent.

Strauss is solicitous of philosophy's esotericism. He seems to count himself among those "so fortunate as to have a natural preference for Jane Austen rather than for Dostoievski," a natural preference that inclined him to Xenophon's view that "It is noble as well as just and pious and more pleasant to remember the good things rather than the bad ones" (*SPPP* 127; *OT* 185). We don't know Nietzsche's response to Emma Woodhouse or Elizabeth Bennet, but we know his response to Dostoievski: gratitude and admiration for Dostoievski's unparalleled psychology and for his willingness to study in the open the bad things of the human soul.

Nietzsche is not at all solicitous of philosophy's esotericism. But from beginning to end he was a student of it, exploring the masks and "hideouts" of the philosophers and their various reasons for employing them (see e.g. *GS* 359). As a student of esotericism, Nietzsche came to hold that some aspects of philosophy's esotericism were simply insurmountable: no matter how great the philosopher's good will to communication, "the pathos of distance" separating the philosopher from the rest of humanity could never be remedied (*BGE* 257). As Zarathustra's career shows, the way in to philosophy is open only to those with inclinations and aptitudes of a peculiar and rare sort. And even for those few, the primary ground of esotericism remains intact: nature loves to hide; we dwell within the natural incomprehensibility of things; even the most gifted intellects pursuing lives of the most spirited inquiry stand before mystery. It therefore belongs to philosophy to be Socratic, to learn its ignorance (*GS* 381).

But the ineluctable obscurity of things is not the only aspect of Nietzsche's esotericism: he chose to retain esotericism's pedagogical function in his characteristic art form, the art of the aphorism. The brevity of the aphorism, its thriftiness, does as little as possible for the reader. But in the little it does, it establishes intimacy between writer and reader, creating accomplices for the writer by forcing readers to make his discoveries, partly at least, on their own. It is the art form of a tempter, a seducer, a corrupter of the young.

But with respect to those chosen forms of esotericism by means of which philosophy had consciously obscured its true character and its true views—with respect to the artful devices of salutary lying—Nietzsche called a halt. He replaced salutary lying with a new probity, a willingness to risk the public exposure of private heresy. He expressed the kernel of his view on this matter in *On the Genealogy of Morals* (3.10).

> Let us compress the facts into a few brief formulas: to begin with, the philosophic spirit always had to use as a mask and cocoon the *previously established* types of the contemplative man—priest, sorcerer, soothsayer, and in any case a religious type—in order to be able to *exist at all: the ascetic ideal* for a long time served the philosopher as a form in which to appear, as a precondition of existence—he had to *represent* it so as to be able to be a philosopher; he had to *believe* in it in order to be able to represent it. The peculiar, withdrawn attitude of the philosopher, world-denying, hostile to life, suspicious of the senses, freed from sensuality, which has been maintained down to the most modern times and has become virtually the *philosopher's pose par excellence*—it is above all a result of the emergency conditions under which philosophy arose and survived at all; for the longest time philosophy would not have been *possible at all* on earth without ascetic wraps and cloak, without an ascetic self-misunderstanding. To put it vividly: the *ascetic priest* provided until the most modern times the repulsive and gloomy caterpillar form in which alone the philosopher could live and creep about.
>
> Has all this really *altered*? Has that many-colored and dangerous

winged creature, the "spirit" which this caterpillar concealed, really been unfettered at last and released into the light, thanks to a sunnier, warmer, brighter world? Is there sufficient pride, daring, courage, self-confidence available today, sufficient will of the spirit, will to responsibility, *freedom of will*, for "the philosopher" to be henceforth—*possible* on earth?—

Has all this really altered? Yes, Nietzsche answered, all this has really altered. Old emergency conditions have died away and made the old ascetic mask no longer appropriate as a public face for a non-ascetic enterprise. Old emergency conditions have been replaced by new emergency conditions that pose a terminal threat to philosophy. As Nietzsche presents it, that threat is found partly in the ascendancy of philosophy's indispensable offspring, science and skepticism; and partly in the exclusive reign of modern virtue, equality and the wisdom of the multitude. Strauss's Nietzsche essay achieves one of its high points when it allows the precise nature of that new threat to be seen.

Faced with the grave new danger posed to philosophy by philosophy's impostors, Nietzsche ran a risk with the truth, with public probity. Part of the risk called for a transformation of the public image of philosophy, metamorphosis of the ugly caterpillar into the beautiful butterfly. This transformation brought philosophy's lying past into the open and made explicit the question of the necessity of noble lying. But this increase in candor brings in its train the fundamental candor, public acknowledgment of what philosophy has known since Socrates: that the highest spiritual enterprise, the most passionate pursuit of knowledge of the whole, is unavoidably accompanied by awareness of the necessary limitations on knowledge.

In judging that there had been a fundamental alteration in the setting for philosophy and that philosophy had to respond, Nietzsche knew that he was playing a game with very high stakes: after completing Part 3 of *Thus Spoke Zarathustra*, Nietzsche had Zarathustra say (in an unpublished fragment), "WE ARE CONDUCTING AN EXPERIMENT WITH THE TRUTH! PERHAPS HUMANITY WILL PERISH OF IT! SO BE IT!" (*KGW* VII 25 [305] Spring 1884). "So be it!" This is no shrug of indifference. It is Nietzsche's acknowledgment of his incapacity to master chance, the incapacity of anyone to spare humanity the uncontrollable consequences of the next phase of its adventure. As Nietzsche presents it, the novel experiment with the truth is simply forced on the contemporary thinker by the history of virtue.

How does Strauss handle Nietzsche's openness? Furtively, in the manner befitting a lover of reserve, for Strauss seems to follow Alfarabi in his "unqualified agreement with Plato's principle of secretiveness" (*WPP* 137).

What does Strauss hide with his calculated obscurity? In part, he hides his own admiring gaze which sees the height Nietzsche achieved, and holds him at that height for the admiration of others who share (if not his own love of obscurity) at least his love of that "very long, never easy, but always pleasant work" (*PAW* 37) required to penetrate a thinker's purposeful obscurity.

How does Strauss's private admiring gaze fit with his public strictures against Nietzsche? More consequentially, how can students of Nietzsche and Strauss adjudicate between Nietzsche's risks and Strauss's reserve—how should the philosophy of the future face philosophy's lying past? These questions can be approached only after Strauss's admiring gaze is fully appreciated.

Chapter Two

How Leo Strauss Read
Nietzsche's *Beyond Good and Evil*

Note on the plan of Nietzsche's *Beyond Good and Evil* that it presents its topics in a descending order of importance. First it deals with philosophy, treating philosophy as the great alternative to religion in the task of providing the grounds for human thought and action. Second it deals with morality, treating morality in both its natural and unnatural forms. And third it deals with the governance of human beings, with the principles of rule or politics. Strauss follows *Beyond Good and Evil* and provides an explicit unfolding of Nietzsche's implicit plan.

However, before Strauss reaches the actual plan of *Beyond Good and Evil,* he must introduce his subject and give it its proper gravity; he must show why the study of Nietzsche is now central to Platonic political philosophy.

Nietzsche's Preface: The Mighty Rivalry

NIETZSCHE AND PLATO[1]

Strauss's first three paragraphs all say the same thing in different ways. They single out *Beyond Good and Evil* from Nietzsche's other works by comparing its unique qualities with those of the other books. The paragraphs differ in that the first paragraph gives Strauss's way of singling out *Beyond Good*

I am grateful to David Frisby for the unstinting help he has given me from beginning to end of my study of Strauss's Nietzsche essay.

1. Strauss's essay is reprinted in the Appendix with the format of *SPPP.* All references to it are to the added paragraph numbers.

and Evil, the second gives Nietzsche's way, and the third gives Strauss's interpretation of Nietzsche's way.

Paragraph 1   *Beyond Good and Evil* "always seemed" to Strauss the most beautiful of Nietzsche's books. But Strauss wonders: Does his impression differ from Nietzsche's own assessment? Nietzsche after all regarded *Zarathustra* as "the most profound" of his books and the "most perfect in regard to language." Does Strauss judge Nietzsche's works from a non-Nietzschean standard? Not necessarily, Strauss will answer; by the end of his paragraph, Nietzsche's reasons for singling out *Zarathustra,* like his reasons for personally preferring *Dawn of Morning* and *Gay Science,* will be seen to be perfectly compatible with Strauss's reasons for singling out *Beyond Good and Evil.* Strauss's emphasis on the beautiful will be seen to be the appropriate one for a reader with Strauss's taste and training.

To illustrate his point about different but compatible standards of measure, Strauss introduces Plato. Immediately, at the very beginning, Strauss does what he will do repeatedly in his essay—introduce Plato in order to measure Nietzsche. The example of Plato "is perhaps not too far-fetched," Strauss says. Though it may in fact seem somewhat far-fetched at first, the unrelenting contrast that Strauss sustains between Plato and Nietzsche will demonstrate that it is not far-fetched at all to measure Nietzsche by Plato and vice versa.

Strauss introduces Plato in order to illustrate his point that "most beautiful" is not identical to "most profound" or "most perfect in regard to language." Once introduced, Plato is used to make an additional point, but this point is one on which Plato differs from Nietzsche: "Plato makes no distinction among his writings." This fact is one aspect of a larger matter on which Plato differs from Nietzsche: Plato "points away from himself whereas Nietzsche points most emphatically to himself, to 'Mr. Nietzsche.'" In pointing away from himself Plato points—as Strauss said in the previous essay—to Socrates (*SPPP* 168). And through Socrates Plato points away from himself to divine nature. In thus pointing away from himself, Strauss says, Plato points away from his "ipsissimosity." But "ipsissimosity" is Nietzsche's invented word (*BGE* 207). And when Nietzsche used it he prefaced it with *accursed:* Nietzsche points to his own accursed ipsissimosity. Nietzsche forces us to gaze at him, to judge him and his accursed ipsissimosity while we are judging his writings: with Nietzsche, the philosopher's humanity becomes the focus of our gaze and not something outside the philosopher to which the philosopher prefers to point, some idealized human, some divine nature.

Has Plato helped us flee our accursed ipsissimosity, directing our attention to some beautified ideal outside ourselves, some göttliche Natur superior to our own accursed nature and an uplifting inspiration to it? And what will be the consequence of Mr. Nietzsche's daring to point to himself and his accursed ipsissimosity? Strauss will go out of his way to show one thing in particular about Mr. Nietzsche, his nobility; he will show that Nietzsche transcended his accursed ipsissimosity in the direction of nobility. That enigmatic final sentence—noble nature replaces divine nature—will come as an answer to the question raised in the very first paragraph and kept before us throughout the essay: Was Mr. Nietzsche wrong to point to himself when our great philosophical model points away from himself to some divine nature?

Strauss judged *Beyond Good and Evil* the most beautiful of Nietzsche's *Paragraph* books. This inadequately expresses, he says, what Nietzsche himself clearly *2* stated about *Beyond Good and Evil* in *Ecce Homo,* the book which points most boldly to Mr. Nietzsche: "Behold the man." *Ecce Homo* contrasts *Beyond Good and Evil* with *Zarathustra:* "In *Beyond Good and Evil* the eye is compelled to grasp clearly the nearest, the timely (the present), the around-us." Strauss emphasizes the result: "the graceful subtlety as regards form, as regards intention, as regards the art of silence are in the foreground in *Beyond Good and Evil.*" The most beautiful of Nietzsche's books was made beautiful by Nietzsche's art of beautification. What is that art? Platonizing.

"In other words": This emphatic little paragraph sums up the reflections *Paragraph* of the first two paragraphs. First Strauss highlights a single characteristic of *3* *Beyond Good and Evil:* it is "the only book published by Nietzsche, in the contemporary preface to which he presents himself as the antagonist of Plato." (Nietzsche had written non-contemporary prefaces to some of his earlier books just after writing *Beyond Good and Evil,* and in some of these he did so as well.) Then Strauss presents the other side of his contrast: in the very book which opens flaunting his antagonism with Plato, Nietzsche "'platonizes' as regards the 'form' more than anywhere else." No wonder *Beyond Good and Evil* always seemed to Strauss Nietzsche's most beautiful book: it is Nietzsche's most platonizing book. Nietzsche's platonizing beautified it in quite specific ways: platonizing gave it a graceful subtlety in form, intention, and the art of silence. Strauss, that master reader schooled in subtleties of form, intention, and the art of silence by master writers from Plato onward, comes to Nietzsche appreciative of his platonizing art.[2]

---

2. In a postcard to Franz Overbeck (22 October 1883) written while he was working on *Zarathustra,* part 3, and reading a book about Plato, Nietzsche expressed astonishment at *"how much* Zarathustra platonizes." Unfortunately, Nietzsche gave no explanation of just how he understood Zarathustra's platonizing.

But how does an anti-Platonist platonize? The next paragraph begins to answer that question by glancing at Plato's platonizing.

PLATO'S PLATONIZING

Paragraph Having brought the antagonists Plato and Nietzsche closer together by sug-
4 gesting that Nietzsche platonized, Strauss now brings them closer together via the opposite route: he suggests that Plato's platonizing hid a view similar to Nietzsche's.

Nietzsche presented himself as Plato's antagonist in the remarkable Preface to *Beyond Good and Evil,* where their mighty agon came to focus on Plato's fundamental error, his invention of the pure mind and the good in itself. Nietzsche presents this as Plato's dogmatism, the dogmatism that held sway over Europe for two millennia to Europe's detriment. But now Platonism "lies on the ground." This is the greatest, most salient fact about our present: the death of Platonism, experienced popularly as the death of God, is the death of our dogmatism, our life-giving dogmatism. Can we survive its death?

But if Platonism was a dogmatism, was Plato himself a dogmatist? This is the question Strauss invites his reader to ask by providing two basic considerations which suggest that Plato was not.

First: Strauss is easily led, he says, from Nietzsche's premise that Plato's fundamental error was his invention of the pure mind and the good in itself to another of Plato's inventions, Diotima's view "that no human being is wise, but only the god is; human beings can only strive for wisdom or philosophize; gods do not philosophize." Strauss leads us to doubt that Plato shared the view of his Diotima. Diotima is one of the great teachers of Platonism but Strauss introduces her for one reason only: to distance Plato from Diotima and draw Plato closer to Nietzsche. Strauss thus disputes Nietzsche's claim in his penultimate aphorism that it is a *novelty* that gods too philosophize: "Plato could well have thought that gods philosophize." Strauss's two references suggest a philosophizing god who, like Nietzsche's Dionysos (*BGE* 295), is not ill disposed toward human beings (*Theaetetus* 151d$^{1-2}$) though he is less a Dionysos than a super-Socrates (*Sophist* 216b$^{5-6}$). If Plato did not share Diotima's conclusion, then for Plato too the gods too philosophize; they do not *possess* wisdom. Pure mind and the good in itself are not what dogmatic Platonism, Diotima's Platonism, had taken them to be, possessions of the highest beings and potential possessions of the highest human beings. Strauss does not openly dispute dogmatic Platonism's claims; instead, he introduces a Platonic character who made those claims and separates *her* from Plato. Plato's platonizing included inventing Diotima and her beautiful dream of a göttliche Natur. Flattering the gods with omniscience (*SPPP* 122) was a piece of platonizing that served Plato's purpose. Plato himself may be spared part of Nietzsche's attack; Diotima could be replaced without replacing Plato.

Second: To further indicate Plato's proximity to Nietzsche, Strauss moves from Nietzsche's "penultimate aphorism" to "the ultimate aphorism of *Beyond Good and Evil*." And Strauss makes it sound as if that final aphorism is the ultimate aphorism of philosophy as such, philosophy's beautiful and wistful speech about the insurmountable gap between speech and truth. Philosophy's ultimate aphorism attests to the impossibility of philosophy itself ever being dogmatic. When Nietzsche underlines the fundamental difference between "written and painted thoughts" and thoughts in their original form, Strauss "cannot help being reminded of what Plato says or intimates regarding the 'weakness of the *logos*' and regarding the unsayable and a fortiori unwritable character of the truth." What Strauss draws from Plato's words suggests again that Plato's view is compatible with Nietzsche's: "the purity of the mind as Plato conceives of it, does not necessarily establish the strength of the *logos*." Strauss does not say how Plato conceives the purity of the mind—though he has suggested that Plato could not have held it in the literal way his Diotima described. Nor does Strauss say just what "the strength of the *logos*" is—though both Nietzsche's statement and the citations from Plato's *Letters* refer to the incapacity of speech to present the most sublime and important matters. But if the purity of the mind as Plato conceives of it does not necessarily establish the strength of the *logos*, then Plato's fundamental error, the pure mind and the good in itself, seems to mask a view that is compatible with Nietzsche's view as presented in the ultimate aphorism. Strauss's whole effort in this paragraph brings Plato close to Nietzsche on the most basic issue of philosophy.

But if Strauss detects a non-dogmatic perspective that Plato shared with Nietzsche, did Nietzsche detect it? Or did Nietzsche misunderstand his greatest antagonist, taking Plato too literally, taking him at his word and therefore failing to see that Platonism may well be a dogmatism Plato did not hold? Did Nietzsche understand Plato's esotericism? Could Strauss's paragraph be an implicit criticism of Nietzsche for failing to understand that his great antagonist stood closer to him than he thought?

Nietzsche was the classical philologist who rediscovered the ancient art of esoteric writing. He was a student of great exponents of that esotericism such as Montaigne and Lessing. He states late in his life that he was first given access to his study of the genealogy of morals by his rediscovery of the "pious fraud" in writers that included Plato: "Neither Manu nor Plato nor Confucius nor the Jewish and Christian teachers ever doubted their *right* to lie" (*TI* Improvers 5). He was made "a complete skeptic about Plato" (*TI* Ancients 2) by long reflection on Plato's use of the necessary lie (*UD* 10) and on the fact that Plato wanted others to believe as absolute truth what Plato himself did not regard as even conditionally true, the separate existence and separate immortality of souls (*KGW* VIII 14 [116] = *WP* 428). Moreover, when Nietzsche set forth the different motives for a philosopher's choice of hideouts, he distinguished Plato's motives, philanthropic motives, he said, from the motives of an Augustine, which Nietzsche found to be rooted in ressentiment and revenge (*GS* 351, 359, 372). And Nietzsche's Plato kept a copy of Aristophanes under his pillow, and for Aristophanes' sake "one forgives everything Hellenic for having existed," including Platonism (*BGE* 28). We must be cautious before concluding that Nietzsche misunderstood his greatest antagonist, or that Strauss criticizes Nietzsche for misunderstanding Plato.

First Main Part: Philosophy and Religion
Chapters 1–3: Philosophy's Rule over Religion

Strauss's account of *Beyond Good and Evil* lays out the book's plan by considering Nietzsche's subtitle, his Preface, and his division of his book into nine chapters. But Strauss takes his own, highly idiosyncratic way through this plan, keeping always to his intention of contrasting Nietzsche with Plato and showing how Nietzsche thinks and acts on the scale of Plato. Strauss's intention, relentlessly pursued, holds before the reader the half-promise, half-challenge with which Nietzsche closed his Preface: "we *good Europeans*, we free, very free minds, we still have it, the whole need of the spirit and the whole tension of its bow! And perhaps also the arrow, the mission, and who knows? the *goal*. . . . ." Out of the death of Platonism arises a new European goal achievable, perhaps, through the very tensions of the spirit, the "need and distress" or nihilism, caused by the centuries-long fight against Platonism.

THE FUNDAMENTAL ALTERNATIVE

Paragraph 5 Before setting out the plan of *Beyond Good and Evil*, Strauss calls attention to philosophy's singular prominence in it, concluding his paragraph by stating that "philosophy is surely the primary theme of *Beyond Good and*

Evil, the obvious theme of the first two chapters." Strauss arrives at this conclusion by beginning with the subtitle, "Prelude to a philosophy of the future." The book is meant to prepare, Strauss asserts, "not indeed the philosophy of the future, the true philosophy, but a new kind of philosophy." This emphasis on the indefinite article could make it seem that the philosophy Nietzsche prepares is only one of many, that Nietzsche's philosophy invites a future relativism marked by a multitude of future philosophies. That this is not at all what Strauss means is indicated by his use, three times in this paragraph, of the phrase "the philosophy of the future." Still, the philosophy of the future cannot be called (and Nietzsche never called it) "the true philosophy," a designation that itself derives from the philosophy of the past. It is "a new kind of philosophy" different from the philosophy held by "the philosophers of the past (and the present)," all of whom, Nietzsche emphasizes, were set on the same track by Plato (aph. 191). The philosophy of the future will follow a different track but it will not be a multitude of tracks.

Strauss adds that Nietzsche does not simply await the philosophers of the future: his book "is meant to be a specimen of the philosophy of the future." But if Nietzsche can already write such a specimen, how does he stand to "the free minds" whom he addresses in his second chapter? He stands as a philosopher of the future addressing those who are still "the heralds and precursors of the philosophy of the future." This is a nice Nietzschean conceit: it has been his lot, he says on many occasions, to return from the most distant futures in order to point even his most advanced contemporaries toward a future that is already a part of his past. Strauss states that it is "hard to say" how Nietzsche's distinction between free minds and philosophers of the future is to be understood, but he asks two questions which suggest how: the free minds are freer than the minds of the philosophers of the future because the latter have arrived at a viewpoint that still lies in the future for the free minds.

In finally setting out the plan of *Beyond Good and Evil*, Strauss empha- *Paragraph* sizes that the primary theme of philosophy requires engagement with the *6* great but lesser themes of religion, morals, and politics. Among those lesser themes a further distinction must be drawn, given the fact that the plan of Nietzsche's book breaks it into two main parts. Philosophy and religion, to which the first main part is chiefly devoted, belong more closely together than do the themes of the second main part, namely, "philosophy and the city," Strauss's summary expression for the topics of philosophy and morals, and philosophy and politics.

Nietzsche's plan for the separation of topics shows how much he differs from the classics on what Strauss calls "the fundamental alternative." For Plato and Aristotle the fundamental alternative was "that of the philosophic and the political life." For Nietzsche it is "that of the rule of philosophy over religion or the rule of religion over philosophy." Has Nietzsche misread the fundamental alternative? Or have our times made a new alternative fundamental such that Nietzsche's difference from Plato and Aristotle is the fitting difference dictated by our times? The issue is simply basic: has the *setting* for philosophy changed fundamentally, requiring that philosophy view a new alternative as fundamental? The issue can be precisely defined: has the historic appearance of revealed religion and its modern heirs so altered the setting for philosophy that a new alternative has become fundamental? Strauss speaks categorically about this issue in *Natural Right and History:*

> The fundamental question, therefore, is whether men can acquire that knowledge of the good without which they cannot guide their lives individually or collectively by the unaided efforts of their natural powers, or whether they are dependent for that knowledge on Divine Revelation. *No alternative is more fundamental than this:* human guidance or divine guidance. The first possibility is characteristic of philosophy or science in the original sense of the term, the second is presented in the Bible. The dilemma cannot be evaded by any harmonization or synthesis. For both philosophy and the Bible proclaim something as the one thing needful, as the only thing that ultimately counts, and the one thing needful proclaimed by the Bible is the opposite of that proclaimed by philosophy: a life of obedient love versus a life of free insight. In every attempt at harmonization, in every synthesis however impressive, one of the two opposed elements is sacrificed, more or less subtly but in any event surely, to the other: philosophy, which means to be the queen, must be made the handmaid of revelation or vice versa. (*NRH* 74–75, emphasis added)

Which will be the handmaid of the other? Which will rule? "No alternative is more fundamental." Great early modern philosophers like Francis Bacon and René Descartes shared this view of the fundamental alternative and they set out to liberate philosophy from the rule of religion to which it had fallen prey and to bring religion under the rule of philosophy.[3] Nietzsche himself is completely explicit about the need for philosophy to rule religion. The need arises from the fact that religion has come to rule philosophy, though now it is *modern* religion, "modern ideas," that determines the future of humanity and threatens the abolition of philosophy.

Strauss states that "for Nietzsche, as distinguished from the classics,

---

3. *NRH* indicates that philosophy's capture by revealed religion in its Christian form necessitated the return to the classics by modern political philosophy (164).

politics belongs from the outset to a lower plane than either philosophy or religion." But what Strauss emphasizes in the relationship between philosophy and religion is itself an issue of politics, the issue of rule. In Nietzsche's view of our history, philosophy conceded rule to its already established rival only for the sake of its own survival. Philosophy had been forced to adopt the appearance of its rival under "emergency conditions" which threatened its very survival (*GM* 3.10). Inwardly, however, the philosophic spirit harbored something quite different from the ascetic, world-denying ideals of the firmly established religious prototypes; inwardly, it was self-affirming and world-affirming, it was erotic and passionate, in love with existence. The new emergency conditions which Nietzsche diagnosed required that philosophy now drop its ascetic pose and abandon its strategic complicity with world-denying religion. Nietzsche risked bringing the fateful rivalry of philosophy and religion into the open in order to ensure philosophy's survival by establishing philosophy's supremacy.

As one way of highlighting the new issue of rule, Strauss says that "in the preface [Nietzsche] intimates that his precursor par excellence is . . . the *homo religiosus* Pascal." Intimates? Pascal is not mentioned in the Preface. Jesuitism, however, Pascal's great enemy, *is* mentioned. What is Jesuitism? In his Preface Nietzsche called it the first attempt in the grand style to relieve the tension of the European spirit caused by the two-millennia-long fight against Platonism. Nietzsche pictures that great spiritual fight as creating a tension of the spirit like a bow drawn taut: with that taut bow we can shoot for the most distant goals. Jesuitism was an attempt to unbend the bow, to dissipate that most promising tension. But with what means? Nietzsche's definition of Jesuitism provides the perfect answer: "the conscious holding on to illusion and forcibly incorporating that illusion as *the basis of culture*" (*KGW* VII 16 [23]). Jesuitism, the spearhead of the militant reformation of Catholic Christianity after the Council of Trent, focused on the priestly magic of the Eucharist, the artistic hosanna of Baroque and Rococo style, the education of an elite loyal to throne and altar—and the conscious rule of religion over philosophy. Jesuitism is a historic and powerful manifestation of that moral phenomenon which so fascinated both Nietzsche and Strauss, the "pious fraud" or manipulative salutary lying endemic to our spiritual traditions. Jesuitism is an explicit form of the rule of religion over philosophy—and, Strauss indicates, Nietzsche's "precursor par excellence" fought it.

But Nietzsche's "precursor," though he gave tortured voice to the European spirit against pious fraud in its newest form, himself spoke in a

Christian voice, the voice of *homo religiosus*, the voice of the profound, monstrous intellectual conscience wounded by surrendering itself to the rule of religion (*BGE* 45). Nietzsche's way of going beyond his "precursor" Pascal is suggested in the aphorism Strauss refers to (45): Nietzsche ascends into that vaulting heaven of bright, malicious spirituality that enables him to survey from above even the heights of Pascal's surrender of mind to heart, of philosophy to religion.

Strauss's little suggestion regarding Pascal amounts to this: Nietzsche stands to the democratic Enlightenment, that other, later attempt in the grand style to unbend the tensed bow of the modern human spirit, as Pascal stood to Jesuitism. Pascal is Nietzsche's "precursor": Pascal too was an actor in the great cultural drama, the fight against the old Platonism of Diotima, the Platonism adopted by Christianity, the religious dogmatism which once bestrode our culture like a monstrous and frightening mask but which now lies on the ground. Pascal himself remained within the horizon of religion whereas Nietzsche claimed to have transcended that horizon, to have transcended all merely religious horizons, viewing them from the perspective of philosophy.

Does Strauss agree with Nietzsche that the fundamental alternative of our time is the rule of philosophy over religion or of religion over philosophy? His essay will show with great rigor just how philosophy has in fact fallen under the rule of modern religion, heir to the revealed religion Christianity. It will show further that philosophy, having been blurred or destroyed by modern beliefs, can be restored by ascending to a position of rule: in the new philosopher, the complementary man, philosophy can be saved from its modern predicament. But in painting this fundamental alternative, Strauss's essay will never forget that Nietzsche's new fundamental alternative claims precedence over the fundamental alternative for Plato and Aristotle. Has this aspect of the Platonic paradigm run its course in Western philosophy? Strauss forces his reader to ask that question.

MEASURING NIETZSCHE PLATONICALLY

Paragraph 7 The guidance necessary for understanding paragraph seven is given only at the beginning of paragraph eight, for here is an occasion on which Strauss indulges himself and practices what he describes so tellingly in other authors: he contradicts himself. It's a small contradiction on a seemingly incidental matter and it's quite flagrant; nevertheless, reflection on it points to the basic matter in Strauss's whole discussion of philosophy and religion in Nietzsche. Paragraph seven opens: "Nietzsche says very little about religion in the first two chapters. One could say that he speaks there on religion only in a single aphorism which happens to be the shortest (37)." But one would be wrong, for paragraph eight opens: "We can now turn to the two aphorisms in *Beyond Good and Evil* I-II that can be said to be devoted to religion (36–37)." What happened to change one to two? Paragraph seven discussed "philosophizing" in Nietzsche and showed the way in which philosophy leads naturally to religion; it showed how the new religion is generated out of philosophy. This relation of dependence, this primacy of philosophy, will be the key issue in Strauss's discussion of philosophy and religion in Nietzsche. Therefore, Strauss's little contradiction indicates that Nietzsche's aphoristic style serves his fundamental argument, it indicates that Nietzsche's aphorisms are often linked—in this case, one aphorism proves to be the corollary of the preceding one, and the new religion is thus shown to be a corollary of the new philosophy. The plan of *Beyond Good and Evil* includes a careful arrangement of linked aphorisms; one becomes two when Nietzsche's aphoristic style is properly appreciated. Fittingly, Strauss later returns to the singular when speaking of religion in the aphorisms of these chapters, for he refers to "*the* theological aphorism occurring in the first two chapters (37)" (paragraph 13, emphasis added).

Strauss's little device of silent self-correction points to another complicating feature of this very complicated paragraph: Strauss does not stand by all his assertions. Instead, his first assertions are often first impressions which require modification upon further reflection. The modifications appear in due time, but they are not trumpeted—one silently becomes two, and the reader is expected to notice. Like that grand master of style, Francis Bacon, Strauss removed the scaffolding from the finished structure of his prose, requiring that the reader perform again the task of the builder.[4]

Perhaps another preparatory remark about Strauss's laconic style may be useful before entering the crucial discussion of philosophy and religion in paragraph seven: Strauss seems to presume that his reader will be familiar with the rest of his work and with the foundations of that work in his own philosophical educators. To fully appreciate Strauss's half-submerged argument on the rule of philosophy over religion in Nietzsche, it helps immeasurably to have in mind another version of that argument set forth by one of those educators, Alfarabi's account of the means of philosophy's rule over religion in *The Attainment of Happiness*.[5] There, the necessity that the genuine philosopher generate the similitudes of religion which persuade the

4. Bacon, *Works, Novum Organum* I. aph. 125.
5. *Alfarabi's Philosophy of Plato and Aristotle,* pp. 41–50.

multitude is presented in somewhat different but completely compatible terms.

"Philosophy is surely the primary theme of *Beyond Good and Evil,* the obvious theme of the first two chapters" (paragraph 5), but Strauss's discussion of philosophy is guided by religion and not by philosophy. Why is this? It seems that Strauss intends to explain what he has just isolated as fundamental in Nietzsche, the rule of philosophy over religion. He looks at the philosophy chapters in order to see how religion fares in them or to show how the new philosophy comes to rule religion. But if Strauss's route into Nietzsche's philosophy follows the question of religion it leads eventually to "the fundamental proposition," "the fundamental fact," will to power. At first—in the present paragraph—the fundamental fact appears as "'only' one interpretation," it appears as measured by the old Platonism; but later—in the next paragraph—it appears as the fundamental fact simply. Strauss gets to what is deepest in Nietzsche's philosophy, will to power, by beginning near the surface. Asking in effect, How does religion fare in the hands of the philosopher who set out to rule it?, Strauss first shows what that philosophy is. Using the mentions of will to power in *Beyond Good and Evil,* spare and few in number as they are, Strauss shows how will to power is Nietzsche's fundamental teaching. After this he will show that a certain kind of religion follows from that philosophy, a religion that philosophy rules quite naturally because it is philosophy's spiritual offspring. Religion thus passes into the care of the new philosophy. In Nietzsche philosophy does not adapt itself to the already existing religious or ascetic spirit with its world-denying, self-denying ways; the new religion will display in a public mode what was always philosophy's inwardness: affirmative, spirited, earthly celebration.

What Strauss demonstrates here strikes me as his most significant contribution to the study of Nietzsche, namely, the recognition that out of the fundamental fact arise new fundamental values, values true to the earth and culminating in the highest value, eternal return. What has been handled so ineptly and arbitrarily by other interpreters of Nietzsche, including especially Heidegger—will to power itself and the connection between will to power and eternal return—is given a masterful reading by Strauss, a philological reading true to Nietzsche's enigmatic texts. The Nietzsche who emerges from these few pages on philosophy and religion is a comprehensive thinker bringing together fact and value in a new and historic way.

Strauss mirrors Nietzsche in being extremely playful on the basic issue. The great metaphysical and epistemological concerns of Nietzsche's thought are entered via the heartfelt, almost desperate question posed by free-minded readers, friends of Nietzsche who cry out after being forced to hear for the first time the full range of his teaching on the will to power: "What? Doesn't this mean, to speak popularly: God is refuted but the devil is not?" (aph. 37). Strauss does not mar Nietzsche's playfulness over the grave trial he forces on his friends, but he does indicate just how dangerous and tempting and blasphemous Nietzsche is in this little dialogue with his friends.

The plan of Nietzsche's *Beyond Good and Evil* includes a strategy for presenting his fundamental teaching, will to power. It is spoken of first—in the early aphorisms (9, 13, 22, 23)—"in the way of bald assertion, not to say dogmatically" (paragraph 8). The reasoning in support of the doctrine is given only later, in aphorism 36. Only there does Nietzsche set forth "with what is at the same time the most intransigent intellectual probity and the most bewitching playfulness his reasons, i.e. the problematic, tentative, tempting, hypothetical character of his proposition" (ibid.). Strauss does not say so explicitly, but Nietzsche's presentation of his new fundamental teaching follows a strategy Strauss had long studied in other philosophers of the first rank: their plans for the presentation of their fundamental thoughts were guided by the conviction that these thoughts need be known only by a very few like-minded readers. Moreover, even these few special readers could make the new fundamental thoughts their own only if they codiscovered them, only if they were tempted into following for themselves the wholly new path opened by the solitary thinker himself. Tempted this way into the new teaching, these few readers became coconspirators in thinking the radical new thoughts for themselves.[6]

Strauss's presentation of will to power retraces Nietzsche's strategy. He begins as Nietzsche began, with the "bald assertions" of the doctrine, and only afterward does he touch the reasoning on its behalf. In addition, Strauss's presentation follows his standard practice of contrasting Nietzsche with Plato. "The will to power takes the place which the *eros*—the striving for 'the good in itself'—occupies in Plato's thought." But Plato's duo of *eros* and pure mind, of driving impulse and the power for insight, are united into one by Nietzsche: "the will to power takes the place of both *eros* and the pure mind." The result is a different description of philosophizing: as the most spiritual will to power, philosophizing "consists in prescribing to nature what or how it ought to be"—whereas for Plato, philosophizing is "the love of the true that is independent of will or decision." Strauss can then

---

6. Strauss, "The Spirit of Sparta or the Taste of Xenophon" 535.

conclude this comparison with a concise formulation: "Whereas according to Plato the pure mind grasps the truth, according to Nietzsche the impure mind, or a certain kind of impure mind, is the sole source of truth."

Is this Strauss's final word on Nietzsche's philosophy, that it "consists in prescribing to nature what or how it ought to be"? Does Strauss think that philosophy as the most spiritual will to power is simply a form of tyranny over its quarry, a whip forcing conformity and obedience on the whipped? Is it the height of anthropomorphization? It is still very early in Strauss's essay, and the formulations presented here will have to be measured by the formulations presented later. Strauss is repeating Nietzsche's procedure: these first formulations about will to power arise from the aphorism in which Nietzsche first mentions will to power in *Beyond Good and Evil*, aphorism 9. Later formulations make it necessary to expand and modify the teaching, correcting the first crass impressions built in to the very term will to power. Only gradually does Strauss exhibit the truth of a statement he had made years earlier that "Nietzsche meant [the will to power] in a very subtle and noble manner."[7]

To elaborate his contrast between Plato and Nietzsche on the love of truth and truth, Strauss now introduces an early statement by Nietzsche on an issue which characterized his investigations from beginning to end, the problem of deadly truth as posed in Nietzsche's *Second Meditation Out of Season*. Strauss is the writer who showed that this very issue of deadly truth had in fact been basic to the whole tradition of Platonic political philosophy, an esoteric tradition whose esotericism flowed, in part, from the recognition that some truths are likely to do harm and that philosophy's social responsibility dictated that philosophy shelter society from the harmful truths. Strauss's Nietzsche essay will emphasize that in Nietzsche's view Platonic lying has been forced into the open by modern probity or honesty, "the youngest virtue," as Nietzsche called it, a virtue Nietzsche did not abandon or ask his friends to abandon.

In stating the great problem of deadly truth on this occasion, Strauss says that "the truth is not attractive, lovable, life-giving, but deadly," and he repeats the three "true doctrines" Nietzsche himself had listed. Strauss then adds, wholly on his own, that the deadly truth "is shown most simply by the true doctrine that God is dead."

Strauss continues by drawing two extreme conclusions which refer in turn to the known and to knowing: "The world in itself, the 'thing-in-itself,'

---

7. Strauss, "Progress or Return" 265.

'nature' (aph. 9) is wholly chaotic and meaningless. Hence all meaning, all order originates in man, in man's creative acts, in his will to power." Does Strauss think these formulations adequately express Nietzsche's views? He makes it clear that he does not, for he immediately adds a consideration that qualifies them and then spells out what the qualification implies. And when he restates this most basic issue in the following paragraph, it is the qualified version that stands. "Nietzsche's statements or suggestions are deliberately enigmatic," Strauss says, referring to the aphorism (40) in which Nietzsche gives the reasons why "every profound spirit needs a mask." But what is enigmatic about the issues Strauss has just been discussing? Presumably that Nietzsche has not stated directly what is suggested by his statements, for that is what Strauss now states directly: Nietzsche does not stop with the deadly truth but "does his best to break the power of the deadly truth." Furthermore, Nietzsche does not stop with a radical, truth-creating relativism but "suggests that the most important, the most comprehensive truth— the truth regarding all truths—is life-giving. In other words, by suggesting that the truth is human creation, he suggests that this truth at any rate is not a human creation." This life-giving, non-created truth will be shown by Strauss to give life in a very specific way: at the historic moment in which "God is dead" because of the modern single-minded pursuit of the truth, Nietzsche's life-giving truth will turn out to be a "vindication of God." Not only that, Strauss will go so far as to suggest that Nietzsche's life-giving truth entails "a relapse into Platonism, into the teaching of 'the good in itself'" (paragraph 14) and that this "relapse" is the unavoidable means of recovering philosophy from the crisis Nietzsche diagnosed.

After suggesting how Nietzsche does his best to break the power of deadly truth, Strauss pictures himself being tempted—and resisting the temptation. "One is tempted to say," Strauss says, "that Nietzsche's pure mind grasps the fact that the impure mind creates perishable truths." This tempting employment of Platonic terms to show that Nietzsche makes a claim impossible on his own terms, this tempting critique of Nietzsche from the side of Plato, is explicitly repudiated: "Resisting that temptation we state Nietzsche's suggestion following him in this manner. . . ." Following Nietzsche and not Plato, Strauss restates Nietzsche's fundamental claim in a way that is more sympathetic and that will open the way to its apparent affirmation (paragraph 8, end). Under the imprint of an old Platonism one is tempted to draw extreme conclusions that seem to refute Nietzsche's claims, but further consideration forces one to set that temptation aside. As Francis Bacon said with respect to the temptation of judging his revolutionary views by the old standards: "I cannot be fairly asked to abide by the decision of a tribunal which is itself on trial."[8]

Nietzsche's way of stating the issue of truth and its discovery is the philologist's way of text and interpretation: "the philosophers tried to get hold of the 'text' as distinguished from 'interpretations'; they tried to 'discover' and not to 'invent.'" Strauss keeps his distance from this formulation—"What Nietzsche claims to have realized"—while stating its further implication: "that the text in its pure, unfalsified form is inaccessible." Strauss draws a most important conclusion: "But for this very reason the text, the world in itself, the true world cannot be of any concern to us; the world of any concern to us is necessarily a fiction, for it is necessarily anthropocentric."[9] Does Strauss stand by this radical conclusion—that the world of concern to us is a human-created world lacking any standard of measure that can reach back to the world as it is, to nature? He shows in the very next paragraph how Nietzsche can claim a standard of measure after all, how the distinction between the world of any concern to us and the world in itself can be abolished. Moreover, at its center, Strauss's essay will turn to nature, and the second half of the essay will show how nature provides a plausible standard for Nietzsche.

After having traced the will to power aphorisms in this way, Strauss speaks of "the lucid, if somewhat hidden, order governing the sequence of aphorisms" in *Beyond Good and Evil* and concludes that "the desultory character of Nietzsche's argument is more pretended than real." Yes, but this is true not only of *Beyond Good and Evil*, it is true of Strauss's essay as well, as a little oddity at just this point makes clear. Toward the end of this paragraph on will to power, Strauss introduces a seemingly extraneous consideration about the relationship between aphorisms 34 and 35: at first glance, Strauss says, there does not seem to be a connection between these two aphorisms but in fact the connection is "a particularly striking example" of the lucid order of the aphorisms. But why refer to 34 and 35 in order to make this general point? These two aphorisms had just been cited in parentheses at the end of the preceding sentence: Strauss seems to assume that his readers have just interrupted their study of his paragraph in order to do what he told them to do: compare 34 and 35 with 32. And now that they've just read 34 and 35, Strauss can invite them to note the connection between them as a methodological clue to reading the whole book: seeing the connection

8. Bacon, *Works, The Great Instauration*, Preface, end.

9. Strauss refers to Plato's *Laws* 716c: "For us, the god would be the measure of all things in the highest degree, and far more so than some 'human being,' as they assert."

between these two—one grave, the other lighthearted, and both concerned with philosophy's search for the truth—they will see that Nietzsche's book is carefully planned to set forth the basic matters with a well-planned mix of gravity and levity.

Aphorism 34 thus enters Strauss's discussion in a way that initially seems arbitrary but in fact is not; and this is the aphorism that will be of special importance for the next paragraph, for what 34 says about "the world of concern to us" will be corrected by what 36 says: the world in itself *is* of concern to us. Nietzsche's self-correction turns out to be the model for Strauss's self-correction. "The desultory character of [Strauss's] argument is more pretended than real": early dogmatic formulations must be corrected in the light of later reasoned ones.

There is another item in aphorism 34 that Strauss may be calling to his readers' attention: Nietzsche speaks there as an *"advocatus dei."* Strauss will emphasize in the next paragraphs that those whom Nietzsche addresses as "my friends" make a serious mistake when they, in alarm, interpret the teacher of will to power as the advocate of the devil (aph. 37). No, Strauss will say five times, Nietzsche's will to power teaching is "a vindication of God," though it is quite understandably mistaken at first for its opposite.

The final sentences of Strauss's paragraph repeat a little playfulness that Nietzsche had indulged in when making his own claims for will to power: Nietzsche let an apparent objection arise in order to claim the very objection as a confirmation of his view (aph. 22). "The doctrine of the will to power cannot claim to reveal what is, the fact, the most fundamental fact but is 'only' one interpretation, presumably the best interpretation, among many." This objection arose in Nietzsche's marvelous little dialogue on will to power (aph. 22) between the old philologist (Nietzsche himself) and the physicists, those colleagues of the philologist made supreme in modern intellectual life by the rise and dominance of modern science. In Nietzsche's aphorism, a mere philologist dares to confront the physicists, charging them with poor philology, poor interpretation of their text, the whole of nature. What Strauss quotes as an "apparent objection" to Nietzsche's claims regarding will to power is the physicists' newly-learned reply to his claims about will to power—their fatal adoption, that is, of the old philologist's new standard: "Well, so much the better," the old philologist responds to their apparent objection that his view too is only interpretation.

Nietzsche did not present to the physicists his reasoning on behalf of the superiority of the will to power view—to them he simply announced his view like just another dogmatist who just "happened to come along." In fact, however, Nietzsche has an argument on behalf of the superiority of the will to power teaching; it is not merely one of any number of interpretations. But Nietzsche delayed the presentation of his reasoning on its behalf until aphorism 36, and presented it then not to the dogmatic physicists secure in the superiority of their interpretation of nature but to the free minds skeptical of any over-all interpretation of nature. Strauss too waits till then to show why "Nietzsche regards this apparent objection as a confirmation of his proposition." Strauss as commentator will provide the useful service of explaining just why the old philologist's ultimate response to the physicists' objection to his view of will to power is more than a little witticism in defense of a trivial relativism, why it is in fact "so much the better" that they take up this "apparent objection" and place all statements about the nature of nature on the level of interpretation: that is the necessary stage for dogmatists on the way to recognizing the superiority of one form of interpretation.

MEASURING NIETZSCHE NIETZSCHEANLY

Paragraph 8 "Now" Strauss can interpret the *two* aphorisms "that can be said to be devoted to religion" in the philosophy chapters (36–37), now that the way has been prepared by the consideration of Nietzsche's earlier statements on will to power. It must be noted that Strauss's procedure does not imply that the teaching on will to power in Nietzsche can itself be reduced to religion. On the contrary, Strauss shows that aphorism 36 presents Nietzsche's "reasoning" regarding will to power and is conducted with "the most intransigent intellectual probity." This aphorism is "devoted to religion" only derivatively in that probity's reasoning shows the way to philosophy's rule over religion, reason's rule over belief.

Nietzsche's plan for the presentation of his fundamental proposition dictated that he begin in the way of bald assertion. Now however, in aphorism 36, Nietzsche sets forth his reasoning in a manner that combines "the most intransigent intellectual probity and the most bewitching playfulness." Nietzsche's reasons reveal "the problematic, tentative, tempting, hypothetical character" of his fundamental proposition; it is the opposite of a dogmatism even though it was first stated dogmatically.

Strauss concentrates on showing how this reasoning modifies what Nietzsche had implied in "the central aphorism" of chapter two, aphorism 34. There Nietzsche had drawn our attention to the distinction between the world which is of any concern to us and the world in itself, a distinction which Strauss had himself emphasized. The will to power teaching and the reasoning on its behalf show that that distinction is not truly fundamental:

"the world as will to power is both the world of any concern to us and the world in itself." Having thus corrected his own emphasis in the preceding paragraph on the fundamental character of that distinction, Strauss now offers an argument on behalf of Nietzsche's claim for will to power which differs from Nietzsche's own.[10] Nietzsche's argument had been tacitly based on the old imperative "Know thyself" and on the demand made by the "conscience of *method*" or the "morality of method" (aph. 36). Nietzsche had earlier referred to this demand as stipulating an "economy of principles," a suspicion of "*superfluous* teleological principles" in the science of biology and "everywhere else" (aph. 13). In aphorism 36, the conscience of method requires the experiment of making do with a single kind of causality and pushing that experiment to the utmost limit. By means of this conscientious method, Nietzsche arrived at his tempting conclusion that "the world viewed from the inside, the world defined and determined according to its 'intelligible character'—it would be 'will to power' and nothing besides.—"

The argument which Strauss puts in place of Nietzsche's argument employs his own earlier distinction between a text and its interpretations: "If all views of the world are interpretations," Strauss says, "i.e. acts of the will to power, the doctrine of the will to power is at the same time an interpretation and the most fundamental fact." Being both, it is superior to any other interpretation: "it is the necessary and sufficient condition of the possibility of any 'categories.'" In this way the will to power teaching can account for itself and for all other interpretations without losing its character as interpretation, without falling into dogmatism. Its character *as* interpretation enables it to claim precedence or to say "so much the better" to all who retort "this too is only interpretation." It remains a claim; it never ascends to certainty. But it has an arguable and plausible superiority as an interpretation, and it is able as well to account for both the world of concern to us and the world in itself.

10. Strauss's refusal to comment on Nietzsche's reasoning on behalf of will to power is consistent with the lifelong practice which he once described in a summary remark at the end of his debate with Kojève: both he and Kojève appear "to turn [their] attention away from Being and toward tyranny." This turn from philosophy to political philosophy occurred while they remained "constantly mindful" of the "fundamental hypotheses" (*OT* 212). Strauss's remark was made in the final paragraph of the original French version of his "Restatement on Xenophon's *Hiero*" (*De la tyrannie*, 1954). Strauss himself deleted this paragraph when he published his English version of this essay in *WPP* in 1959 and kept it out when he republished it in a "Revised and Enlarged" edition of *OT* in 1963. The editors of the "Revised and Expanded" edition of *OT* (1991) translated the French paragraph and restored it to the end of Strauss's essay without any indication in the text that they were rescinding Strauss's decision and shifting from Strauss's English to their own (see *OT* vii).

Strauss's brief treatment of the decisive argument on the will to power, the most basic matter in Nietzsche's philosophy and "the whole doctrine of *Beyond Good and Evil*" (paragraph 9), includes references to aphorisms 34 and 35; a study of those aphorisms guided by Strauss's comments adds essential elements to his argument. The "grave" and "central" aphorism 34 discussed the peculiar form which the most serious problem of human knowledge had assumed in contemporary or post-Kantian philosophy: the distinction between the world which is of any concern to us and the world in itself had become a distinction between an apparent world quite evident to us and a true world in no way accessible to us. The problems caused by this seemingly fundamental distinction between the apparent and true worlds had proven insoluble, Nietzsche argues in aphorism 34, partly because the distinction had been understood naively, and it had been understood naively partly because of an innocent faith in grammar transmitted to us by our nannies and schoolmarms. If our investigations of the world are ever to move beyond innocence in the hope of grasping the world in itself, they will have to renounce other innocent faiths as well—and one of those faiths is exposed in aphorism 35, the faith typified by that old schoolmarm Voltaire which holds that the way to the true can only be found through a love of the good. The connection between aphorism 34 and 35 indicates that the way to the world in itself has been blocked by our need to believe that the true must accord with our learned sense of the good. We have been "too human" about "the search for the truth," Nietzsche suggests (35), suggesting by implication that there is going to be something inhuman or inhuman-sounding in any true interpretation of the world. Thus the essential link between 34 and 35 prepares the way for 36, where Nietzsche arrives at what purports to be a true interpretation of the world, having left behind innocent notions of the good. But because his readers' sense of the true continues to be governed by their all-too-human sense of the good, this new account of the true is bound to strike them as inhuman. In this way, the link between 34 and 35 prepares the way for the link between 36 and 37, for Nietzsche's new interpretation of the true elicits in 37 a shocked response even from the very audience he has done his best to prepare. When Strauss finally turns to aphorism 37, it is only after he has prepared his own audience to understand it by his quiet references to 34 and 35 and their indications about Nietzsche's subtle mode of argument.

Paragraph   Nietzsche's manner of presenting the will to power was intended to
9   tempt some of his readers, Strauss says. Which ones? Strauss refers to aphorism 30, devoted to that favorite among Strauss's themes, "the difference

between the exoteric and the esoteric, formerly known to philosophers." Nietzsche tempts those readers for whom he really writes, those attuned to the difference between exoteric and esoteric and willing to follow a writer's implications. Nietzsche had begun aphorism 30 by stating that his "highest insights must—and should!—sound like follies and sometimes like crimes when they are heard without permission by those who are not predisposed and predestined for them." Nietzsche's highest insight is the insight into will to power, and his tempting presentation of it makes clear that at first it sounds like a crime even to those for whom it is intended, those whom it tempts. But if it sounds like a crime at first, it can come to sound differently if those for whom it is intended—free minds attuned to the esoteric, the high—can free themselves of their lingering prejudices, free themselves of the sway still exercised over their unfree minds by their all-too-human sense of the good. Only then will they be able to understand that what sounds like a crime is in truth a vindication of God. And now Strauss can move at last to the wonderful little aphorism that has, with remarkable thrift, governed his whole presentation of the chapters on philosophy.

Nietzsche has just revealed the full extent of the will to power teaching. He has addressed it to his special audience of free minds, those "friends" whose way in to the fundamental teaching has been prepared by the plan of *Beyond Good and Evil*. And now, at this high point, Nietzsche allows his friends to give voice to their shocked response: "What? Doesn't this mean, to speak popularly: God is refuted but the devil is not?" Doesn't your will to power teaching commit the highest crime, robbing us of everything high and sacred while endorsing and loosing what is lowest and base? Isn't your philosophy just an inhuman reversal of what has prevailed in the popular mind? Aren't you a teacher of evil, the advocate of the devil?

Strauss gives Nietzsche's whole marvelous reply: "On the contrary! On the contrary, my friends! And, to the devil, what forces you to speak popularly?" Strauss's little commentary on this little exchange offers an enticing fragment of a complete interpretation of just what "On the contrary" means: "the doctrine of the will to power," Strauss says, "is in a manner a vindication of God." Yes. And Strauss will emphasize this affirmative implication by saying it five times, thus insisting that so far from being the advocate of the devil, Nietzsche has just demonstrated himself to be what he promised he was at the beginning of aphorism 34: *advocatus dei*. But while emphasizing this affirmative half of what is implied by Nietzsche's emphatic "On the contrary," Strauss neglects to mention the other, negative half—namely, that Nietzsche's manner of vindicating God almost utters the ultimate blasphemy against the God of our fathers. For if half of "On the contrary" states that God is vindicated, the other half states that the devil is refuted.

The reaction of Nietzsche's friends to his will to power teaching shows that they need new lessons in divinity because their thinking about the divine is still dictated by the dead God in whom they no longer believe. Trapped in that conception, even free minds hear the will to power teaching as demonic. Let their lesson in divinity begin starkly with a mere reversal of God and devil. The devil refuted by the will to power teaching is the God of our fathers, that transcendent, all-powerful being whose sovereignty made all of us his slaves.

This unmentioned half of Nietzsche's implied conclusion is, of course, not at all a new idea to Strauss, for Strauss had had his fun with it on other occasions, most notably when he called attention to Machiavelli's subtly stated blasphemy that "God is a tyrant" (TM 49, 187–88, cf. 185, 231).[11] And it seems to be implied as well when Strauss described the principles on which Socrates based his actions: they did *not* include "a categorical imperative demanding passive obedience" (WPP 33).[12] By the Machiavellian standard made so entertaining by Strauss, not only is Nietzsche a great blasphemer, Nietzsche knows how to blaspheme best:

> When a man openly utters or vomits a blasphemy, all good men shudder and turn away from him, or punish him according to his deserts; the sin is entirely his. But a concealed blasphemy is so insidious, not only because it protects the blasphemer against punishment by due process of law, but above all because it practically compels the hearer or reader to think the blasphemy by himself and thus to become an accomplice of the blasphemer. [He] thus establishes a kind of intimacy with his readers . . . by inducing them to think forbidden or criminal thoughts (SPPP 224–25).

Nietzsche's lovely little dialogue in response to the one reasoned presentation of will to power in his book shows him establishing intimacy, corrupting his friends. And Strauss? Neither shocked nor deterred, Strauss helps his readers enter Nietzsche's blasphemy in the fitting way; by refusing to lay out the concealed blasphemy, he compels his readers to think out the blasphemy on their own and become accomplices to the blasphemer.

The devil—to speak popularly—is our old God, the God who forced

---

11. Nowhere is this blasphemy more finely put than in the central essay of the third and final part of Montaigne's *Essays,* entitled "Of the disadvantage of greatness" (iii.7). Montaigne's essay assails the supposed greatness of the sovereign God and follows the advice of its opening sentence: "Since we cannot attain it, let us take our revenge by speaking ill of it."

12. On monotheism and tyranny see TM 207 and Nietzsche's GS 143, entitled "The greatest advantage of polytheism."

us to judge the world demonic by placing the world under the powers of the Prince of Darkness, the Prince of this World. With Christianity, as Nietzsche said, "'world' becomes a term of abuse" (*CW* Epilogue; *BGE* 195). In Nietzsche's contrary view, this abused world becomes the place of divinity. Strauss's three references at the end of his paragraph refer to Nietzsche's advocacy of the earthly god Dionysos. Any vindication of God, however, that points to earthly Dionysos can not long tolerate loose speech about the devil made popular by the old God. For this reason, Nietzsche's lesson in divinity continues by showing that earthly religion has no place for the concept devil. After Nietzsche himself has employed the popular idiom to make his main point, he says to his friends: "And, to the devil, what forces you to speak popularly?" What but that old Devil himself, dead but not gone, present still as a gruesome shadow of our only language of divinity (*GS* 108)? As long as his friends speak popularly, employing the categories of an old Platonism for the people, Nietzsche can simply invert God and devil to indict the old God and vindicate the new. But such simplistic polarities will have to be replaced in the religion arising out of the new philosophy.[13]

In the final sentence of this paragraph, the sentence taking leave of the philosophy chapters, Strauss mentions as an aside that will to power is "the whole doctrine of *Beyond Good and Evil*." Strauss himself has used this doctrine to make a single point about the philosophy chapters, namely, how the new philosophy comes to rule religion. But that doctrine lies at the base of everything said in *Beyond Good and Evil*. The will to power teaching will necessarily make its reappearance in Strauss's discussion of other points in *Beyond Good and Evil* because it is the ultimate ground of all those points.

When Strauss says five times of the doctrine of the will to power that it is a vindication of God, does he mean to praise Nietzsche's basic doctrine or to blame it? The fundamental issue that Strauss has isolated is the rule of philosophy over religion or of religion over philosophy. In the terms set down by this alternative, a doctrine is bad insofar as it leaves philosophy in tutelage to religion and good insofar as it frees philosophy from religion or, more precisely, enables philosophy to rule religion. Strauss's essay shows that the manner in which the will to power doctrine vindicates God sets what

13. Nietzsche shares with certain forms of ancient gnosticism the view that the creator God of Genesis is the devil, but he is as far as possible from being a gnostic: *his* judgment against God is not based on the view that the world is so fallen that its creator must be evil. Instead, Nietzsche's judgment is based on the experience that the world is good as it is, uncreated, unfallen, and unredeemed. From a Nietzschean perspective, gnosticism is merely an intensification of the biblical sense of the world, plausibly extending its revulsion at the world to the world's creator.

is high, religion, under what is highest, philosophy. Or, in slightly different language, the will to power doctrine finds a way to align the good with the true; it frees the true from an all-too-human standard of the good and begins the long process of teaching humanity to find the true good.[14]

HOW PHILOSOPHY RULES RELIGION

Paragraph Strauss begins his account of Nietzsche's chapter "Das Religiöse Wesen" by
10 stating why it is not entitled "Das Wesen der Religion." This odd procedure is in fact perfectly reasonable: without saying so, Strauss is again contrasting Nietzsche and Plato. The search for the essence of a thing, its idea, is obsolete, replaced by the Nietzschean search, a form of inquiry which Strauss immediately describes: the history or genealogy of a thing. The essence or idea of religion, that unattainable grail of an obsolete Platonism, "is not or should not be of any concern to us." It has already been established that the world of concern to us is the whole world, the totality of things as will to power; that world does not include the essences or ideas of things.[15]

Strauss notes on the plan of the chapter on religion that it is divided into

---

14. In a valuable introduction to *SPPP* that repays close attention, Thomas Pangle asks why Strauss would place his Nietzsche essay "at the very center of his last work" and suggests that it is because Nietzsche radicalizes and makes permanent Christianity's capture of philosophy (24–25). Pangle argues that the essay is in the right place after "Jerusalem and Athens" because it shows how Nietzsche extended Christianity's capture of philosophy and prepared the way for Heidegger's replacement of political philosophy by god or the gods. For Pangle, therefore, Nietzsche is a mere step in the eradication of the Socratic procedure which had successfully preserved the refutability of religion while maintaining religion's popular necessity. Pangle thus interprets Strauss's repeated phrase "the doctrine of the will to power is in a manner a vindication of God" as indicating that for Strauss Nietzsche advanced the rule of religion over philosophy. As I see it, there are three primary difficulties with this interpretation. First, Strauss's text makes "reasoning" foundational to Nietzsche's view and makes the new religion derivative from that reasoning. Second, in the latter half of his essay Strauss shows that what truly endangers philosophy in the modern age is modern secular religion, and that Nietzsche set out to emancipate philosophy from this now dominant religion. Third, if Strauss in fact held that Nietzsche allowed philosophy to pass into the tyranny of religion, if he in fact criticized Nietzsche for this most fateful of turns, why shelter such a conclusion? He did not shelter it in the case of Heidegger. It seems a frivolous exercise to hide a useful truth if it fully accords with the public stance and would help illuminate that stance.

15. How little Strauss's world included the Platonic ideas in any traditional sense is indicated by his discussion of them in *CM*: not only does Strauss say that the doctrine "is very hard to understand; to begin with, it is utterly incredible, not to say that it appears to be fantastic"; he also implies that its rhetorical utility is dependent upon prior beliefs in gods like *Dike* and *Nike* or, better still, in gods like those of the theology of the *Republic* (*CM* 119–21). Strauss's own use for the doctrine seems to be indicated by what he says of Socrates: Socrates "viewed man in the light of the unchangeable ideas, i.e., of the fundamental and permanent problems" (*WPP* 39). The doctrine of the unchangeable ideas proves changeable indeed.

three parts: religion hitherto, the religion of the future, and Nietzsche's appraisal of religion as a whole. Strauss completely ignores the third, highly charged part with its account of "what religion is good for" (aph. 58) and permits his discussion to end on the religion of the future.

In analyzing the first part, religion hitherto, Strauss addresses one of his own great themes, "Athens and Jerusalem." He raises the old Greeks to "Old Greeks," putting them on a level with the "Old Testament." And he claims that Nietzsche's two aphorisms on the Old Greeks and the Old Testament interrupt the aphorisms on Christianity in order to measure Christianity and judge it from a superior height. But Strauss seems to ignore the aphorism on Greek religion. Noble Greeks, Nietzsche says (aph. 49), created a religion that exudes an enormous abundance of gratitude. Later Greek religion, post-noble Greek religion, became a religion of the rabble which trafficked in fear and prepared the way for Christianity. Nietzsche's more extensive descriptions of this historic Greek shift away from Homer indict Plato: Plato is the Greek philosopher most responsible for the success of base religion with its just gods and immortal souls, the religion not of gratitude but of revenge. For Nietzsche himself, it seems that the "old Greeks" measure not so much Christianity as Christianity's precursor, Plato.

Strauss makes use of Nietzsche's two "interrupting aphorisms" to draw his own conclusion about "the distance or rather opposition" between Athens and Jerusalem. Concentrating on the aphorism on the Old Testament, Strauss, unlike Nietzsche, emphasizes what distinguishes the Old Testament from Greek theology, namely, "the conception, the creation of the holy God." Strauss's reference to *Dawn of Morning* aph. 68 makes his implied point even stronger: the holy God is shared by Old and New Testaments, marking both testaments off from the Old Greeks and their Homeric theology. Jerusalem in both its creations, holy God and holy man, differs radically from the noble religion of Old Greeks based in gratitude.

Strauss ends his paragraph on what is, in a way, "Das Wesen der Religion": human will to power, the creative source of both noble religion and base religion. The will to power as the way of all beings and of human beings is of concern to us because it provides the ultimate explanatory principle for phenomena that might otherwise be taken to be fundamental or self-explanatory—"*superfluous* teleological principles" (*BGE* 13).

But there is something peculiar about Nietzsche's vindication of God: *Paragraph* "Nietzsche's vindication of God is then atheistic, at least for the time being." *11* At least for the time being, as Nietzsche recognizes, atheism is the only possible response to the death of the old God. Those liberated by that death into the pleasures of a free mind no longer like to hear of God or gods, as Nietzsche admits to them when he forces them to hear of Dionysos and Ariadne (aph. 295). Strauss's paragraph reflects on the aphorism "Why atheism today?" (53). Though for a time theism "was true, i.e. powerful, life-giving," it has lost its power. Nietzsche gives a lovely, lighthearted account of the reasons that moved his contemporaries to atheism, and Strauss observes that "Not a few of his better readers will justifiably think that those reasons verge on the frivolous." Those better readers would have included a kind that Nietzsche thinks has now become rare, those few who are reluctant to advocate atheism because they still know "what religions are good for" (aph. 58). Although "it is not quite clear" whether the reasons Nietzsche gives are directed against a natural (rational) theology or revealed theology, it is completely clear that the most powerful argument is against revelation, against the very possibility of revelation. There might be a place, therefore, for a kind of natural or rational theology after the current atheism has run its course, for our atheism is the completely reasonable response to the long sway of the God of revealed religion. That wretched communicator now stands completely exposed, found wanting by our refined moral and intellectual standards, as one of the aphorisms in *Dawn of Morning* (91) cited by Strauss shows: "A god who is all-knowing and all-powerful and who does not even make sure that his creatures understand his intention—could that be a god of goodness?"

Strauss emphasizes a crucial but neglected point in Nietzsche's account of religion: the current and necessary atheism is not the final stopping place for the philosophers of the future; "atheism is only a transitional phase." To what? Strauss answers this question in a subtle, lighthearted fashion by telling a Nietzschean joke, a joke that makes a fine contribution to the continuous theme of the essay, the contrast of Nietzsche and Plato. But Strauss adds to the joke—he alters it by one iota. Strauss asks whether "a certain kind of non-atheism belongs to the philosopher of the future who will again worship the god Dionysos or will again be, as an Epicurean might say, a *dionysokolax* (cf. aph. 7)." Well, an Epicurean might say that. But if we do what we're told and "cf. aph. 7" we find that what Strauss's Epicurean might say is ever so slightly different from what Epicurus himself actually said. Nietzsche says he knows "of nothing more venomous than the joke Epicurus permitted himself against Plato and the Platonists: he called them *dionysiokolakes*." Epicurus's venomous pun added a single iota to the popular name for an actor, *dionysokolax*—flatterer of Dionysos. Plato and his Platonists, says Epicurus, they're not only actors, devotees of Dionysos, they're actors who flatter the tyrant Dionysios. Epicurus's venom, Nietzsche suggests, could well be the spite that a garden god, retired from politics, directed against a mighty rival who refused to retire behind the garden wall and whose public actions required that he tie the future of philosophy, or of his philosophy, to a tyrant's favor. Of course no Epicurean could say of Nietzsche that *he* is a *dionysiokolax*. But Strauss suggests that an Epicurean might well say that "the philosopher of the future will *again* be" a *dionysokolax*, that Nietzsche, like Plato, belongs to Dionysos's company as an actor. Strauss subtracts the venom from Epicurus's joke by subtracting the single iota Epicurus added. And in this way he makes a little joke of his own: from an Epicurean point of view, looking out over the garden wall, Plato and Nietzsche can be seen to belong together, both *dionysokolakes*, actors who argue philosophy's case outside the garden wall, pursuing a philosophic politics geared to remake that outside world by turning a world hostile to philosophy into one friendly to philosophy. Plato played the risky game by flattering the tyrant. Nietzsche played the risky game without such flattery.

What will the religion of the future be like? The past and present of *Paragraph* philosophy can help supply an answer because the religion of the future has *12* a rationale; it is no accident that it arises at just this point in our spiritual history and that it takes the form that it does. Strauss focuses on Nietzsche's next aphorisms (54 and 55), dealing with modern philosophy and its consequence, nihilism. The "anti-Christian but not anti-religious" character of modern philosophy (54) does not "point to something reminding of the Vedanta philosophy" but to "a more Western, a sterner, more terrible and more invigorating possibility" (55). This possibility, intrinsic to our own tradition, appears as a consequence of the final rung of religious cruelty, the sacrificing from cruelty of God himself. Strauss calls this cruel sacrifice "the will to power turning against itself." He will later follow Nietzsche and describe this spiritual mechanism of cruel self-deprivation as the work of the youngest virtue, honesty.

Aphorism 55 claims that sacrificing God prepares a next phase: "the worshipping of the stone, stupidity, heaviness (gravity), fate, the Nothing. . . . All of us already know something of this." Strauss credits Nietzsche with a primary insight into our times, for "the better among the contemporary atheists will come to know what they are doing." They will not be shallow optimists like Engels, a stand-in for the whole Hegelian school who believe in the End of History as the age of grace. The "better among contemporary atheists . . . will come to realize that there is something infinitely more terrible, depressing and degrading in the offing" than the *foeda religio*, the shit religion, faced by Roman philosophers[16] or the infamous thing Enlightenment thinkers wanted to erase. What will these contemporary thinkers face that is so much worse than Christianity? "The possibility, nay, the fact that human life is utterly meaningless and lacking support." This of course is not a strictly modern realization: Strauss's reference to Anaxagoras implies that this possibility was faced by the better ancients as well. Nevertheless, moderns will face the basic cosmological fact in a more direct way. This is one of the facts, one of the deadly truths, within which the whole of Nietzsche's thought occurs, and Strauss indicates this constant in Nietzsche's thought by referring to the little parable with which Nietzsche began a very early unpublished essay ("On Truth and Lie in an Extra-Moral Sense," 1873), the parable of the clever animal on an obscure planet who invented knowledge, eventually the knowledge of its own and its planet's ultimate extinction.

Paragraph 13   But Strauss knows very well that Nietzsche does not belong even to these nihilists, to "the better among the contemporary atheists": "Nietzsche does not mean to sacrifice God for the sake of the Nothing." Strauss's Nietzsche is no nihilist. Instead, Nietzsche thinks nihilism through to its depths and glimpses a new ideal. In this way, Strauss follows Nietzsche's route into aphorism 56, the one aphorism in *Beyond Good and Evil* that provides access to what Nietzsche said was his most important teaching, eternal return. Strauss's pursuit of the religion of the future culminates in reflection on eternal return. And the reflection on eternal return that begins here in the appropriate way, by following Nietzsche's lead into the logic of its affirmation, will be carried forward through the rest of the essay. What is implied in affirming eternal return? Is such an affirmation defensible? Strauss will show why it is defensible by showing why it is necessary. And why its affirmation achieves philosophy's rule over religion.

Nietzsche is no nihilist: he aims "to discover in the depth of the deadly truth its opposite." In this way too—as with the will to power teaching— Nietzsche "does his best to break the power of the deadly truth" (paragraph 7). Strauss describes Nietzsche's self-presentation in aphorism 56: Nietzsche "grasped a more world-denying way of thinking than that of any previous pessimist." Yet precisely by following that route of world-denial, Nietzsche was able to open his eyes to the opposite ideal, "the ideal belonging to the religion of the future." Strauss's determined pursuit of the question of the rule of philosophy over religion in the first chapters of *Beyond Good and Evil* now reaches its final stage: Nietzsche's philosophy achieves insight into

16. In *CW*, Epilogue, Nietzsche says, "Noble Romans experienced Christianity as *foeda superstitio*."

the fundamental fact of will to power, and that very insight, seemingly so world-denying, flowers into a new religion whose ideal is the opposite of the world-denying ideal that has prevailed in our culture till now. Nihilism, "adoration of the Nothing," proves to be what Nietzsche always said it could be, "the indispensable transition from every kind of world-denial to the most unbounded Yes: the eternal Yes-saying to everything that was and is." Strauss's immediate comment on this affirmation is nicely ironic: What a conservatism!, he says in effect, a conservatism "beyond the wildest wishes of all other conservatives." But this conservatism is "serviceable for revolutionary purposes"—and the second half of the essay will reveal the historical roots of this revolution and point to the present as its decisive moment.

Strauss ends his presentation of Nietzsche's most important thought Nietzscheanly, ambiguously, by reflecting on the final ambiguous words of aphorism 56: "And this would not be *circulus vitiosus deus?*"—a vicious circle made god? god is a vicious circle? the circle is a vicious god? Nietzsche's "atheism is not unambiguous," Strauss says, but then he provides a possible key to the ambiguity: "The conclusion of the present aphorism," Strauss says, "reminds us, through its form, of the theological aphorism occurring in the first two chapters (37)." Perhaps the likeness of form conveys a likeness of content, for just here Strauss repeats that the doctrine of will to power is a vindication of God. Is eternal return a vicious circle made god? The likeness of form between the aphorism that ends on this question and aphorism 37, Strauss seems to suggest, implies that its question too can be answered as the earlier question was answered: "On the contrary! On the contrary, my friends!" This time the contrary is that eternal return transforms the apparently vicious circle of dying and rising life into something divine; the circle of eternal return is the circle denoted religiously by dying and rising Dionysos. The new religion celebrates life as the highest. In this way, the religion of the future grows naturally out of the philosophy of the future as an earthly religion that affirms life.

A RELAPSE INTO PLATONISM

Strauss now brings his reflections on philosophy and religion in Nietzsche *Paragraph* to a dramatic conclusion by showing how eternal return, that oddest and *14* most enigmatic of Nietzsche's teachings, in fact has an altogether appropriate grounding in philosophy. The argument given here on behalf of eternal return ties it to the fundamental fact; a second argument, given later, will tie it to its historic moment, our moment, in the history of the human spirit.

The paragraph is surely one of the finest in Strauss's essay: dramatic, urgent, demanding, hiding a whole world of philosophical debate in a few questions, it plunges inexorably to a most surprising conclusion. Beginning with what confronts us now—the possible rise of the religion of the future out of contemporary nihilism—it raises the most challenging issue in a series of six separate questions that end in a decisive if somewhat veiled answer. The questions pass from a vulgar Nietzscheanism—Isn't this mere willfulness?—to the answer of a profound Platonism—No, it is love for the most lovable beloved. And the questions and answers intimate the fundamental argument that can be made on Nietzsche's behalf: Nietzsche is linked to Plato on the primacy of eros; he too is a comprehensive thinker who affirms in love the object of his thought.

The paragraph reflects further on the event described in aphorism 56, the sudden transformation of the most world-denying pessimism into the unbounded Yes-saying to everything that was and is. Strauss's questioning confronts "the fact that the vindication of God is only the inversion of the sacrificing of God to stupidity, to the Nothing, or at any rate presupposes that sacrificing." Nietzsche's vindication of God presupposes the modern choice against God, probity's sacrifice of ˜God, its willingness to live or die without that comforting life-supporting lie. But even if the transformation presupposes this conscious choice of nihilism, even if it presupposes "our virtue" of the most uncompromising honesty, do we not have to say that the inversion itself is an affront to honesty, that it is mere willfulness dependent upon the heart tricking the mind to yield to new gods?

Strauss's first question asks: "What is it that suddenly, if after a long preparation, divinizes the Nothing?" Two possibilities are presented by the series of five more questions that follow, and they are reminiscent of the possibilities presented by Socrates' question in the *Euthyphro* (10a), "Is the pious loved by the gods because it is pious, or is it pious because it is loved?" The second and third questions ask if the transformation of the world is merely the result of willing eternity, if the world is simply at the disposal of a powerful will. They thus evoke the fourth question: "Is beloved eternity divine merely because it is beloved?" In answer, Strauss poses the opposite possibility as something that would initially seem contradictory to a Nietzschean view of will and world: "If we were to say that it must be in itself lovable, in order to deserve to be loved, would we not become guilty of a relapse into Platonism, into the teaching of 'the good in itself'?" Has Strauss isolated a fatal incoherence in Nietzsche's thought? Does saying Yes to everything that was and is involve *either* a mere willfulness contrary to our probity *or* a Platonism contrary to Nietzsche's essential teaching?

"But can we avoid such a relapse altogether?" Strauss's opening "But" requires that the previous question be understood as already answered: Yes, we would be guilty of a relapse into Platonism. But can we avoid it? No, we cannot avoid such a relapse and Nietzsche does not avoid it. The questions are over and Strauss ends his paragraph with two sentences of assertions. "For the eternal to which Nietzsche says Yes, is not the stone, the stupidity, the Nothing which even if eternal or sempiternal cannot arouse an enthusiastic, life-inspiring Yes." To what does Nietzsche say Yes? To the very thing his inquiry into the stone, the stupidity, the Nothing had finally led him, to the world as will to power; *that* can arouse an enthusiastic, life-inspiring Yes: "The transformation of the world-denying way of thinking into the opposite ideal is connected with the realization or divination that the stone, the stupidity or the Nothing to which God is being sacrificed, is in its 'intelligible character' the will to power (cf. aph. 36)." Strauss keeps his distance from this crucial point—"realization or divination"[17]—but the argument is clear: the Yes of eternal return is based on the insight that the world in its intelligible character is will to power and nothing besides. The most unbounded affirmation of the world derives from the most comprehensive insight into the world and its intelligible character. The highest ideal, the highest value, is an affirmation that flows from insight into the fundamental fact.

Is this profound complex of insight and affirmation fully visible in *Beyond Good and Evil?* Strauss's isolation of the fundamental topics of will to power and eternal return certainly makes the inner connection between them more prominent than *Beyond Good and Evil* by itself ever does. Strauss does not state here but he intimates later that this complex of insight into will to power and affirmation of eternal return is the dramatic core of Nietzsche's most important book, *Thus Spoke Zarathustra,* the book which Strauss's opening paragraph pointed to as his most profound. The poetic form of *Zarathustra* depicts a lover in pursuit of the highest beloved. Who is that beloved? Is it Wisdom? Or is it Life? The philosopher Zarathustra at first confuses the two, but Life gradually wins her proper precedence and does so by revealing her secret: "Life is will to power." Granted insight into that secret, Zarathustra moves to the ultimate affirmation of eternal return. When Life, now divined as who she is, finally hears from her lover the affirming words, "Eternally return," Life takes the name Eternity. The marriage song of Zarathustra and Eternity sung at the climax of *Thus Spoke*

---

17. Perhaps Strauss has in mind Nietzsche's definition of divination: "The power of understanding with only the least assistance, at the slightest suggestion, 'intelligent' *sensuality* (*Sinnlichkeit*)" (*KGW* VIII 14 [117] = *WP* 800).

Zarathustra celebrates in a new form the marriage of Dionysos and Ariadne, the sacred marriage that celebrates earthly life.[18] *Zarathustra* exists to display the inner logic of insight and affirmation at the core of Nietzsche's thought, and *Beyond Good and Evil* was planned as a strategic book, a fishhook that would catch contemporaries and draw them almost unawares into that profound core (*EH* Books *BGE*). Eternal return belongs to Nietzsche's thought as its affirmative culmination: life is lovable as it is. Strauss's little essay depicts that inner logic of love in his own chosen sobriety, with constant reference to philosophy's other great erotic, Plato. Is Nietzsche's thought a relapse into Platonism? Philosophy cannot avoid such a relapse. Philosophy is a lover's passion for the greatest of beloveds.

Nietzsche is guilty of a relapse into Platonism. Strauss thus begins to suggest that Nietzsche recovers and makes explicit the essential passionate core of philosophy that has made every great thinker a "Platonist," an erotic in love with the world.

The whole history of philosophy must be reconsidered from this affirmative Nietzschean perspective, for the lover's passion can be seen to be present throughout, from philosophy's first beginnings in the tragic age of the Greeks, through the emergency conditions that forced it to cower in a falsifying ascetic dress, up to the present dangerous situation which compels it to come into the open as self-affirming and world-affirming. Discerning such a continuity, a Nietzschean history of philosophy could say with Lessing, "there is no other philosophy than that of Spinoza" (*PAW* 182).[19]

Nietzsche's relapse into Platonism is expressed, at its peak, in the eternal Yes-saying to everything that was and is. Eternal return is the new highest ideal and can therefore be understood as a form of edification, an affirmation of the world that ennobles the world by being "the highest formula of affirmation that is at all attainable" (*EH* Books *Z*). At the end of *Thoughts on Machiavelli* Strauss had said, "For while 'philosophy must beware of wishing to be edifying,' it is of necessity edifying" (*TM* 299; see *LAM* 8). In his Nietzsche essay, Strauss indicates that Nietzsche was not moved by the wish to be edifying. Instead, he was a thinker "prompted by 'some enigmatic desire'" to think pessimism through to its depth and to liberate it from the delusions of morality that had hitherto prevented it from reaching its depth. As a consequence of this exercise of thought, Nietzsche "grasped a more world-denying way of thinking than that of any previous pessimist" (para-

18. For a detailed account of these events see Lampert, *Nietzsche's Teaching*.
19. I return to the theme of a Nietzschean history of philosophy below, pp. 121–26.

graph 13). If Nietzsche then found his eyes opened to the opposite ideal, he did so *"without intending to do this"* (emphasis added). Nietzsche did not set out to be edifying; he set out to inquire, to pursue inquiry with the most intransigent intellectual probity wherever it would lead. In the fundamental words Nietzsche had employed earlier to criticize philosophy's subjection to edification, Nietzsche himself did not "seek the true only to do the good" (aph. 35)—he sought the true. And if the good—a new sense of the good, an opposite ideal—clarified itself at the deepest point of his inquiry, it was not for the sake of that discovery that Nietzsche had first set out or persisted in his inquiry. It was philosophy and not religion that guided Nietzsche fundamentally; only in the end, only with eternal return, did he discover a new and natural link between philosophy and religion. Nietzsche ended with an edifying teaching because ultimately inquiry is of necessity edifying— philosophy arrives at a love of the whole that necessarily edifies, even if its edification is not always evident to the otherwise pious. Eternal return is philosophy's *natural* edifying teaching; it does not comfort itself or others with the next world ostensibly more perfect than our own; it says of the only world there is, or rather it "shouts insatiably" (aph. 56) to the world as it is: Be what you are, be eternally what you are.

In his final paragraph on religion, Strauss calls attention to something *Paragraph* he will not speak about because he has "no access" to it: "an important in- *15* gredient, not to say the nerve, of Nietzsche's 'theology.'" Strauss avows no access to Dionysos and Ariadne about whom Nietzsche had the nerve to speak as if they actually appeared to him, as if he actually participated in those dialogues on Naxos. Strauss is resolute on this matter: "I have not spoken and shall not speak." This refusal on Strauss's part seems to be something more than the reflex of apparent loyalty to a wholly different religious tradition. It seems to be Strauss's confession that he is in no position to make a judgment about the viability of this aspect of Nietzsche's attempt to bring religion under the rule of philosophy, Nietzsche's attempt amid the ruins of revealed or otherworldly religion to initiate in its place a naturalistic religion based on gods who philosophize, who love the earth, and who are well disposed toward humanity (*BGE* 295). (Though if Strauss had *no* access to this issue, he hardly seems to be in a position to judge that it had been "worthily treated" by Karl Reinhardt.)

But even though Strauss avows no access to Dionysos and Ariadne, he has exhibited the crucial matter: being the last disciple and initiate of the god Dionysos is not the incidental preoccupation of an aesthete enamored with antique religion. It is instead one of the ways in which the philosophy of the future sets out to rule religion: by reviving the earthly religion akin to its own profound eros. Dionysian or earthly religion belongs to the new philosophy as its corollary in another mode, the mode of god-creation that has always formed a part of the human picturing of the world with respect to the highest and best things. The vindication of God implicit in the teachings of will to power and eternal return points to a particular, non-theistic conception of gods, one with a long tradition predating our particular theistic conceptions, though a tradition now long dead thanks to the predatory tyranny of the religion of the jealous God, a grave, centuries-long event in our history, the most fateful event since the advent of philosophy. Despite its gravity, Nietzsche could transform this event into his best joke: "One of the gods announced one day, 'There is only one God. Thou shalt have no other gods before me,' and all the other gods—died laughing" (Z 3.8 "On Apostates"). The death of that presumptuous deity presages the rebirth of the laughing gods.

Strauss's argument on philosophy and religion in Nietzsche shows how the philosophy of the future, the new understanding of the whole, flowers into the religion of the future, a world-affirming religion with a new highest ideal. Only later in his essay will Strauss add the other essential dimension to his argument, the historical considerations which show how the contemporary crisis, the virulence of modern ideas, necessitated Nietzsche's dramatic step. This much, however, can be said already: Nietzsche sets out to accomplish philosophy's rule over religion by generating values true to the earth, opposite values to those employed by Plato in his successful accomplishment of philosophy's rule over religion.

It seems reasonable to suppose that Strauss was aided in gaining insight into this most comprehensive matter of rule in Nietzsche by his study of Alfarabi, the great Medieval Platonist who was one of Strauss's philosophical masters. "Religion is an imitation of philosophy," Alfarabi says, for philosophy grasps the ideas of things with the intellect by means of certain demonstrations, while religion grasps similitudes of things with the imagination by means of persuasive methods.[20] The true philosopher is a legislator (section 57) who possesses both the theoretical sciences and the faculty for exploring them for the benefit of all others according to their capacity (54). Those others, *all* others besides the philosopher (51), are the multitude, and the multitude assents to the images of things which take hold of their souls and dominate them so that they are unable to resolve to do anything except what those images dictate (59). Knowing the difference between himself and the

---

20. *Alfarabi's Philosophy of Plato and Aristotle*, "The Attainment of Happiness," section 55.

multitude to be a difference between knowledge and opinion or between philosophy and religion, the true philosopher "is the one who invents the images and the persuasive arguments [for the multitude], but not for the sake of establishing these things in his own soul as a religion for himself" (59). Alfarabi credits Plato with establishing this view of the philosopher as a commander and legislator who creates values or who rules the multitude through religion. It is identical to the view that Strauss, student of Alfarabi, finds in Nietzsche as well as in Plato.

Given Strauss's refusal to assess this aspect of Nietzsche's work, it seems fitting to ask at the end of his paragraphs on philosophy and religion: Is Strauss the Epicurean who might say that Nietzsche is a *dionysokolax?* Is he the observer who watches from behind the protection of his own garden wall and sees what Plato and Nietzsche share in their daring attempts to bring philosophy to rule through a new religion?

Interlude: "Sayings and Interludes"
Chapter 4: Centering Nature

KNOWLEDGE AND SELF-KNOWLEDGE

According to the plan Strauss gives, chapter 4, "Sayings and Interludes," separates the two main parts of *Beyond Good and Evil*, the first devoted chiefly to philosophy and religion, the second devoted chiefly to morals and politics (paragraph 6). To begin his account of the "about 123 'Sayings and Interludes,'"[21] Strauss suggests that it is possible but not likely that they have no order, "that there is no rhyme or reason to their selection and sequence." But then he offers a temptation, not to say a provocation: "a few observations which are perhaps helpful to some of us." Which ones? And "us"? Could Strauss himself have been helped by these observations? Strauss's observations ascribe a very tight sequential order of argument to Nietzsche's aphorisms. But the argument is extremely cryptic and its point extremely dark; nevertheless, some of Strauss's implications seem clear enough. *Paragraph 16*

The rhyme or reason Strauss finds in the aphorisms or attributes to them consists of a series of inferences tracing a single topic: the knowledge sought and attained by that very special knower who seeks knowledge of nature. Nature is made the central theme of the Sayings and Interludes in *Paragraph 17*

21. "About" because chapter 4 contains the aphorisms numbered 63 to 185; 123 aphorisms except for the fact that there are two 65s and two 73s.

this the 17th paragraph—and "17 stands for nature."[22] Strauss's account of chapter 4 thus serves a preparatory function: nature will be the one great theme of the second part of his essay, the foundation of the morals and politics to which Nietzsche points.

Nietzsche's opening aphorism (63) draws Strauss's attention "to the paramountcy of being-oneself, or being for oneself, of 'preserving' oneself (cf. aph. 41)," but only because the aphorism itself draws attention to the opposite, to one who exists for others, the teacher who exists for his pupils. Not aphorism 63 but aphorism 41 speaks directly of the paramountcy of being-oneself; there Nietzsche's subject is the person "destined for independence and command," the one forced by his nature to play "the most dangerous game" of never sticking fast in any localism or loyalty. This, apparently, is the subject of Strauss's reflection, the thinker driven by inquiry to sever all attachments of the heart; such a person "must know how to preserve oneself: the hardest test of independence" (41).

The paramountcy of being for oneself and never sticking fast means that knowledge cannot be good for its own sake: Strauss's second sentence refers to Nietzsche's second aphorism as if it were a conclusion drawn from his first; it treats Nietzsche's first two aphorisms as if they were related by implication. And Strauss carries the conclusion beyond what is actually stated in the second aphorism: "knowledge is justifiable only as self-knowledge." Strauss's interpretation of this Socratic injunction to know thyself leads him to draw a further conclusion on his own: "being oneself means being honest with oneself, going the way to one's own ideal." Honesty and Nietzsche's own going the way to his ideal will be major themes in Strauss's account of the following chapters. Strauss's sequence of inferences now culminates in the final inference he draws: "This seems to have atheistic implications." The atheistic implication leads Strauss to count—to miscount. He says there are nine references to God, one to nature (126) and "instead" of more references to nature, nine to woman and man. There is in fact only one reference to nature, but there are ten references to God and there are five references to woman and man, and five to woman as *Weib*, and two to women as *Frauen*. The arbitrary symmetry invented by miscounting creates an odd troika that allows nature to stand singled out at the center surrounded by an equal number of references to God and to woman and man, to divine nature and noble

---

22. Strauss, "How to Begin to Study *The Guide*" xxx. On this and other references to numbers, it is useful to remember Strauss's statement about "the significance of the number *seven* in" Maimonides: "Considerations of this kind are necessarily somewhat playful," *WPP* 165. Consider also what Strauss says about "hints" in that essay, 162, 166.

nature, perhaps. Would anyone care to believe that Strauss believed that this is the order *Nietzsche* gave to his chapter?

But not only has Strauss miscounted and centered the theme of nature, he has shown why he used the word "seems" when he spoke of the "atheistic implications" of being for oneself: among the nine references to God is one to "Nietzsche's own theology": Nietzsche's seeming atheism remains an ambiguity because his thought clearly harbors a theology about which he has a fitting reluctance to speak. This ambiguity preserves the character of Nietzsche's thought as an experiment or temptation (paragraph 11).

Strauss now moves to firmer ground, leaving behind imaginative counting and ambiguity: "Surely" is the first word of the next sentence. "Surely the knower whom Nietzsche has in mind has not, like Kant, the starred heaven above himself." (This is a reference to aphorism 71, though it is not cited by number.) Surely the seemingly atheistic knower is unlike the theist Kant; the knower Nietzsche has in mind is not moved to self-diminishment in the face of the starred heaven, he does not place the heavens "above" himself. Strauss draws a noteworthy conclusion from this order of rank between humans and the heavens which distinguishes Kant and Nietzsche: "As a consequence" of this "demoting or degrading of heaven and the heavenly lights,"[23] the knower Nietzsche has in mind "has a high morality." A seeming atheism that demotes heaven leads to a high morality.

Just what is this high morality that is derivative from the paramountcy of being for oneself and demoting heaven? The second half of Strauss's essay will describe this new morality in detail, grounding it in nature, the subject Strauss is now making central. It will not be a Kantian morality that defers to some supposed moral law within in order to rescue human dignity from its supposed diminishment under the starred heaven, a heaven full of idols. It is—Strauss continues—"a morality beyond good and evil and in particular beyond puritanism and asceticism." Puritanism and asceticism, moralities of good and evil, are the almost indispensable instruments for educating and ennobling an ascendant race working its way up to rule—so says aphorism 61, an aphorism not referred to here by number. In addition to describing puritanism and asceticism as historic preparations for rule, aphorism 61 describes some aspects of the high morality of the philosopher himself, the morality of the one with the most comprehensive responsibility for the overall development of humanity.

The high morality of the knower Nietzsche has in mind requires free-

23. See "Jerusalem and Athens" (*SPPP*) 153; *PAW* 20; Kant, *Critique of Practical Reason,* "Conclusion."

dom and bondage at the same time: "Precisely because he is concerned with the freedom of his mind, he must imprison his heart (87, 107)." For the mind to rule the heart, for philosophy to rule religion in the commonwealth of one's own being, the heart must be bound as Odysseus was bound before hearing the Sirens' song. But in presenting this thought from aphorism 87, Strauss has added a reference to aphorism 107, and aphorism 107 says that it is a sign of strong character that one closes one's ears even to the best counterargument once the decision has been made. "Therefore," Nietzsche concludes, "an occasional will to stupidity." Strauss then states the ground for such stupidity, for tethering one's heart to what the mind has chosen and listening to no more reasons: "Freedom of one's mind is not possible without a dash of stupidity (9)." This reference is to the aphorism which calls philosophy "the most spiritual will to power, to the 'creation of the world.'" Creation of a world seems to be what happens around a god according to the one aphorism on Nietzsche's own theology to which Strauss has just called attention (150).

The first part of Strauss's final sentence paraphrases what Nietzsche stated in the aphorisms Strauss cites (80–81, 231, 249): "Self-knowledge is not only very difficult but impossible to achieve." Knowledge may be justifiable only as self-knowledge, but pursuit of self-knowledge ultimately recognizes an impenetrable ignorance: it knows it does not know. The aphorism to which Strauss refers last (249) states this conclusion in terms of the virtues: "The best that one is, one knows not, one can not know." Strauss's relentless sequence of conclusions in pursuit of the knower in this chapter seems to point to one special conclusion: Nietzsche has not avoided a relapse into Socratism. Nietzsche shares with Socrates a clear recognition of the limitations of knowledge, a recognition that may, with Nietzsche too, appear to be atheism but is not, a recognition that carries with it high moral responsibility that can lead to the creation of a world by something like a god.

Strauss's final phrase is not a paraphrase of what Nietzsche said in any of these aphorisms: "man could not live with perfect self-knowledge." This cannot mean that such knowledge is deadly and better avoided lest man perish of torment, unable to bear knowledge of his defective nature, for perfect self-knowledge is impossible to achieve. But Strauss has made it obvious that it is neither impossible nor undesirable to seek to achieve it. Man of necessity philosophizes. Self-knowledge is not forbidden, it is commanded by a great stupidity; and the highest, most spirited natures obey that command. Man would no longer be man if he were able to attain perfect self-knowledge; he would be like Diotima's imaginary gods.

Self-knowledge is commanded by Apollo according to one of the aphorisms Strauss refers to last, aphorism 80. But what, Nietzsche asks, did Apollo mean by his command "Know thyself!"? Because "a matter that becomes clear stops being of concern to us," could Apollo have meant, "Stop being of concern to yourself! Become objective!"? And Nietzsche adds, enigmatically: "And Socrates?—And the 'scientific man'?—." Nietzsche himself seems to hold that man can never become so clear to himself that he ceases to be of concern to himself. Aphorism 81 suggests this interpretation of aphorism 80, for the two aphorisms are linked, as Strauss indicates by placing a dash and not a comma between their numbers. Adrift on an ocean of truth never fully to be fathomed, man can at least preserve himself from salting that ocean and depriving it of its capacity to quench his ever-renewed thirst for self-knowledge (aph. 81). Nietzsche seems to be addressing an injunction to Socrates and the "scientific men" to stop interpreting clear-eyed Apollo as if he were commanding them to "Stop being of concern to yourself," as if he were commanding them to look away from their accursed ipsissimosity to some fathomable good in itself. Whatever the enigmatic god might have meant, it is time for humans to turn toward themselves and drink deeply of their inexhaustible knowability.

Strauss would surely not follow Nietzsche in this particular judgment against Socrates; but by giving his own account of self-knowledge and its responsibilities, Strauss seems intent on bringing Nietzsche and Socrates closer together.[24]

Second Main Part: Morals and Politics

Chapter 5: The Nietzschean Turn in Morals

Strauss devotes more space to chapter 5, "Toward the Natural History of Morality," than to any other chapter. He highlights two themes in Nietzsche's treatment of morality: nature and reason. At the end of his discussion the contest between Nietzsche and Plato breaks into the open again, for Nietzsche's view of nature and reason in morality exposes him to new charges, crimes against the morality championed by Socrates and Plato.

24. Dashes end the discussions of chapters 2, 3, and 4, thus isolating the discussions of religions and of the sayings and interludes by separating them from the discussions of philosophy and of nature. Apart from the possibility that Strauss intended to separate those topics from the united themes of philosophy and nature, I can see no reason why dashes would appear here and nowhere else in the essay. Strauss employed dashes in *CM* as well: 29, 41, 45, 62. See *Philosophie und Gesetz* 10.

Strauss defends Nietzsche against the new charges, but he leaves open the great question he himself had formulated with precision: Is it possible that the Nietzschean turn in morals is both natural and rational? The remainder of his essay pursues the answer to this question, finally intimating that the answer is Yes, the Nietzschean turn in morals is both natural and rational.

The second half of Strauss's study thus demonstrates the internal coherence of Nietzsche's teaching as a whole; it shows how a consistent morals and politics arises out of the new philosophy, the new understanding of nature, and how that consistent view of nature, morals, and politics is contrary to Plato's account of morals and politics. A coherent naturalism distinguishing high and low as noble and base emerges as a now reasonable alternative to the old antinaturalism or supernaturalism which called the high göttlich and eternal and the low earthly and mortal.

CENTERING NATURE AGAIN

Paragraph 18 We are nearing the center of Strauss's essay, and Strauss liked such occasions. He has just centered nature by the arbitrary miscounting practiced on chapter 4. Now, in the tiny eighteenth paragraph, Strauss calls attention to the fact that chapter 5 is Nietzsche's central chapter, and he associates nature with that center by noting that the central chapter is the only one whose heading refers to nature.

Strauss asks: "Could nature be the theme of this chapter or even of the whole second part of the book?" Nature is most certainly the theme of the whole second part of Strauss's essay. And because the second part of Nietzsche's book is devoted "chiefly to morals and politics," Strauss's study turns to the place of nature in Nietzsche's morals and politics. Could Nietzsche really have achieved the naturalization of morals and politics he claimed?

Paragraph 19 This is the final paragraph of the first half of his essay, and Strauss pauses before pushing forward into the second main part of Nietzsche's book and the place of nature in Nietzsche's morals and politics. Fittingly for a final paragraph, it looks backward over the first main part to review the place of nature in it by referring to "the most important or striking" mentions of nature in the first four chapters. As Strauss reports them, these are Nietzsche's distinctions between nature and life and between nature and "us." Strauss comments that life's opposite, death, "is or may be no less natural than life." On the other hand, "the opposite of the natural is the unnatural," and Strauss gives some of Nietzsche's characterizations of the unnatural in the first half of the book: "the artificial, the domesticated, the misbegotten (62), the anti-natural (21, 51, 55)," and explains his point: "i.e., the unnatural may very well be alive." It seems that Strauss is suggesting that the unnatural and anti-natural break out among " 'us' (human beings)" and that they do so because of the natural phenomenon, death. These considerations set the theme of the second half of Strauss's essay: Nietzsche's advocacy of the natural must combat the very much alive unnatural and antinatural that broke out so long ago among us human beings that they have come to seem natural. Advocacy of the natural now appears unnatural; consequently, it will have to develop a politics to achieve its ends.

THE STUDY OF MORALITY: A FIELD FOR A WHOLE ARMY OF WORKERS

"In the introductory aphorism"—these are Strauss's opening words for *Paragraph* this paragraph: he begins his second half in a fitting manner. *20*

Strauss contrasts what Nietzsche does in this introductory aphorism (aph. 186) with what he had done in the aphorism introducing the chapter on religion (aph. 45). There, Nietzsche "led us to suspect" that the true science of religion is for all practical purposes impossible. Here, Nietzsche simply states that a "science of morals which teaches the only true morality" is impossible. Strauss concludes: "It would seem that he makes higher demands on the student of religion than on the student of morality." Nietzsche seems to demand the impossible of the student of religion while sparing the student of morality that demand.

A glance at the two introductory aphorisms themselves shows what Strauss means, for they show why a science of religion and a science of morals differ with respect to their possibility. The empirical study of religion is a psychology, a study of the heights and depths of the human soul. Who is fit for such a study, Nietzsche asks, while lamenting, "Only one hunter, alas, a single one!" To say that the true science of religion is "for all practical purposes impossible" means therefore that it is impossible as a science for scholars, those "well-trained hounds" which the one hunter would love to send into "this primeval forest" in search of *his* quarry, "to round up *his* game." But the science of religion is therefore not *simply* impossible, and Strauss will show that the one hunter, the man of the highest spirituality called the "complementary man," in fact fulfills the requirements set out in this paragraph for this most demanding, most solitary study of the soul: the complementary man will be "familiar with the religious experience of the most profound *homines religiosi* and at the same time . . . be able to look down, from above, on these experiences."

But if it is possible for that one hunter to pursue the true science of religion, it is impossible for anyone ever to achieve the old goal of philosophical ethics, a science of morals which would teach the only true morality. The empirical psychology of religion studies an existing entity, the human soul, and needs to be furthered even if it can be pursued only by the smallest number; a philosophical ethics, on the other hand, pursues a postulated but nonexistent entity and it can be abandoned by science. The same criteria, however, dictate that an empirical study or description of the various historical moralities *is* possible as a shared public science pursued by an army of workers who necessarily lack the singular experiences of the one hunter. The many scholars, the well-trained hounds, *can* be of use in this different kind of inquiry, and Nietzsche's introductory aphorism to the natural history of morality invites his readers to take up this important empirical study with a single goal in mind, the development of a "typology of morals" useful to a high morality beyond good and evil.

The higher demands placed on the student of religion turned Nietzsche into a solitary. The lower demands placed on the student of morality turned Nietzsche into a colleague, if a commanding one: Nietzsche often spoke of his efforts to enlist others in the cooperative scientific effort of developing a natural history of morals, his friend Paul Rée for instance, or the combined faculties of philology, history, philosophy, physiology, and medicine (*GM* Preface 7, *GM* First Essay, end note).

NATURE AND REASON IN MORALITY

Paragraph The philosophers' impossible science of morals claimed to have discovered
21 the foundation of morals either in nature or in reason. Opposing this "gratuitous assumption" that morality can be either natural or rational, Nietzsche argues that every morality is based on some tyranny against nature and reason, and that "everything of value, every freedom" arises from that tyranny. But then "Nietzsche asserts that precisely long lasting obedience to unnatural and unreasonable *nomoi* is 'the moral imperative of nature.'" So Nietzsche bases *nomos* on *physis* after all. Nietzsche's critique of attempts to ground morals in nature itself grounds morals in nature. Strauss is not above speaking Greek in order to make Nietzsche's nice ironic point. Greek spares him from saying directly that Nietzsche claims to have understood the basic imperative of nature and to have grounded his own imperatives on nature's imperative. And Greek ties Nietzsche's thought to Greek philosophical moralists, the first thinkers to confront the *nomoi* with *physis* and attempt to reform the *nomoi* in the light of *physis*.

The moral imperatives to which Nietzsche turns in this chapter arise out of nature itself, whose basic moral imperative he claims to have read correctly. Strauss concludes his paragraph by saying that nature "has become a problem for Nietzsche and yet he cannot do without nature." Nature has become a problem because it always seems to be only "nature," nature so-called. Nietzsche's own critique of the knowledge claims of the philosophers makes it seem that knowledge of nature itself is simply impossible. And yet Nietzsche cannot do without nature because the imperatives of his own great moral turn presume to base themselves on nature and not only on "nature." A judgment will have to be made about the validity of Nietzsche's claim, and Strauss will not shrink from making it: at the very apex of his inquiry into nature and morals in Nietzsche (paragraph 35), Strauss will repeat his sentence that nature "has become a problem for Nietzsche and yet he cannot do without nature," and his repetition will show how Nietzsche solved the problem.

Strauss knows very well that Nietzsche was not a skeptic about the knowledge of nature. Speaking of the current climate of philosophical skepticism, Nietzsche himself said that "if a philosopher these days lets it be known that he is not a skeptic . . . everyone is annoyed" (aph. 208). Strauss is not annoyed. He takes with the utmost seriousness Nietzsche's conclusion that the world viewed from the inside is will to power and nothing besides; and he takes with a corresponding seriousness Nietzsche's derivation of a morality from this view of the world, a morality whose guidance comes from the highest, the most noble: in the aphorism under discussion (188),[25] Nietzsche speaks of "'die Natur,' wie sie ist, in ihrer ganzen verschwenderischen und *gleichgültigen* Grossartigkeit, welche empört, aber vornehm ist"— "'nature' as it is, in all its wasteful and *indifferent* magnificence, which appalls, but is noble." Because vornehme Natur appalls us, we have tried to replace it by the unnatural or antinatural. But if vornehme Natur is ever to replace göttliche Natur, then nature as it is, appalling nature in its whole prodigal and indifferent magnificence, will have to be faced, and even, ultimately, celebrated. When Nietzsche first described nature this way in *Beyond Good and Evil* (aph. 9), he emphasized what looked like the impossibility of living in accord with nature so construed: "How *could* you live

25. In his seminars on *BGE* Strauss gave special emphasis to aph. 188: "You must always consider 188 as a very important section for understanding Nietzsche's whole position" (transcript of 1967 seminar, lecture 12, p. 4). It is perhaps worth noting that the transcripts of Strauss's two courses on *BGE* contain nothing essential that is not also in his Nietzsche essay. The carefully polished essay is, in my opinion, far richer in suggestion and nuance, far bolder in its claims and implications. It seems evident that the essential forum for Strauss's communication of his thoughts is his writings and not his classes.

according to this indifference?" Nietzsche said to the Stoics, whose injunction "Live according to nature" actually meant "Live according to our unnatural construal of nature." "How *could* you live according to this indifference?" How indeed? It is now becoming apparent that this is just what the new Nietzschean morality will demand.

Repetitions, like Strauss's repetition of his sentence on nature becoming a problem for Nietzsche, are an authorial device to which Strauss called attention in other writers (*PAW* 16, 62–64). Other little authorial devices are on display in this paragraph. Strauss notes that in aphorism 188 Nietzsche put nature in quotation marks every time but the final time, when speaking of "the moral imperative of nature." Strauss himself will play with quotation marks in just this way when describing "our" virtues (paragraph 31), thereby forcing his reader to ask and answer the question of just where Strauss himself stands with respect to "our" virtues. A more general device is also employed here: in his discussion of this chapter, Strauss only occasionally cites the number of the aphorism he is paraphrasing or employing—it seems to be understood that the serious reader will have Nietzsche's book open and will search out Nietzsche's words in order to judge Strauss's use of them.

Paragraph 22   "As for rationalist morality": Strauss now turns from *nature* as the foundation of morals to the other foundation presupposed by the philosophers, *reason*. At issue is Nietzsche's view of Socrates and Plato, founders of the rationalist tradition in morals. Strauss will here depart from the text of *Beyond Good and Evil* in order to deepen and broaden the contrast between Nietzsche and his antagonist Plato on the issue of reason and morals, and he will concentrate the radical difference between Nietzschean and Platonic morality on one issue alone: the philosopher's relationship to "the large majority of men." One question will become central, even urgent: could Nietzsche be right in realigning philosophy against "the morality of the human herd"? Could the Nietzschean turn in morals be in accord with reason?

Strauss uses aphorisms 190 and 191 to advance the contest between Nietzsche and Plato, forcing it to focus on a Nietzschean joke about the Platonic Socrates. How could the patrician Plato have taken over the Socratic teaching, "for which," Nietzsche says, "he was really too noble"? The teaching of the Platonic Socrates was utilitarian, identifying the good with the useful and pleasant. "The Platonic Socrates is a monstrosity," a Homeric monster as Nietzsche puts it, setting his joke in a line of Homeric Greek and substituting his nouns for Homer's (*Iliad* 6.181): in front Plato in back Plato and in the middle Chimera. Homer's line ran: in front a lion in back a snake

and in the middle a she-goat—the unnatural monster Chimera. Plato, Nietzsche's little joke suggests, sheltered that Homeric monster Socrates within a
civil front and back provided by the noble Plato himself. By referring to
Nietzsche's Greek joke as a riddle, Strauss makes it sound as if Nietzsche
wins power over Plato by solving his riddle, for Strauss draws the following
inference from the riddle: "Nietzsche intends then to overcome Plato not
only by substituting his truth for Plato's but also by surpassing him in
strength or power." To unriddle the Platonic Socrates is to peer through the
Platonic front and back to the hidden Homeric monster within, to peer
through the platonizing art which created a new ideal, a göttliche ideal, out
of the human, all too human. And thus to unriddle the Platonic Socrates is
to win power over Plato, to surpass him in strength and power. But Plato's
strength and power was such that it forced all philosophers and theologians
after him onto the same track (aph. 191). To surpass Plato is to put all philosophers and theologians of the future on a new track.

Strauss now moves directly to the mighty agon, Nietzsche versus Plato.
Now he will show just how Nietzsche overcomes Plato by surpassing him,
how vornehme Natur ersetzt göttliche Natur. How could Nietzsche surpass
Plato in strength and power? Citing *Twilight of the Idols* (Ancients 2),
Strauss says: "'Plato is boring' . . . while Nietzsche surely is never boring."
Strauss's answer seems to verge on the frivolous. But Strauss says that this
is only one "among other things"; he does not mention those other things,
but he cites the passage in which Nietzsche does. "Plato is boring," Nietzsche
says—and also says that he is "a complete skeptic about Plato" and that his
"mistrust of Plato extends to the very bottom." Nietzsche is suspicious
about Plato because Plato turned away from the fundamental instincts of the
older Hellenes, noble instincts exhibited in Thucydides, Nietzsche's cure for
Platonism. Nietzsche prefers to speak of Plato not merely as boring but as
the "higher swindle," an "antecedent Christian" whose strategic lies about
God and the soul prepared the way for the great calamity of Christianity:
Nietzsche surely is never boring.

Could it be that Strauss signals the gravity of this indictment of Plato
by making a little blunder with Nietzsche's title, the very sort of blunder he
was pleased to find in other writers? Strauss mistitles Nietzsche's book, calling it *Twilight of the Gods* just here where he is referring to the passage in
which Nietzsche charges that Plato was an antecedent Christian, the philosopher whose elevation of "the concept 'good' as the supreme concept" prepared the way for the Christian God, the God whose growing supremacy

marked in fact the twilight of the gods. Is the twilight of the gods—as Nietzsche thought—part of *Plato's* work, a twilight followed by the dawn of the Ideas and the Good? To surpass Plato would be a work appropriately entitled *Twilight of the Idols*, for it is a work which makes the Ideas and the Good visible as decadent values which replaced the noble virtues of the older Hellenes and which prepared the way for Christianity. A few pages later, Strauss refers to Nietzsche's work again, this time assigning it its correct title, *Twilight of the Idols*, and the context suggests that Nietzsche's work marks the twilight of the idols of Platonism by an ascent to nature (paragraph 33). Curiously enough, it may be that this little blunder with Nietzsche's title simply completes Strauss's play with this title begun in *Socrates and Aristophanes:* when referring to "the problem of Socrates," Strauss titles Nietzsche's book *Dawn of Idols*, an alternative way of titling Plato's work, as the daybreak of a new ideal (*SA* 315 n. 6, see pp. 6–8).[26]

Nietzsche intends to surpass Plato by advocating instinct over reason. Strauss says that both Socrates and Plato follow not only reason but implicitly take the side of instinct as well: reason is their passion, as Nietzsche said; philosophy is the highest eros, as Plato's Diotima said. Nietzsche, however, explicitly takes the side of instinct against reason; he takes the side of nature, of what can be expelled but always comes back (*BGE* 264); he takes the side of the fundamental instinct, will to power. But Strauss adds an additional consideration here by saying that Nietzsche also sides with the religious instinct, the "god-forming instinct." Why mention that here as a seeming aside? Presumably because it points to the one great difference between Plato and Nietzsche with respect to religion: Plato employed all his strength (aph. 191) "to prove to himself that reason and instinct of themselves tend toward one goal, the good, 'God.'" Whereas Nietzsche holds (in the aphorism introduced here by Strauss, *WP* 1038) that the god-forming instinct is many-sided: "How many gods are still possible! How differently, how variously, has the divine always made itself open to me!" So this is how Plato is boring: his track leads everyone to the unitary, the uniform, the universal, the boring. Nietzsche refuses the tyranny of the univocal. In popular form, that tyranny came to be exercised by the God of the monotheisms of revealed religion. Monotheism was "perhaps the greatest danger that has yet confronted humanity" precisely because of its tyranny, because it dictated

26. Strauss's handwritten version of the Nietzsche essay has *Twilight of the Idols* throughout, suggesting that the change of title was no slip of the pen but a little subtlety added late.

"one normal type and ideal"; "the great advantage of polytheism" is found in its permission to behold "a plurality of norms" (*GS* 143).

Beyond Good and Evil teaches that it is high time for religion once again to pass into the care of philosophy, only now it is high time that religion pass into the care of a not boring philosopher who follows a new track, whose instincts or nature rebel at the tyrannical notion that there exists some universal, unitary rule to which everything must be obedient. Plato, and all philosophers and theologians since Plato, are on the same boring track leading to the universal, to the uniform, to monotheism, to what Nietzsche—forcing God and the boring to share a single word—named *monotonotheism* (*TI* Reason 1). Whether the monotone is a unitary Good beyond being in dignity and power and grounding all beings in its unchanging splendor, or a unitary God directing all things by his will, or the single vision of mechanical or technological science directing a universal and autonomous herd, it follows Plato and is, "among other things," boring. Nietzsche, who surely is never boring, undertakes to replace Plato by setting himself against the tyranny of the univocal.

The final sentence of Strauss's paragraph draws the moral consequence from the contest of reason and instinct elaborated in the paragraph and adds Strauss's own inference. Employing Nietzsche's statement that Socrates had finally "seen through the irrational in moral judgments" (whereas Plato was "more innocent in such matters"), Strauss draws a consequence Nietzsche himself did not explicitly draw: there "cannot be any universally valid moral rules: different moralities fit, belong to, different types of human beings." This conclusion prepares the discussion of morality in the next paragraphs, because one must ask, How many types of human beings are there? And what moralities fit them? Strauss will provide Nietzsche's graphic answers. "The large majority of men," the human herd in Nietzsche's impolite words, constitute one type, and the morality that fits them tends toward the universal because the large majority stands in fear of the exception or the exceptional. The large majority, needing the comfort of the universal, utilizes the power of the universal to rule over and eventually rule out the threatening exception. Moreover—and this will be a major point—Platonism served the morality of the large majority. Universally valid moral rules, valid for all peoples at all times, can support themselves on the Platonic rational principle founded on the Good, on God—on some cosmic spider in Nietzsche's language. The contest between Plato and Nietzsche regarding morality takes on a historic dimension: Plato's strength and power supported a moral teaching that sided with the large majority and set all subsequent philosophers and theologians on the same track. But now the sway of that teaching elicits a philosophic protest that advocates a new moral teaching, one that sides with the other moral type, the *only* other type, the exceptions.

A TYPOLOGY OF MORALS WITH ONLY TWO MORAL TYPES

Paragraph 23 Strauss continues his discussion of morality by searching out Nietzsche's next use of the word *nature* (aph. 197) and employing it to make his own contribution to what Nietzsche there dissects, "Morality as Fearfulness." At issue in this aphorism are the two moral types: "predatory beings" on the one hand, the "dangerous, intemperate, passionate, 'tropical'" men, and their judges on the other hand, those who condemned the predatory as "almost all moralists" so far have done. The moralists' judgment against the predatory beings condemned them as defectively natural but Nietzsche takes the opposite view: it was the defective nature of the moralists, their fearfulness or timidity, which prompted their false judgment. Strauss is at pains to point out that the moralists did not themselves *originate* the morality stemming from fearfulness, for that is the morality of "the large majority of men." The morality which fits or belongs to the large majority fears the exceptional natures and judges them defectively natural. The moralists simply endorsed and grounded the already present prejudice of the majority, a prejudice stemming from their fear of beings unlike themselves, superior beings, uncontrolled, unpredictable, and powerful.

"The utmost one could say"—Strauss begins his final sentence of the paragraph with these words which introduce a defense of the moral philosophers. But in response to what does Strauss say the utmost one can say in defense of moral philosophers? Strauss's sentence begins without identifying its antecedent; the reader must reenact the implied dialogue, supplying what Strauss omits by reconstructing the logic of the paragraph. Nietzsche has just pronounced an indictment on the moral philosophers who took the side of the large majority, "the moral philosophers (and theologians)" who had all been on Plato's track (aph. 191). Strauss speaks up in their defense: the utmost one could say in defense of the moral philosophers and their Platonic morality, a morality of fearfulness in Nietzsche's words, of "judicious conformity" in Strauss's own more polite words (*WPP* 153), the morality, in any case, which takes the side of the large majority—the utmost one could say in defense of the moral philosophers is this: they "tried to protect the individual against the dangers with which he is threatened, not by other men, but by his own passions." This is in fact what Nietzsche himself said in the next aphorism (198), another entry "for the chapter 'Morality as Fear-fulness.'" Turning from the predatory beings to "recipes for the passions" of the large majority, Nietzsche himself offered this defense of Platonic morality: it was, in its way, public-spirited; it provided a means of controlling the passions for those endangered by their own passions.

But if this is the utmost Strauss can say in paraphrasing Nietzsche's point, what did Nietzsche himself say? Strauss's words stop just short of the most telling aspect of Nietzsche's judgment: What is this alleged rational science of morals, this Platonic public-spiritedness on behalf of the large majority threatened by its passions? It is, Nietzsche says, "prudence, prudence, prudence mixed with stupidity, stupidity, stupidity." Fearful philosophic moralists led by Plato made prudent compromises with popular stupidity. It is characteristic of these stupidities, Nietzsche says, that "all of them speak unconditionally" because all of them need to rule out the exception. The philosophers who made this prudent compromise with stupidity ran a great risk with the human future, and in Nietzsche's view the risk was unnecessary: Nietzsche sides with Epicurus and "with all the profound natures of antiquity" who shared a disgust at "the philosophers of virtue" who sprang from Socrates and his moralizing (*KGW* VIII 14 [129] = *WP* 434).

Even the utmost one could say in defense of Platonic morality and its historic encouragement of popular stupidity does not absolve it of ultimate if unwitting responsibility for the present moral situation. And in the next paragraphs Strauss follows Nietzsche to show that modern Europe has fallen under the universal sway of a stupidity grown so powerful that it is now able to rule out all exceptions through its universally valid moral rules. What may once have been defensible as prudent public-spiritedness can now be seen to have contributed to the exclusive sway of stupidity, the "autonomy of the herd."

Strauss now traces the historic consequences of Platonism's prudent *Paragraph* compromise with stupidity, distilling the main points of aphorisms 199 and *24* 201 without supplying the reference. At issue is the great Nietzschean theme of the genealogy of conscience, the history of morals that lays bare our spiritual past as the conflict between an instinct to obedience and an instinct to command. These two instincts define the two basic types of human beings and the two different moralities that fit or belong to them. If our history can be read in terms of their conflicts and compromises, our present gives evidence of the historic victory of the instinct to obedience, what Zarathustra described as the reign of the last man.

Strauss emphasizes that the morality of the large majority now "successfully claims to be the only true morality." Success in this claim means obliterating the one competing morality, the morality of those marked by independence, superiority, and inequality, the morality of those who command. Though they were always a threat, the exceptions were nevertheless esteemed because they were useful for the common good of the tribe as its fearless leaders and defenders. But in contemporary Europe they are no longer needed, so they no longer have to be tolerated; the "ultimate consequences" of herd morality render them superfluous. For the herd to become "autonomous" means that it no longer needs superior leaders. When Strauss speaks, with Nietzsche, of herd morality abolishing its only remaining ground of fear, he speaks of rendering the "criminals" harmless. He cannot mean mere thieves and murderers: the true criminals are those high criminals the aphorism described, those few whose crime is opposition to the morality of the large majority, natural masters whose abolition defines the ultimate consequences of the morality of the large majority or its ascent into "the autonomous herd." Strauss ends his paragraph affixing his own label to the new idea of the good which justifies fearfulness and the abolition of the great criminals: he calls the new good "indiscriminate compassion."

Crime in the sense here implied is one of the great themes of Strauss's lifelong study, philosophy and law. The great philosophers—the great Platonic political philosophers—set out to become secret spiritual rulers while recognizing that philosophy in their sense must be judged a crime by the merely moral. The philosophers agreed with one another in knowing themselves to be the greatest criminals; they move the boundary stones; as new lawgivers, they are unavoidably called evil by those with the laws on their side, the large majority, or, as Nietzsche said, "the farmers of the spirit" who work the old fields in the old ways (GS 4). But now the instinct to obedience can successfully threaten these few exceptions, those whose high spirituality is marked by independence, superiority, and inequality. The ultimate consequence of Plato's compromise with the morality of the large majority, of prudence with stupidity, threatens the very existence of philosophy through the universal sway of stupidity.

FOLLOWING LEADERS

Paragraph
25

Strauss's argument on the natural history of morals now comes to its fitting conclusion: the history of morals has resulted in a new homogeneity that threatens all difference. Who are the truly different? The examples begin with Napoleon, Alcibiades, and Caesar, but they end with the new philosophers, "men of the highest spirituality, of the greatest reason." The turn in morals, the great Nietzschean turn, is a turn away from "the autonomy of the herd" and toward "the rule of the philosophers of the future." They are the ones who act in accord with nature, their own high spirituality, and who act in accord with reason, for it is reasonable that philosophy now become what it has never yet been, faced as it is with an unprecedented threat, the ultimate consequences of Platonic morality.

This argument of course is Nietzsche's. By presenting it as he does here, Strauss prepares the ground for the rest of his essay, for now the trajectory of its whole second half opens before our view. First, while considering just who the true leaders are, Strauss once again pictures himself faced with temptation. He had resisted the previous temptation (paragraph 7), but he seems to give in to this one: the fundamental Nietzschean step in morals is, "we are tempted to say, to the highest degree according to nature" and "to the highest degree according to reason." Then, in the following paragraphs, Strauss puts the Nietzschean temptation on trial, and he speaks for the defense (paragraph 26). Finally, the trial having resolved all the issues but one—namely, whether a natural or rational morality is at all possible for Nietzsche, Strauss places all the weight on the very issue Nietzsche himself chose to make decisive, the morality of eternal return (paragraph 27). This issue subsequently guides Strauss's consideration of the next two chapters and is resolved, finally and affirmatively, at their end (paragraph 35).

In the present paragraph, "the victory of the democratic movement" is treated as already past, its victory marking the end of moral variety. This movement to uniformity prides itself on—it even defines itself by—its tolerance of variety. Nietzsche, however, treats even its opposite extremes, anarchists and socialists, as embodiments of a single moral type. The democratic movement is morally homogeneous; its apparent tolerance of variety masks its intolerance of the one moral difference that matters. This modern narrowing of the moral horizon means that "moralities other and higher than the herd morality" are no longer known.

Just after speaking of "other moralities," Strauss mentions Nietzsche's examples, Napoleon, Alcibiades, and Caesar, emphasizing the difference between Caesar and Alcibiades from the point of view of herd morality. Nevertheless, Strauss follows Nietzsche by speaking of "men of such a nature," submerging the great differences to which he has just called attention and highlighting their sameness of nature by contrasting it to "men of the opposite nature." Strauss notes that this view of human nature as consisting of two kinds continues throughout Nietzsche's fifth chapter even though the word "nature" is no longer used. Abolition of one of the two kinds would amount to a change in human nature, or, because ejected nature always returns, to a social contract contrary to human nature.

Without noting it explicitly, Strauss turns to the final aphorism of "Toward the natural history of morality." Nietzsche himself had just described the faith and hope of "the automous herd" in aphorism 202, and he begins the final aphorism by speaking of "We, the we who are of a different faith." The hope attendant to this faith is a hope for new philosophers (aph. 203). Strauss says that Nietzsche makes an appeal "from the victorious herd morality of contemporary Europe to the superior morality of leaders (*Führer*)." This appeal to a morality no longer known is rendered even more alien and repugnant by Strauss's insistence on Nietzsche's German word *Führer*. But who are these *Führer* after all? Their task is to "counteract the degradation of man which has led to the autonomy of the herd." An opposition to modern morality on this scale cannot be led merely by "men born to rule like Napoleon, Alcibiades and Caesar." Strauss defines the true leaders able to counteract the modern degradation of man by using a combination of Nietzsche's terms from this aphorism: "They must be philosophers, new philosophers, a new kind of philosophers and commanders, the philosophers of the future." In then saying, "Mere Caesars, however great, will not suffice," Strauss suggests that they will at least be like Caesar in the one way to which he has called attention, the way which distinguished Caesar from glory-seeking Alcibiades whom even Socrates could not tame: they will perform "a great historic function," not merely for Rome but for humanity; they will be, as it were, functionaries of human history. They will, as Nietzsche said, be those few with the highest responsibility who "have the whole history of humanity on their conscience" (aph. 61).

Nietzsche ends the aphorism that began with a new faith and hope by speaking of "a new task" assigned by that faith and hope. It arises from the natural history of morals, and Strauss ends his account of this chapter describing the new task. "The new philosophers," Strauss says, paraphrasing aphorism 203, "must teach man the future of man as his will." By taking up that new future, humans "put an end to the gruesome rule of nonsense and chance which was hitherto regarded as 'history.'" The true history "requires the subjugation of chance, of nature (*Genealogy* II. n. 2) by men of the highest spirituality, of the greatest reason." By adding the phrase "subjugation of nature" to Nietzsche's own account of the task, Strauss supplements aphorism 203 with a parallel description of the man of the highest spirituality from the *Genealogy of Morals*. Both of Nietzsche's passages make it perfectly clear that the "subjugation of nature" is not to be understood in the sense of a popular Baconianism. Strauss in no way follows Heidegger into the ridiculous notion that Nietzsche voices the metaphysics of the technological mastery of nature. That mastery, as its founder and prophet Francis Bacon understood perfectly, is an instrument for the large majority by means of which they could diminish natural difference or overcome to a degree the arbitrary dispensations of fate. Strauss may be referring to that Baconian sense of subjugation when he cites "a Marxian distinction" which had been used to advance the Baconian subjugation of nature. But whether that is the case or not, the subjugation of nature of which Strauss primarily speaks here is the act of the highest or "sovereign" man directed in the first instance over himself and only then over "nature" defined as "all the more short-willed and unreliable creatures"—humans, that is, whose nature is different from that of the sovereign (GM 2.2).

Strauss's whole argument on this chapter requires that the subjugation of nature by the highest natures be understood as a response to the already existing attempt to subjugate nature, primarily the modern moral attempt to subjugate *human* nature to the imperatives of one type of human being. As Strauss said in *On Tyranny*, we are now brought face to face with a new form of tyranny because of "'the conquest of nature' and in particular of human nature" (OT 27). Nietzsche's new task is the task made imperative by our history of the subjugation of our nature. The new task does not subjugate human nature; it sets out instead to conquer the already far-advanced rage to subjugate human nature through the elimination of its supreme forms. To achieve its end, the new task grants sway to the predatory beings, to "men of the highest spirituality, of the greatest reason," those who act in accord with their nature and in accord with reason.

The drift of the argument is clear (though it will be made still clearer in the climactic paragraph 35): the present moral moment requires that those of the highest spirituality and the greatest reason act on behalf of human nature for the human future. Translated into Nietzsche's language, this says that philosophy no longer has the luxury of a prudent compromise with stupidity; philosophy may no longer make concessions to the natural morality of the large majority. What is needed is a new politics for philosophy undertaken by those of the highest spirituality and greatest reason, a politics for philosophy that self-consciously opposes the Platonic compromise because it now stands within the ultimate consequences of that compromise and knows where it stands. "The subjugation of nature depends then decisively on men who possess a certain nature." Nietzsche "cannot do without nature" (paragraph 21) because Nietzsche's whole appeal is to a certain kind of nature.

Strauss does not resist the temptation to say that the new philosophers are or act to the highest degree according to nature and to the highest degree according to reason: his whole discussion on nature and reason in morals comes to this affirmative conclusion. But one cannot yet say that Strauss simply assents to this anti-Platonic view that looks back on Platonism and judges its compromise with stupidity to have had disastrous consequences— for the next paragraphs raise the appropriate objections and hesitations.

In his final sentence before the objections break out, Strauss links the present argument from the history of morals to the earlier argument from philosophy and religion: the historic turn in morals from the autonomy of the herd to the rule of the philosophers of the future is, he says, "akin" to the historic transformation of the worship of the nothing into the unbounded Yes to everything that was and is. Where does the kinship lie? It would seem that the reasonableness of the turn in morals attests independently to the reasonableness of the transformation of nihilism into the affirmation of eternal return.

This is a capital point: besides its own inner logic as the Yes arising out of the insight into will to power, eternal return has a *historic* logic that links it to the turn from the autonomy of the herd to the rule of the philosophers of the future. The teaching of eternal return arises reasonably, within a historical trajectory that can now be plotted in the natural history of morals. Eternal return arises as the world-affirming ideal opposite to the ideal of world-denial natural to the fearful morality of the large majority and encouraged in them by prudent philosophers following Plato. The opposite ideal arises at just that historic moment in which the very notion of a morality different from that of the large majority appears as scandalous, as an immoral relic of brutal societies. At this historic moment, the turn to the rule of the philosophers of the future is reasonable. The opposite ideal arises, therefore, as the implement of their rule, spiritual rule modeled on Plato's rule, rule achieved by inculcating an ideal but the opposite one to the old ideal of world-denial. The philosophers of the future rule in the only way philosophers have ever ruled, through a new highest ideal. Because it is new, and because it is the opposite ideal, it appears in the only way that fundamental novelty can ever appear—as a crime. Nevertheless, at this point in our moral history it is a reasonable crime.

NIETZSCHE ON TRIAL

Paragraph 26 Strauss's readers, Strauss's friends, have had just about enough. So Strauss lets them have their say, as Nietzsche let his readers have their say in aphorism 37; he lets them vent their anti-Nietzschean ire. That prejudiced ire pours forth as a series of objections cascading down to a mindless fight between Nietzsche and Plato, the very fight Strauss's study has elevated to such high-mindedness. Each of the objections is something Strauss might have expected from readers trained in his writings, but each is met by a quiet or quieting answer that directs the objection into deliberation: the mighty agon between Nietzsche and Plato cannot be settled by prejudiced ire. Still, the contest that breaks out here shows that if the objections can be answered, the objectors can't. They know the ugly truth about Nietzsche, and no mere argument will sway them.

The objections arise at the point in the argument where Strauss has yielded to the temptation to view the historic turn from the autonomy of the herd to the rule of the philosophers of the future as natural and rational, and they open charging contradiction: "But what becomes then of the irrationality of the moral judgment, i.e. of every moral judgment (aph. 191)?" Hasn't Nietzsche contradicted himself, the teacher of the irrationality of every moral judgment advocating as rational the historic moral turn from the autonomy of the herd to the rule of the philosophers of the future?

"Or does it cease to be rational merely because one must be strong, healthy and well-born in order to agree to it or even to understand it?" This subtle response admits of two answers and each in its way is a defense of Nietzsche against the superficial charge that it is self-contradictory to regard the Nietzschean turn in morals as reasonable or rational.

—Yes. It *does* cease to be "rational" in any universal, "Platonic" sense of rationality. Therefore Nietzsche has not contradicted himself: the reasonableness of his turn to the rule of the philosophers of the future is suitably "irrational"—it is not universal but fits or belongs to a certain moral type.

—No. It does *not* cease to be rational in the Nietzschean sense of rationality, namely, the high spirituality that wins its own perspective on events, the perspective of the moral type threatened with submersion under the modern tide. Therefore Nietzsche has not contradicted himself: the reasonableness of his turn to the rule of the philosophers of the future is suitably rational.

The decisive presence of the irrational in every moral judgment is found in the irrationality of its source, namely, the mere accident of a person where there are two types of person. This does not mean that every moral judgment simply ceases to be rational. The rationality or reasonableness of the Nietzschean turn in morals must be measured by its source and by its circumstances. Its claimed source is the high spirituality to which philosophy has always laid claim. Its circumstances are a world in which such claims are impermissible or unrecognizable, a world in which philosophy is supplanted by the true view well known to everyone.

"Yet can one say that Nietzsche's praise of cruelty, as distinguished from Plato's praise of gentleness, is rational?" This question seems to have come from nowhere. But the way it is framed, its beginning with *Yet*, implies that the Nietzschean turn has just been successfully defended and that new grounds must be found on which to attack the turn. And what better grounds than the shocking things everyone already knows about Nietzsche—his praise of cruelty, for instance? Moreover, the abrupt introduction of Plato implies that Nietzschean rationality has just been defended against Platonic rationality; Plato, already introduced by this implied contrast, can readily be invoked to defend the high ground everyone knows Plato defends.

"Or is that praise of cruelty only the indispensable and therefore reasonable corrective to the irrational glorification of compassion (cf. *Genealogy*, preface, nr. 5 end)?" This is one of the most telling sentences in Strauss's whole essay. Can Strauss actually speak in defense of Nietzsche's praise of cruelty? First he reduces the charge Nietzsche faces: the charge is not cruelty as such, but what appears as cruelty in our setting of the irrational glorification of compassion. Then he shows that other philosophers are guilty of the same charge: his reference to the *Genealogy of Morals* is to a list of philosophers who do not share the contemporary overevaluation of compassion—and Plato heads that list. Strauss can go so far as to call in Plato in Nietzsche's defense against the charge of cruelty. And finally, what are we to make of Strauss's phrase "the irrational glorification of compassion"? With this fine phrase Strauss dramatizes his contribution to Nietzsche's defense, summarizing the Christianized, softened setting for Nietzsche's call to hardness, and casting back on the accuser the whole question of what is rational or reasonable on the volatile issue of cruelty.

Once raised, the issue of cruelty will not easily disappear; it remains an important consideration for the remainder of Strauss's essay, right up to the final paragraph on virtue. That Nietzsche is not the mad advocate of cruelty inflicted on others will be made clear by Strauss when he discusses the intellectual conscience: cruelty in Nietzsche's sense is the refusal of mad comforts, the refusal of stupidity. Cruelty in Nietzsche's sense is the surrender of easy pleasures for far more difficult and painful ones.

For the defense of Nietzsche on cruelty, Strauss could have called in Machiavelli, except that such a witness would not be thought a witness for the defense, given Machiavelli's reputation as a teacher of evil.[27] Neverthe-less, there is a small curiosity about the fact that cruelty arises as an issue just here in Strauss's essay, a curiosity which seems, in the fittingly sly fash-ion, to introduce Machiavelli after all: the theme of cruelty, introduced with-out warning here in paragraph 26 as a means of condemning Nietzsche, ap-pears as the theme of the 26th chapter of Machiavelli's *Discourses*—as Strauss shows in his account of the use of the number 26 in Machiavelli ("Machiavelli" *SPPP* 224).[28] In his 26th chapter, Machiavelli spoke of the necessity of cruelty in the founder, the wholly new prince in the wholly new state: "His means must be cruel and inimical, not only to every Christian manner of living but to every humane manner of living as well." Strauss adds: "The new prince cannot avoid acquiring a reputation for cruelty." And Strauss makes it perfectly clear that the most princely are the few genuine philosophers who introduce new modes and orders, like the cruel Machia-velli or the cruel Nietzsche (*TM* 49, 187; see *SPPP* 223). If not Machiavelli himself, then Machiavelli's 26th chapter serves as a defense of Nietzsche where Nietzsche's setting is a radicalization of Machiavelli's setting, an irra-tional glorification of compassion.

"Furthermore, is not Nietzsche's critique of Plato and of Socrates a grave exaggeration, not to say a caricature?" "Furthermore"—this final question simply ignores Strauss's mitigation of the charge of cruelty and broadens the charge against Nietzsche, first by bringing in Socrates and then by question-ing Nietzsche's critique of both Plato and Socrates. Here is an issue that Strauss made central to understanding the whole history of philosophy, Nietzsche's critique of Socrates, Nietzsche's "question of the worth of what Socrates stood for" (*SA* 6). What does Strauss, the great contemporary stu-dent of Socrates, have to say about Nietzsche's critique of Socrates when that critique is raised against Nietzsche as grounds for condemning his teaching on morals?

The considerations that follow all focus on the Platonic Socrates. They are not introduced with "Or . . ." as were the two previous responses to charges against Nietzsche; they do not refute the charge but elaborate it, specifying the reasons why Nietzsche's critique might be misplaced. Do they then simply confirm the charge of "caricature"? The logic of the paragraph

27. Strauss might also have called in Xenophon for the defense of Nietzsche on cruelty: see Strauss's statements on "the problem of justice" in his commentary on the cruelty of the com-mander Xenophon, "Xenophon's *Anabasis*," *SPPP* 127–28.

28. But why does the discussion of 26 and cruelty appear in the 27th paragraph of Strauss's essay on Machiavelli? On the number 26 see *TM* 48ff. In *TM*, the chapter on *The Prince*, a book of 26 chapters, contains 26 paragraphs.

forbids this interpretation, for the considerations are followed by this state-ment: "To considerations such as these one is compelled to retort"—and the retort raises a new and final charge against Nietzsche, namely, that Nietz-sche's turn in morals cannot be natural or rational because Nietzsche, unlike Socrates, denied that there is a nature of man. Because they evoke this final charge in *retort*, Strauss's considerations must contribute to the defense of Nietzsche. How do they do that? They bring Socrates closer to Nietzsche; they show that Socrates is more Nietzschean than Nietzsche himself might have thought.

Strauss's considerations begin by inviting a study of Plato's *Protagoras* and *Gorgias* in order to see that Socrates was not a utilitarian in Nietzsche's sense. Strauss then goes out of his way to point out that "in the same chap-ter" in which Nietzsche spoke of Socrates as a utilitarian, Nietzsche also said that "Socrates did not think that he knew what good and evil is." In the passage Strauss refers to (aph. 202), Nietzsche discusses the uniform moral standpoint that has come to dominate Europe, and he makes a statement especially arresting to a reader of Plato like Strauss: "Obviously, one now *knows* in Europe what Socrates thought he did not know and what that fa-mous old serpent promised to teach—today one 'knows' what good and evil is." In his ironic scorn for the alleged modern knowledge of good and evil, Nietzsche appeals to the difference between what Socrates knew and what he promised to teach, to Socratic ignorance masked by feigned knowledge. Strauss's first consideration thus raises the suspicion that Nietzsche's critique of Socrates as a utilitarian is far from the whole story, for Nietzsche knew that Socrates' knowledge of ignorance precluded knowing that the good is "identical with 'useful and agreeable'" (aph. 190).

"In other words"—Strauss's next sentence interprets the suspicion about the old serpent Socrates that is raised by Nietzsche's own texts: "In other words, 'virtue is knowledge' is a riddle rather than a solution." Strauss at-tempts a solution to this Socratic riddle by offering two comments. Each of them involves an "awareness," a kind of knowledge, and each of them comes from Nietzsche himself as an awareness he had attained for himself: Strauss's point seems to be that Nietzsche and Socrates shared awareness of the same phenomena.

The riddle, Strauss says first, "is based on awareness" of a certain fact to which Nietzsche called attention, a fact which shows that virtue and knowledge do *not* coincide: "Socrates' enigmatic saying is based on aware-ness of the fact that sometimes 'a scientific head is placed on the body of an ape, a subtle exceptional understanding on a vulgar soul' (aph. 26)." Nietzsche's aphorism 26 concerns one aspect of the philosopher's self-knowledge, his secret inward awareness of the difference between himself and the average man; and it speaks of how that awareness can be attained: "The long and serious study of the *average* man constitutes a necessary part of the life-history of every philosopher"—as it constituted the most prominent part of the public life-history of the Platonic Socrates. Study of the average man is greatly aided, Nietzsche said, by cynics who dare to speak openly of the animal man. Attending to the revealing speech of cynics can lead to the awareness that sometimes "a scientific head is placed on the body of an ape, a subtle exceptional understanding on a vulgar soul." To have gained this awareness is to know that "virtue is knowledge" is not simply true, and Socrates, Strauss says, gained this awareness.

Socrates was aware of a second matter made prominent by Nietzsche, for his enigmatic statement that virtue is knowledge "implies awareness of the complexity of the relation between *Wissen* and *Gewissen,* to use a favorite distinction of Nietzsche which in this form is indeed alien to Socrates." Nietzsche's form of expressing this shared awareness of complexity is alien to Socrates because the history of morals since Socrates has provided Nietzsche with both a different vocabulary and clearer evidence: according to Nietzsche's historical view, conscience had been sharpened and deepened over two millennia by the unwavering presence of an all-knowing, all-punishing God, and conscience had come to be defined exclusively by those whose experience was of *bad* conscience, the self-condemnation arising from their inability to do the good they thought they knew. (For Nietzsche's account of the new, affirmative conscience as a form of "virtue is knowledge" possessed by "the sovereign human being," see *GM* 2.2.)

Strauss has here used the resources of *Beyond Good and Evil* to bring Socrates and Nietzsche closer together; he has used Nietzschean materials to show that Socrates and Nietzsche shared an awareness that Nietzsche dared to express openly and that Socrates hid behind a riddle. Nietzsche knew that Socrates was a "great ironic, so rich in secrets" (aph. 191); he knew that the Platonic Socrates was a riddle, Plato in front Plato in back and in the middle Chimera (aph. 190). Strauss thus suggests that Nietzsche knew that Socrates knew his own "accursed ipsissimosity" (aph. 207), and that Socrates pointed away from it by employing riddles like "virtue is knowledge," or inventing fictions like a teacher who taught him that "the gods do not philosophize but are knowers," or by promising to teach a knowledge of good and evil he did not himself possess (aph. 202).

"To considerations such as these"—considerations which bring Socrates and Nietzsche close together in their awareness of the enigma of knowledge and self-knowledge—"one is compelled to retort. . . ." And the retort stipulates that the argument on Nietzsche's behalf is still open in one basic respect. Strauss's argument so far has concerned the place of nature and reason in the new Nietzschean morals. It has just mounted a defense of the natural and rational character of Nietzsche's basic turn in morals in the face of an attack based on indignation at Nietzsche and trust in the classics, blind trust in an ironic Plato and an ironic Socrates. But now the final objection is raised: Nietzsche's turn can be neither natural nor rational "because he denies that there is a nature of man." This objection is elaborated as a demand that the inconsistent Nietzsche be consistent. Nietzsche is forbidden his affirmations because they contradict his denials: "the denial of any cardinal difference between man and brute is a truth, if a deadly truth; hence there cannot be natural ends of man as man: all values are human creations."

Strauss had said that Nietzsche "does his best to break the power of the deadly truth" (paragraph 7). Was his best not good enough? Is the human animal capable only of arbitrary creations lacking all ground in nature or reason, as this retort charges? Or could the animal man have a natural end? And could a certain kind of value creation be reasonable? The next main argument shows that the new understanding of nature as historical opens a way to understand the human animal through its genealogy. Furthermore, this historical understanding will be able to argue plausibly that the Nietzschean turn in morals is reasonable at this moment in human history. The crucial argument therefore continues into chapters six and seven: Is Nietzsche's turn in morals founded on nature and reason? And that argument will now have to address the unresolved question: Does Nietzsche deny that there is a nature of man?

Paragraph 27   Apparently, one additional matter must be highlighted as preparation for those chapters, another seeming objection to the great Nietzschean turn from the autonomous herd to the rule of the new philosophers. This turn, Strauss says, "is in perfect agreement with his doctrine of the will to power," but he adds that "it seems to be irreconcilable with his doctrine of eternal return." Strauss then spells out the seeming difficulty: How can the demand for something completely new, "this intransigent farewell to the whole past. . . be reconciled with the unbounded Yes to everything that was and is?" Strauss immediately hints at the solution to the difficulty he has raised by suggesting that "toward the end of the present chapter Nietzsche gives a hint regarding the connection between the demand for wholly new philosophers and eternal return." Nietzsche's hint in aphorism 203 is that "the philoso-

phers of the future . . . must be able to endure the weight of the responsibility for the future of man." Strauss then makes that weight basic to the
teaching of eternal return by citing the heading of the aphorism in which
Nietzsche first made eternal return public, "*Das grösste Schwergewicht.*"
Strauss himself will display in the coming paragraphs just how the teaching
of eternal return requires that philosophers of the future assume responsibility for the future of humanity by assuming the weight of responsibility
for the whole of the past, everything that was and is. The responsibility
implied in the new teaching is therefore the very opposite of a "farewell to
the whole past," however much its new ideal leaves behind the ideal of the
past. Strauss's argument, prepared by the seeming difficulty and the hint that
leads to its solution, will continue to focus on the reasonableness of the
Nietzschean turn. Now, however, it will focus in particular on the reasonableness of willing eternal return, until eventually Strauss will be able to
conclude that the Nietzschean turn in morals is in perfect agreement with
both fundamental doctrines, will to power and eternal return.

Strauss has extracted Nietzsche's hint from a passage rich in implications
for the new stage in the natural history of morality. It occurs at the very end
of the central chapter on nature and describes the qualities necessary to effect
the great turn in morals without describing the content of the turn. Speaking
of the weight of responsibility that the philosophers of the future have to
endure (aph. 203), Nietzsche named their overall task "a transvaluation of
values." That transvaluation exerts what Nietzsche calls "a new pressure and
hammer" under whose force "a conscience would be forged [*gestählt*—
steeled], a heart transformed into bronze." Only such a steeled conscience
and hardened heart would make it possible for the philosopher of the future
to accept the responsibility for the new turn in morals. Strauss will now
follow the plan of Nietzsche's book into a description of the steeled philosopher of the future (chapter 6) and the transvaluation of values he effects
through the teaching of eternal return (chapter 7).

Chapter 6: Nature and Philosophy

> It is certainly not an overstatement to say that no one has ever spoken so
> greatly and so nobly of what a philosopher is as Nietzsche.
>
> Strauss, *RCPR* 40

Strauss's account of chapter 6, "We Scholars," continues the great theme of
nature, but in application now to philosophy. How are nature and philoso-

phy related? Strauss puts the focus where Nietzsche put it, on the few genuine philosophers as distinct from the many philosophical laborers. Just who
the genuine philosopher is is central to Strauss's lifelong investigations in the
history of philosophy, and on this issue too Nietzsche presents the greatest
challenge to Plato. For Strauss's life work shows that Platonic political philosophy had labored to keep obscure the natural order of rank which placed
the genuine philosopher at the very pinnacle of nature. Rather than flaunt
that fact, Platonic political philosophy had sheltered philosophy within existing conceptions of the order of rank, surrendering supremacy to preten-
ders. Nietzsche's view of the philosopher is not different from Plato's except
that Nietzsche forced philosophy to shed its sheltering skin, its prudent conformity, and come into the open as what it is, the highest union of mind and
heart, intellect and spirit.

Why did Nietzsche abandon philosophy's prudent modesty? Was it
mere bravado, blind courage, a failure to grasp what Platonic political philosophy saw most clearly, philosophy's endangered place in the world? On
the contrary, Strauss shows that it was precisely Nietzsche's recognition of
an unparalleled threat to philosophy that forced philosophy's advocate into
the open. Philosophy's advocate is nature's advocate: against the modern
claims to correct nature and human nature by machining away natural difference through a new social contract, Nietzsche brought the natural order
of rank into the open, risking offense in the cause of philosophy by flaunting
its greatness, its natural nobility. The historic turn in morals now being completed, the turn to the autonomy of the herd, required a new politics for
philosophy. Leo Strauss, the contemporary advocate par excellence of Platonic political philosophy, here confronts the greatest challenge to that view,
Nietzsche's open proclamation that there are genuine philosophers whose
natural nobility lifts them far above science and scholarship and whose
achievements attest to the true ground of the dignity of man and therewith
the goodness of the world (LAM 8).

Strauss's account of chapter 6 links chapters 5, 6, and 7 as the presentation of Nietzsche's essential argument in the second main part of Beyond
Good and Evil, the argument relating nature to morals and politics. Crucial
to chapter 6 is the distinction between the genuine philosopher and philosophical laborers. It is imperative that the philosophical laborers, the scholars
and scientists of philosophy, understand this distinction or understand the
rank of the genuine philosopher because the faith and hope expressed at the
end of chapter 5 hinges entirely on the achievements of the genuine philosopher. After making this distinction clear, Strauss will go on to show that the

genuine philosopher is the complementary human being of chapter 7, the thinker whose task Strauss will go out of his way—out of *Beyond Good and Evil*—to describe. Description of that task will mark the culmination of Strauss's whole argument on the second main part of *Beyond Good and Evil*: successful accomplishment of the task of the genuine philosopher or complementary human being effects the turn from the autonomy of the herd to the rule of the philosopher of the future.

PHILOSOPHICAL LABORERS AND GENUINE PHILOSOPHERS

Philosophical laborers, "professors of philosophy," ought to be subservient to philosophy as its handmaidens, but instead, they have experienced "emancipation" from philosophy. Apparent emancipation, however, came at the cost of actual servitude, for philosophical laborers have become the servants of modern democratic politics. Emancipated from the naturally high that they ought by right to serve, they—we—are indentured to a politics whose comprehensive goal is the emancipation of the low from subordination to the high. This is "the degeneration of the modern scholar" of which Nietzsche often spoke (*GS* 358). *Paragraph 28*

Nietzsche's charge of enslavement is most unwelcome, for it is addressed to the very ones who suppose themselves emancipated. Moreover, in the very same breath Nietzsche claims for himself real emancipation from the scholars' so-called emancipation while claiming as well that such emancipation is impossible for any but the very few. Nietzscheans, if there came to be any, would in a certain way resemble Platonists: they too would be philosophical laborers without thinking it a slur, they too would recognize an order of rank between philosophy and science and see in themselves the scientists of philosophy. Strauss speaks in his own name to state his agreement with Nietzsche on the danger presented to philosophy by the apparent emancipation of science: "The things which we have observed in the 20th century regarding the sciences of man confirm Nietzsche's diagnosis." The correctness and importance of Nietzsche's diagnosis of philosophy's loss of rank occupies Strauss in the next two paragraphs.

Strauss calls attention to the irony of Nietzsche's title, *Wir Gelehrten*. As the only chapter title that uses "the first person of the personal pronoun," it places Nietzsche among the scholars, it places Nietzsche himself on one of the steps on which the scientific laborers of philosophy must remain standing but which the genuine philosopher must step beyond. Strauss thinks he knows what Nietzsche "wishes to emphasize" by his use of this title, namely, "that apart from being a precursor of the philosophers of the future"—and just what high office is assigned to the precursor remains to be seen—"he belongs to the scholars and not, for instance, to the poets or the *homines religiosi*." Poets and *homines religiosi* follow high callings in Nietzsche's view, high callings of spiritual servitude: they are always the valets of some morality or some divinity. In a book addressed to scholars who take themselves to be free minds, it is only politic of Nietzsche to emphasize that he belongs among the scholars and not among those whom the scholars themselves regard as unfree minds. Still, toward the end of his book, Nietzsche will risk the disclosure that he is the last disciple and initiate of the god Dionysos, knowing full well that the scholars will not want to hear it (aph. 295). Furthermore, he will end his aphorisms with a reflection on the necessary poetry of philosophy and add last a poem which names "friend Zarathustra, that guest of guests," Zarathustra, inspiration for a poetic work in which Nietzsche presents a scholar taking a few nibbles of Zarathustra's poetry and announcing: "Zarathustra is no longer a scholar" (Z 2.6). What Nietzsche wishes to emphasize is only one of many possible ways in which he could appear.

Strauss's paragraph is concerned with Nietzsche's true identity as well as the identity he wishes to have assigned to him, for Nietzsche's true identity is one of the main issues of his book. Nietzsche's many feints and masks complicate and deepen the issue, making its resolution a challenge for his reader: discovering Nietzsche's true identity educates the reader on what is possible for a human being, or what a genuine philosopher is. Does Nietzsche really belong to the scholars, as he wishes to emphasize?[29]

Paragraph   Toward the end of aphorism 207, in the midst of a long discussion of the
29   scholar's maiming but necessary objectivity, Nietzsche drops a small remark

29. Does Strauss make a little blunder here in order to help call attention to this question of identity? Strauss says: "The chapter devoted to [philosophical laborers] is entitled '*Wir Gelehrten*'; it is the only one in whose title the first person of the personal pronoun is used." Is it? The title of the next chapter is "Our Virtues," and when he turns to this chapter Strauss calls attention to the connection between the two titles by saying of "Our Virtues" that "the 'we' whose virtues he discusses there, are not 'we scholars'" (paragraph 31). In the transcript of his 1967 seminar on *Beyond Good and Evil* at the University of Chicago, Strauss spoke of "the only *two* cases in which the first person plural—or for that matter the first person—occurs at all in a chapter heading" (Lecture 9, page 1 emphasis added). In the next lecture Strauss says, "Book 6 dealt with 'We Scholars'; chapter 7 deals with 'Our Virtues.' Are the two 'we's' identical or different?" (Lecture 10, page 2). When Strauss writes of this pair in his essay he isolates one as "the only one in whose title the first person of the personal pronoun is used." Is "our" a personal pronoun? It is used here as a possessive adjective but does a personal pronoun used in the possessive case as an adjective cease to be a personal pronoun? If this is an intentional blunder on Strauss's part, it is fully in keeping with Nietzsche's playfulness about his identity when speaking of *we* and *our* in these chapters.

about the only way in which the scholar "is still 'nature' and 'natural.'" Strauss is evidently still in pursuit of Nietzsche's every use of the word *nature*, for he springs on this first use of the word in this chapter[30] to begin his discussion of its specifics even though Nietzsche's little remark occurs more than a third of the way through the chapter. Using this remark, Strauss constructs a whole paragraph on the issue of nature and history, or the modern replacement of nature by history. This too is an important theme of Strauss's life work. He had directed unrelenting criticism against radical historicism, the dissolving of nature into history, of what lasts into what passes. He defined radical historicism as follows: "All understanding, all knowledge, however limited and 'scientific,' presupposes a frame of reference; it presupposes a horizon, a comprehensive view within which understanding and knowing take place" (*NRH* 26). Unlike Strauss's own historical studies of philosophy, which he once called contributions to a sociology of philosophy (*PAW* Introduction), historicism is incompatible with philosophy. It is a resignation into skepticism in the face of the great difficulties that philosophy had uncovered regarding the possibility of knowledge. Is Nietzsche a radical historicist? The school Strauss generated characteristically assumes that the answer is Yes, for it has taken to speaking of "Nietzsche and Heidegger" as if this were the long name of some German philosopher born in 1844 and buried in 1976. Did Strauss himself think that Nietzsche was nothing more than a stage in the dialectic of modernity? When this question had arisen in Strauss's earlier discussions of Heidegger and Nietzsche, he seems to have been very careful to leave the question open with respect to Nietzsche (e.g., *WPP* 53–55; *NRH* 26; *SPPP* 33–34). And now?

Strauss speaks of a shift in philosophy away from the identification of the natural and the genuine: Plato endorsed the identification, but Rousseau set out to eradicate it. And Nietzsche? Strauss says that "Nietzsche prepares decisively the replacement of the natural by the authentic": Nietzsche himself does not make this replacement; he does not himself fall into what he prepares. But is what he prepares, Heidegger's teaching on authenticity and radical historicism, simply the necessary unfolding of Nietzsche's thought? Strauss does not answer this question. Instead of looking to the consequences of Nietzsche's thought, he considers its causes, the setting to which it responded. He chooses to give his own explanation of the direction Nietzsche took, "that" and "why" Nietzsche's reflections on nature took the

---

30. In aphorism 206, Nietzsche had used the word "natures" in a different sense, speaking of the lynx-eyes which scholars possess for "*das Niedrige solcher Naturen*" whose heights they cannot reach.

course they did. Strauss says Nietzsche faced a situation dangerous to philosophy, a grave situation not of his own making. Philosophy, the highest
pursuit and prone to danger, faced in Nietzsche's time "a greater danger"
from historical study than from "natural science." Natural science posed the
great danger to philosophy in *Socrates'* time, according to Plato's *Phaedo*,
and that danger had forced Socrates to set out on his second sailing, a turn
away from natural science to the logoi, the turn that became the hallmark of
Plato's Platonism. That great turn was designed, Socrates said, to save philosophy from misology and misanthropy; it was the "safe way" for philosophy in response to the hatred of reason caused by unrealistic hopes in
reason's ability to explain everything. The danger to philosophy faced by
Nietzsche was analogous to the danger to philosophy faced by Socrates, but
it was nevertheless a peculiarly modern danger arising from the fact that
"historical study had come to be closer to philosophy." The danger Nietzsche
faced, Strauss says, was "a consequence of . . . the historicization of philosophy," Hegel's teaching that reduced philosophy to a mere function of place
and time. Strauss makes clear in the next paragraph that Nietzsche opposed
Hegel, that he did not reduce philosophy to its place and time.[31]

For Nietzsche himself, it is not the case that history "takes the place of"
nature. Rather, one form or understanding of nature takes the place of another form or understanding of nature. For Strauss, Nietzsche seeks "a way
of thinking and living that transcends historicism" (paragraph 31). "Historicism is the child of the peculiarly modern tendency to understand everything in terms of its genesis"—but then Strauss quotes Locke's view that
"nature furnishes only the almost worthless materials as in themselves."
The two passages from Nietzsche to which Strauss had just referred, *BGE*
213 and *Dawn of Morning* 540, make it clear that Nietzsche is very far from
this view of human production. Nietzsche is no child of Locke. He does not
allow philosophy to succumb to the danger posed by modernity's elevation

---

31. Worth considering in this context is the extremely enigmatic final sentence of the essay
"Political Philosophy and History," *WPP* 77: "For historicism asserts that the fusion of philosophic and historical questions marks in itself a progress beyond 'naive' non-historical philosophy, whereas we limit ourselves to asserting that that fusion is, within the limits indicated,
inevitable on the basis of modern philosophy, as distinguished from pre-modern philosophy or
'the philosophy of the future.'" That final phrase, so odd in this setting but an inevitable re-
minder of Nietzsche, brings together Nietzsche and pre-modern philosophy against a common
foe, historicism. Furthermore, it associates Nietzsche with what must now be added to pre-
modern philosophy in order to overcome historicism: we need "a special kind of inquiry" to
keep alive what was lost by modern teachings, we need the "philosophic inquiry" Strauss calls
"the history of philosophy or of science" (end of the two previous paragraphs). "The philosophy of the future," Strauss indicates, meets this need of a history of philosophy or of science.

of history, its myth of human self-making. (This fiction is one of the targets of Nietzsche's critique of modernity in *GS* 356.) Nietzsche's focus is on natural man, and the proper understanding of natural man cannot ignore history or transcend history into the divine, into some supposed timelessness. History must be integrated into nature, as Strauss puts it (paragraph 34); the study of nature must become natural history, genealogy, the intimate tale of the human family.[32]

THE COMPLEMENTARY MAN

How did Nietzsche respond to the danger philosophy faced, now that it had been usurped by philosophical laborers laboring in the service of Locke and Hegel and reducing philosophy to history? He risked stating openly that the genuine philosopher is the peak of nature. Strauss does Nietzsche the courtesy of referring to the genuine philosopher with the term used in *Beyond Good and Evil* rather than the one used early in *Zarathustra*. And by calling him "the complementary man" rather than "the superman," Strauss spares Nietzsche the opprobrium that still clings to the latter term—spares him fittingly, for Nietzsche himself abandoned that term, never having used it in a sense remotely like what we necessarily hear in it. Strauss will say "the complementary man" five times, leading up to the final time where he describes what the complementary man must do, the values he must create (paragraph 35). *Paragraph 30*

The philosopher "strictly speaking" or "in the precise sense" is the complementary man, the philosopher of the future, as Nietzsche also calls him. What Strauss then goes on to say about the complementary man exhibits Nietzsche's opposition to radical historicism, for the complementary man "is the peak which does not permit and still less demand to be overcome." "Have there been such philosophers yet?" Nietzsche asks, and Strauss indicates that the answer is Yes, there were philosophers of the future in the past, the very few philosophers who have had the whole future of humanity on their conscience (*BGE* 61), and that Plato is central. But, Strauss asks, "does it remain true that we must overcome also the Greeks?" Strauss's two references for this question are to *The Gay Science*, to "the dying Socrates" (340) and to "the Madman" (125) who heralds the death of God, the death

---

32. An essay on "Relativism" published in 1961 culminates with the judgment "that Nietzsche may be said to have transformed the deadly truth of relativism into the most life-giving truth" (*RCPR* 26). But why was it necessary that Strauss then go on to state Nietzsche's case in his final paragraph "with all necessary vagueness"? Strauss ends by referring to Nietzsche's "relapse into metaphysics or . . . his recourse to nature," pregnant phrases judging by their parallels in his Nietzsche essay.

of the göttliche Natur born in Plato's writings. The two references therefore apply the consistent theme of Strauss's essay—Nietzsche contra Plato—to the issue of the complementary man or the philosopher of the future. The content of these aphorisms indicates that one philosopher of the future must overcome another without the type itself being overcome, the type being a natural human type, the rare peak achievements of humanity. If there is such a natural human type, radical historicism cannot be true; humanity is not fully malleable at the hands of time—as Strauss will go on to demonstrate, the charge that Nietzsche "denies that there is a nature of man" (paragraph 26) is false.

"The philosopher as philosopher belongs to the future." Strauss confirms that there were philosophers of the future in the past, for the genuine philosopher "was . . . at all times in contradiction to his Today." They were never "the sons of their times" as the historicist philosophical laborer Hegel thought; they were always the "step-sons" of their times as Nietzsche thought; they transcended their times toward a future they aimed to bring about.

In his final sentence of this paragraph, Strauss turns to the great task that faces the "precursors of the philosophers of the future." These precursors are identified in the following paragraph as "we free minds." They too are no longer enslaved to their place and time but are its step-sons; they too have high concerns, "the excellence of man in general" and "the preservation of Europe." But only the philosophers of the future can perform the creative task that would meet these concerns; they alone "must become the invisible spiritual rulers of a united Europe without ever becoming its servants."

Chapter 7: Nature, History, and the Complementary Man

> By becoming aware of the dignity of the mind, we realize the true ground
> on the dignity of man and therewith the goodness of the world.
>
> Strauss, *LAM* 8

Strauss's insistent pursuit of the theme of nature in *Beyond Good and Evil* now yields its greatest reward, for here natural man, the complementary man, "solves the highest, the most difficult problem" (paragraph 35). Himself the product of a high morality, the complementary man must perform an act still higher than morality, an act beyond good and evil: he must create the new values that complement nature and bring to a fitting culmination the history of non-sense and chance that is the history of humanity till now. The new values complement nature by assigning limits to the conquest of nature; they preserve natural difference by maintaining the order of rank both among things and among human beings. Based in nature, wholly natural, the complementary man is historical to the core; part of a natural order fated to pass, he learns to love what passes and he learns to teach mortal beings love of the mortal.

HALF-BARBARIAN MORALISTS

Hidden within the sober topics and sonorous tone of this long, winding paragraph on "Our Virtues" one discovers a little game, a Nietzschean game played with quotation marks. What began as "our" virtues, the virtues of the free minds Nietzsche addresses, becomes our virtues when they are identified as the historical sense and intellectual probity. Does Strauss wordlessly abolish the distance between the free minds and himself? Surely his is a free mind possessed of the historical sense and intellectual probity. How far does he go with these virtues? *Paragraph 31*

The chapter "Our Virtues," Strauss says, turns from scholars (the theme of "We Scholars") to free minds, minds freed of enslavement to their place and time, made step-sons of their place and time by their historical sense and their intellectual probity. But the virtues of the free mind have their attendant vices. To learn the remedy for those vices is, perhaps, to learn how to understand the distinction between the free minds and the philosophers of the future. Earlier Strauss had said it was "hard to say" how this distinction is to be understood: "are the free minds by any chance freer than the philosophers of the future? do they possess an openness which is possible only during the transitional period between the philosophy of the past and the philosophy of the future?" (paragraph 5). Yes, Strauss now answers, that temporary openness is a barbarity that can be made civil by the philosopher of the future.

The virtues and vices of the free mind represent progress in morality, but for the free minds to take pride in their progress would be incompatible with another moral gain, increased delicacy in moral matters. Besides, Strauss immediately emphasizes, such pride is sobered and tempered by the clear recognition of the limitations of the free mind because the very highest escapes it. Strauss thus prepares for his elucidation of the civilizing role played by the complementary man.

Strauss treats it as a "concession," as something Nietzsche "is willing to grant," that only the moral progress leading to the free minds has made possible that further step in moral progress, the step to the complementary man. Strauss then paraphrases the soaring passage in which Nietzsche set forth the spiritual grandeur and magnificence of the complementary man (aph. 219). His "high spirituality (intellectuality) is the ultimate product of moral qualities"; though itself beyond good and evil, "it is the synthesis of all those states which one ascribes to men who are 'only moral.'" Strauss drains Nietzsche's aphorism of its playful taunting of the "merely moral," those "free" minds whose very moralism arms them against their spiritual superiors by enabling them to deny the existence of any height beyond their own severe morality. But rather than outrage the merely moral by sharpening the distance between them and that higher spirituality, Nietzsche chooses to honor them by conceding that this high spirituality is itself the ultimate product of their moral qualities. Strauss then quotes Nietzsche's definition of that high spirituality in aphorism 219, the definition that will eventually pour forth its content in Strauss's own account of what the complementary man must do. This high spirituality "consists in the spiritualization of justice and of that kind of severity which knows that it is commissioned to maintain in the world the order of rank, even among the things and not only among men."

Every aspect of Nietzsche's definition will be utilized by Strauss in the coming paragraphs. The *spiritualization* of justice and the *spiritualization* of severity will be the core, even if the core is somewhat masked by Strauss's use of the terms *suffering* and *cruelty* to describe what Nietzsche advocates. Just what grants the commission to shoulder this awesome responsibility will come to light as nature itself, not some romanticized or humanized fiction of nature but nature seen Nietzscheanly. And the maintenance of the order of rank among things and humans will be shown to depend upon values created by the complementary man which endorse natural difference, natural rank, and which are grounded in gratitude for that difference, not in revenge against it.

Light is cast on the meaning and gravity Strauss assigns to Nietzsche's word *spiritualization* by a definition Strauss offers in an essay written shortly before his Nietzsche essay. In his introductory essay for Hermann Cohen's *Religion of Reason out of the Sources of Judaism* (1972), destined to be the final chapter of *Studies in Platonic Political Philosophy*, Strauss says that Cohen "interprets Jewish thought by 'idealizing' or 'spiritualizing' it." He then offers this expansion and explanation of the activity of spiritualizing an already existing phenomenon: "thinking it through and . . . understanding it in the light of its highest possibilities" (*SPPP* 235). Just how the complementary man spiritualizes justice and severity by thinking them through and understanding them in the light of their highest possibilities will be shown by Strauss in the rest of his essay.

How does the complementary man stand to us? "Our virtues" are not the virtues of the philosopher of the future; he has a "superior morality." Three moralities are in play here: first, the reigning moralities (defined as altruism, the identification of goodness with compassion, and utilitarianism); second, our moral critique of these reigning moralities; and third, the superior morality which flows from the critique. Our virtue is the second of these, embodied in the historical sense which Strauss describes as both a novel and an "ambiguous phenomenon." Rooted in a lack of self-sufficiency, it expresses the self-criticism of modernity. Our virtue therefore has a defect which Strauss expresses in Nietzsche's words: "measure is foreign to us; we are titillated by the infinite and unmeasured." Strauss comments in his own words, using the first person plural for the first time without quotation marks: "hence we are half-barbarians." The superior morality arising out of mere critique would remedy this defect and teach us measure; it would civilize us half-barbarians who have no way of knowing how to assign a measure. It would teach us how to limit the historical sense or to stop its plunge into radical historicism bereft of measure; it would teach us how to assign limits to the conquest of nature—the crucial aspect of our barbarism isolated in the culminating paragraph. Historicism's lack of measure "points to a way of thinking and living that transcends historicism," the way that Strauss has, till now, left abstract or contentless as the "superior morality" of the complementary man.

Strauss points to what he takes to be a little plan in the order of the aphorisms presenting the historical sense, drawing the conclusion that the historical sense mediates or falls between the two types of morality in Nietzsche's typology, the morality of the large majority which aims at abolishing suffering and "the opposite morality which goes together with awareness of the great things man owes to suffering."

Following Nietzsche, Strauss emphasizes the irony that "we immoralists" are "men of duty" true to our virtue; our immoral virtue is our intellectual probity. But Strauss does not mention what Nietzsche emphasizes: such men of duty will always appear to the moral as simply *im*moral: "Whatever we do, dolts and appearances speak against us—'These are men *without* duty'—we always have dolts and appearances against us" (aph. 226). Intellectual probity is therefore "evil" in the sense Nietzsche always emphasized when daring to parade himself as a teacher of evil. "Evil is what goes against custom" (*HH* 96). "What is new is always *evil*. . . . The good men are in all ages those who cultivate the old thoughts . . . the farmers of the spirit" (*GS* 4).

The virtue of intellectual probity has its limits, and to display them Strauss turns—without mentioning it—to the next aphorism (227), another little debate between the honest and the dolts which aims to give heart to the honest. Because it points to the past rather than to the future, intellectual probity needs to be supplemented by "our most delicate, most disguised, most spiritual will to power." Will to power with the qualities of delicacy, disguise, and spirituality is described by Nietzsche as part of the equipment necessary for "coming to the assistance of our 'god' with all our 'devils.'" Any god of probity served by such devils of will to power will of course be misunderstood in the way will to power is characteristically misunderstood:

> They will say:
>   "Their 'probity'—that's their devilry and nothing else!"
> —Who cares?[33]

But even more threatening than the old charge of siding with the devil is a temptation that comes from within, the temptation Strauss refers to in his final sentence of this paragraph, probity's temptation to a pride that "would lead us back to moralism (and to theism)"—and away, therefore, from the most disguised, most spiritual will to power. Nietzsche's own playful words at the end of aphorism 227 fill in the content of this temptation to return to the surface rather than descend to the depth:

> Every virtue inclines toward stupidity, every stupidity, toward virtue. "Stupid to the point of holiness," they say in Russia. Let us take care that out of probity we do not finally become saints and bores. Isn't life a hundred times too short—for boredom? One really would have to believe in eternal life to —

To what? To return to the boring, to moralism (and to theism), to Platonism, to that compromise with stupidity which held that having dolts and appearances against us meant that we had to look like saints and moral bores for our very survival—and theirs.

---

33. Kaufmann's translation omits Nietzsche's little dialogue. This is most unfortunate because Nietzsche's economy in speaking about his most basic thought ("the whole doctrine of *Beyond Good and Evil*," paragraph 9) suggests that he surely has in mind here the contexts of his earlier little dialogues on the "most spiritual will to power" (9) and on the charge uttered by the free minds that a comprehensive teaching of will to power refutes God but not the devil (36–37).

CRUELTY

Cruelty now reappears, and it does so because Strauss engineers a helpful *Paragraph* contrast between "our virtue" and "the morality preached up by the English *32* utilitarians." Making use of elements from aphorisms 228, 229, and 230, Strauss shows that the two moralisms share egoism but that utilitarianism, because it lacks insight into will to power, fails to realize that egoism can include cruelty directed toward oneself, cruelty "effective in intellectual probity, in 'the intellectual conscience.'" Strauss pursues this form of cruelty in the next paragraph. It is the cruelty basic to Nietzsche's great lesson on the spirit and spiritedness in aphorisms 229 and 230, the cruelty of the seeker after knowledge who "forces his spirit to recognize things against the inclination of the spirit, and often enough also against the wishes of his heart," who desires "to hurt the basic will of the spirit which unceasingly strives for the apparent and superficial" (229).

Why emphasize cruelty? Because "to recognize the crucial importance *Paragraph* of cruelty is indispensable if 'the terrible basic text *homo natura*,'[34] 'that *33* eternal basic text' is again to be seen, if man is to be 're-translated into nature.'" Nietzsche's essential task requires that the indispensability of cruelty be faced, that it not be wiped away by the "praise of gentleness," that sop to the basic will of the spirit which permitted its stupidities to become dominant. Further evidence in Nietzsche's favor relevant to the trial of paragraph 26 is here introduced: insistence on cruelty, cruelty in the service of intellectual probity, is not the blamable idiosyncrasy of an incautious or perverse thinker bent on the malign; insistence on cruelty is necessary to recover and preserve human nature.

In order to supplement the argument of aphorism 230 that Nietzsche's task was the recovery of the natural in humanity, Strauss departs from the text of *Beyond Good and Evil* and gathers a series of references clarifying Nietzsche's task of naturalization. It is a task on behalf of the future made necessary by the present and past not only of philosophy but of the whole of humanity. The human species has never yet been natural, but in Nietzsche's evolutionary view humanity could be made natural through a new view of nature, and Strauss quotes the important aphorism 109 of *The Gay Science* that describes the new view of nature as a refusal to attribute to nature any humanizing myth, any shadow of the dead god of aphorism 108. Unlike other species, the human species is not yet fixed, has not yet acquired its final character, and Strauss quotes Aristotle in confirmation of Nietzsche's

---

34. Unfortunately Kaufmann's translation omits *schreckliche* (terrible).

point. Nietzsche can speak of a "return to nature" only in the sense of an ascent to the peak of humanity, the philosopher of the future, the truly complementary man—"return" to the rare exceptions, or to the recognition that there are such exceptions, whose occasional appearance belongs to human nature as its crown.[35] Here, where the process of naturalization requires that Strauss define the task of the truly complementary man, he does so by drawing together two basic arguments from his essay:

One: The complementary man "is the first man who consciously creates values on the basis of the understanding of the will to power as the fundamental phenomenon." Just what those values are Strauss is going to make clear—they are in no way arbitrary, they are not invented or created in order to celebrate mere inventiveness. Such creativity for its own sake counts for less than nothing in Nietzsche, *less* than nothing because mere creativity is the modern way, the way of the actor, the way Nietzsche most opposes: Nietzsche contra Wagner. Understanding the will to power as the fundamental phenomenon *generates* values of a precise sort, natural values, naturalizing values. Insight into the fundamental fact gives birth to new highest values.

Two: The complementary man, by his act of creating values that complement nature, "puts an end to the rule of non-sense and chance (aph. 203)." This shorthand reference invokes the natural history of morals that Strauss had just laid bare: the values created by the truly complementary man facilitate the reasonable turn from the autonomy of the herd to the rule of the philosopher of the future.

Strauss then makes a statement that could cause considerable confusion: the naturalization of man, he says, "is at the same time the peak of the anthropomorphization of the non-human (cf. *Will to Power* nr. 614)." How far does Strauss extend this matter of anthropomorphization? Does he suppose that Nietzsche holds all knowing to be anthropomorphization? *Will to Power* 614 runs in full: "To 'humanize' the world, i.e., to feel ourselves more and more masters within it—" (*KGW* VII 25 [312]). If Strauss reads these words as Nietzsche's wish, he has misread them; for they imply instead a critique of the whole history of wishful interpretations of the world. So far from endorsing any wishful humanization, Nietzsche takes it to be a major part of his task to terminate it. Another note states this unequivocally: "My mis-

---

35. In this context of a return to nature, Strauss cites Nietzsche's title correctly; the return to nature is the *Twilight of the Idols*, the twilight of the göttliche super-nature.

sion: the dehumanization (*Entmenschung*) of nature and then the natural-ization of the human after it has gained the pure concept 'Nature'" (*KGW* V 11 [211] Spring–Fall 1881). In a related note Nietzsche says, "Humanity and philosophy have hitherto poetized the human into nature—let us de-humanize nature!" (ibid. [238]). This *de*-anthropomorphization of nature is the task Nietzsche set out in *The Gay Science* 109, an aphorism to which Strauss had referred in this paragraph. Strauss himself, however, seems to extend willful anthropomorphism to the important aphorism 9 of *Beyond Good and Evil*, for he says in reference to it that "the most spiritual will to power consists in prescribing to nature what or how it ought to be." Does this implicate Nietzsche in the willful humanization he criticizes in this very aphorism? Has Strauss missed the nice irony implied in aphorism 9 by the spectacle of Nietzsche himself offering a description of nature in the very aphorism criticizing philosophy for tyrannizing nature, for creating the world in its own image? Nietzsche surely intended the reader of aphorism 9 to challenge him: What status can your own purported description of nature have if you yourself say philosophy is the most spiritual will to power which creates the world in its own image? That Nietzsche's description of nature as will to power claims for itself a status beyond mere anthropomorphization is shown gradually in aphorisms 13, 22, 23, and then finally, definitively, in aphorisms 36 and 37, the aphorisms to which Strauss drew attention as the core of Nietzsche's argument that will to power is the fundamental fact.

Nietzsche's own perspective on anthropomorphizing is stated with great clarity in the very aphorism Strauss is here discussing, 230. Humanity is to stand before humanity, Nietzsche says, in the very way it now stands before "the *rest* of nature," before non-human nature: with respect to its own na-ture too, humanity must grow hard under "the discipline of science"; it must see its own nature as it is, and it must allow its own nature to be as it is. And to do this, humanity must overcome also the Greeks, even the greatest of them, Oedipus and Odysseus: it cannot pluck out its eyes at the sight of what it is and has done but must gaze on itself "free of shock"; and it must put wax in *its own* ears in order to resist the temptation of a special brand of Sirens, "old metaphysical bird-catchers" who, like Odysseus himself, put wax in their friends' ears lest their friends fall prey to the Sirens. Those old metaphysical bird-catchers, those Platonists, have piped all too long at hu-manity, "You are more, you are higher, you are of a different origin." Not the anthropomorphizing of nature and human nature but their *de*-anthropomorphizing is Nietzsche's goal; and in part that can be achieved under the discipline of science, whose intellectual probity now forces humanity to be cruel with itself and view its own nature as it is.

Has Strauss misunderstood Nietzsche on this altogether basic matter of anthropomorphization? The answer is No. Just what *anthropomorphization* means here can be understood only if we take our bearings by Strauss's essay: Where are we in Strauss's essay? We stand just before the crucial paragraphs that will speak of eternal return, the heart of the new, consciously created values. And Strauss has just reminded his reader that that creation takes place "on the basis of the understanding of the will to power as the fundamental phenomenon." When, after this reaffirmation of the fundamental phenomenon, he goes on to talk of anthropomorphization, he does not mean that the fundamental phenomenon, will to power, is *itself* an anthropomorphization. That point Strauss had already settled earlier in his essay where the theme was explicitly will to power. Now, however, after the stage has been properly prepared by the lengthy consideration of the history of morals with its focus on the precise turning point to which that history has brought us, *now* is the time to introduce the created values generated by the insight into the fundamental phenomenon. These values, like all values, necessarily anthropomorphize; these values, like all values, express human passion and longing. But they do so on the grounds of an insight into nature that is not an anthropomorphizing; and they do so by affirming to the highest degree possible just what nature is.

Strauss's essay thus faithfully follows the economy of Nietzsche's thought as a whole. First, a cruel act of *de*-anthropomorphizing must occur: wishful humanity must cease to misread nature on the basis of its old antinatural wishes stemming from one of the two moral types, wishes for a supernatural realm where it could shelter itself and its treasures. Then and only then can nature as it is be seen as it is. But nature itself, relieved of the condemnation based on wishful dreaming, could then gradually be seen as noble in its prodigal and indifferent magnificence. And finally, human love of the natural could ascend to its highest pitch in the affirmation of a new highest good, the opposite ideal, as Nietzsche called it (aph. 56), the ideal of a lover moved to say to the beloved, "Be what you are, be eternally what you are!" This would now be the highest wish of the wishful beast. And a whole new poetry, a whole new beautification of nature, would learn to sing the transience of things; the best parables would now be parables of time and becoming (Z 2.2). This new song would, in its way, be a humanization of nature; it would give voice to the human will to eternalize the beloved (GS 370).

INTEGRATING HISTORY AND NATURE

Each sentence in this paragraph is supplied with a logical connective that *Paragraph* gives a palpable sense of dialogue to the whole and forces the reader to think *34* through the logic connecting the sentences.

—"However": The first sentence refers back to the decisive claim of the previous paragraph that the action of creating values by the truly complementary man puts an end to the rule of non-sense and chance. "The necessary condition for the subjugation of non-sense and chance" turns out to be the very rule of non-sense and chance, "the history of man hitherto."

—"That is to say": "The *Vernatürlichung* of man presupposes and brings to its conclusion the whole historical process." This conclusion is no End of History as the culmination of some hidden logic in the rule of non-sense and chance; such a historical argument, the continued theologizing of history, is used to justify the autonomy of the herd. The turn to the rule of the philosophers of the future or the completion of history in the naturalization of humanity is "by no means necessary but requires a new, free creative act."

—"Still": Even though this completing act lacks necessity, "in this way history can be said to be integrated into nature." The completing act of history integrates history into nature. With this statement, Strauss's investigation of nature in Nietzsche comes to one of its terminal points. Nature is not transcendent to history, being is not transcendent to becoming; nature is not properly represented mythically in some göttliche Natur revealing the truth of timeless nature. The very history of the unnatural beast that refused nature through its invented anti-natural values and elevated itself beyond the merely natural to some supernatural status now makes possible the integration of history into nature.

—"Be this as it may": Strauss flaunts neutrality on this great claim of *Vernatürlichung* as he moves to the next, necessary point, just what the creative act is that integrates history into nature. To affirm the philosophers of the future requires affirming the past that made them possible, the history responsible for the generation of such natures.

—"Yet": There is a great difference between *this* affirmation of the past—this past, this once, affirmed as what makes the completing act of philosophy possible—and "the unbounded Yes to everything that was and is, i.e. the affirmation of eternal return." Why is it necessary to affirm eternal return? This is the question Strauss's essay has been moving toward. It is not a question *Beyond Good and Evil* has been moving toward: the plan of Strauss's essay and not the plan of Nietzsche's *Beyond Good and Evil* makes the answer to this question the peak of the investigation. Strauss acts as if the logic of aphorism 230 required Nietzsche to answer this crucial question, for he says (to begin the next paragraph):

—"Instead" of answering that question, Nietzsche indicated something else, namely, that this affirmation, "the highest achievement," "is in the last analysis not the work of reason but of nature." "In the last analysis" it is not the logic of a historical argument but the disposition of a certain kind of being that is the key to the necessity of affirming eternal return according to what Nietzsche himself indicates. Nevertheless, by his repetition of the phrase "in the last analysis," Strauss seems to indicate that there are other factors at work in this affirmation, that it is also the work of reason: it is reasonable now to turn from the autonomy of the herd to the rule of the philosophers of the future whose nature, whose "unteachable deep down," makes it necessary to affirm eternal return. Strauss thus ends his own argument by adding the essential historical reason for affirming eternal return to the primary reason already given in the first part of his essay, namely, that it is the natural affirmation of the highest natures, their unavoidable relapse into Platonism subsequent to their insight into will to power as the fundamental fact.

SOLVING THE HIGHEST, THE MOST DIFFICULT PROBLEM

Paragraph 35 Strauss goes out of his way to provide what Nietzsche did not provide at this point of *Beyond Good and Evil,* an explicit argument explaining why it is necessary to affirm eternal return. The historical argument that culminates Strauss's presentation of *Beyond Good and Evil* is, at best, latent in *Beyond Good and Evil.* Its main elements as an argument in favor of eternal return are in fact imported from *Thus Spoke Zarathustra,* and they are employed here in the service of Strauss's own consistent theme: how philosophy comes to rule religion in Nietzsche's thought. There is no suggestion on Strauss's part that the absence of this argument is an oversight on Nietzsche's part: *Beyond Good and Evil* is a satellite of *Zarathustra.* The most beautiful of Nietzsche's books provides access to the most profound. Nietzsche platonizes in order to provide an entry to his Platonism.

The argument Strauss supplies is based on nature, the theme made prominent by Strauss's relentless pursuit of it in the second half of his essay. The argument he supplies is also based on history, the history of human views of nature that has brought us to the present point in the history of culture. Strauss's explanation of why it is necessary to affirm eternal return demonstrates the profound unity and cohesion of Nietzsche's thought, for the will to power, the complementary man, the genealogy of morals, and eternal return all belong together as aspects of the solution to "the highest, the most difficult problem."

Strauss concludes Nietzsche's particular argument before making his own more general one. Aphorism 230 leads beautifully into 231, where the theme of nature in human nature receives a marvelous treatment. Why have knowledge at all (230)? Why submit oneself to the cruel rigors of an intellectual conscience that cause such suffering for the basic will of the spirit which wants only ease? Because one is fated to it by one's nature (231), that "great stupidity," that "*unteachable* deep down." By asking his reader to compare aphorism 8 to aphorism 231, Strauss suggests that this is the point at which Nietzsche's conviction is reached, here that animal from comedy, that ass of his own philosophy, appears on stage—for the only answer Nietzsche can give to the great, historic question, Why have knowledge at all when knowledge forces cruelty and suffering on us, is this: It belongs to our nature, and rather than alter nature we choose obedience to our nature.

Strauss's way of treating this culmination to Nietzsche's great lesson on spiritedness and spirituality turns it into a tool for his own argument on behalf of eternal return. The "highest achievement" is here a synonym for affirming eternal return, and like all earlier high achievements affirming eternal return "is in the last analysis not the work of reason but of nature"; it depends on something unteachable "deep down." Drawing this conclusion, Strauss again makes explicit his essay-long contrast between Nietzsche and Plato (or at least a popular Platonism): the ground of all worthwhile understanding, he says, seems to be "the nature of the individual, the individual nature, not evident and universally valid insights."

What Strauss now provides at last renders the postponed verdict in the trial of paragraph 26 and renders it in Nietzsche's favor. For the one charge left open at the end of the series of charges in paragraph 26 was "that for Nietzsche there cannot be a natural or rational morality because he denies that there is a nature of man." The charge is false. Nietzsche does not deny that there is a nature of man, though of course he denies that it is timeless or even that it is now unalterable: the very threat to human nature in one of its forms requires that Nietzsche act. And that act, with all the cruelty it involves, is founded on the nature of man, though of course Nietzsche puts it playfully and impolitely; human nature is that "fundamental stupidity" way deep down, what is given or granted, that to which one must be obedient. Strauss's clarifying little repetition makes his point about Nietzsche and the nature of man, for Strauss speaks of "the nature of the individual, the individual nature": the nature of the individual is to be understood as the individual nature; the nature of the individual is to be understood Nietzscheanly and not Platonistically, not somehow transcendent to the individual nature.

At this point Strauss takes off on his own to sketch Nietzsche's view of the nature of man and to exhibit the morality implied in it. And his way of doing so confirms the indispensability of the teaching of eternal return, for Strauss shows that from a historical perspective, the reasonableness of affirming eternal return is a corollary to the reasonableness of the turn to the rule of the philosophers of the future. Affirming eternal return is a means of effecting the rule of the philosopher of the future and forestalling the threatened autonomy of the herd.

"There is an order of rank of the natures," Strauss says, and at its summit stands the complementary man. His claim to be the summit of the natures is not empty, for it is based on an essential achievement; "his supremacy is shown by the fact that he solves the highest, the most difficult problem." That problem is the problem of nature faced by modern humanity, a problem that has arisen out of the history of humanity. Strauss, quite explicitly, repeats himself: "As we have observed, for Nietzsche nature has become a problem and yet he cannot do without nature." Nietzsche cannot and does not magically dispense with nature, transporting himself into some radical historicism that supposes it can solve the problem of nature by treating nature as a conceptual fiction. Nietzsche does not conquer nature conceptually, denying its sway and affirming the modern fiction of our radical power to make ourselves whatever we fancy. Nor does Nietzsche surrender to nature under another name, affirming the radical subjection of our minds to the shifting power of what is given, to Being, say.

But what *is* the problem of nature? Here, at the culminating point, Strauss gives, quite explicitly, his own definition of it: "Nature, *we may say,* has become a problem owing to the fact that man is conquering nature and there are no assignable limits to that conquest" (emphasis added). Nature was not always a problem. It *became* a problem because of a fact, something that arose in our history, the willful conquest of nature. Once again, this is no random complaint about the Baconian–Cartesian conquest of nature through an infinity of devices.[36] Strauss's essay has shown that nature has become a problem because of the conquest of *human* nature in a very precise sense, namely, elimination of one of the two natural human types. The

36. See on paragraph 25, "the subjugation of chance, of nature," pp. 76–77 above.

Baconian–Cartesian technological conquest of nature is only a means, if an indispensable means, to the achievement of the ideal of the large majority, universal comfortable self-preservation, which makes the other type expendable.

The victory of the autonomous herd *is* the highest, the most difficult problem, the problem presented to the philosopher by our history. How can the problem be solved? Nietzsche cannot do without nature; he must reinstate nature or assign limits to its conquest, where the relevant conquest is the abolition of the order of rank of the natures. How is this to be done? Through the creation of a new morality, the new good and bad which will provide a new sense of what is ultimately worth doing and what is no longer permitted. With *this* conscious creation of values the truly complementary man fulfills the commission granted him to maintain in the world the order of rank. For the new morality conserves by initiating the most radical reform: overthrow of the dominant morality which has so little respect for nature that it knows no limits to its abolition of the natural order, and establishment in its place of a morality that will conserve the natural order of rank. This is why it is necessary to affirm eternal return. This is also why eternal return will be perceived as the "evil" teaching: its abolition of the old morality will force it to speak an immoral language advocating suffering, inequality, cruelty, difference—advocating nature.

Strauss's way of stating this argument on behalf of eternal return employs the appropriate categories of his essay. Because of the reckless hopes generated by the modern promise to conquer nature, "people have come to think of abolishing suffering and inequality." People dream of the End of History, the universal sway of slave morality, as Hegel taught, everyone free and wised-up and at ease, the view Strauss so eloquently opposed when it was stated in ruthless grandeur by Hegel's twentieth-century spokesman, Alexandre Kojève. Strauss states Nietzsche's counter-view: "Yet suffering and inequality are the prerequisites of human greatness (aph. 239 and 257)." Suffering and inequality must here be thought Nietzscheanly, not crassly or atavistically, as if Nietzsche advocated a return to old brutalities and old slaveries. Strauss is quite clear on this: "Hitherto suffering and inequality have been taken for granted, as 'given,' as imposed on man"—granted, given, imposed: what comes by grace or chance came to be seen as needing correction; nature was viewed as niggardly or cruel or unfair. And it was precisely the order of rank of the natures that caused the deepest suffering: envy and self-hatred. These twin fountainheads of revenge were the moving force behind the human will to correct faulty nature. This disguised "second and more refined atheism," as Nietzsche called it (*BGE* 22), is hatred directed against anything favored by grace or chance; "neither God nor master" is one of its rallying cries (*BGE* 22, 202).

Strauss states Nietzsche's case for hardness: "Henceforth, [suffering and inequality] must be willed." And he defines just what it means to will suffering and inequality or how humanity must be naturalized by willing what it heretofore sought to conquer. (Before considering that definition it is useful to recall that when Strauss first introduced the theme of nature, he had emphasized the aliveness of the unnatural: "The opposite of the natural is the unnatural: the artificial, the domesticated, the misbegotten (62), the antinatural (21, 51, 55); i.e., the unnatural may very well be alive" (paragraph 19). The unnatural, very much alive in the modern moral context that Strauss has now laid out, threatens death to nature; Nietzsche's new natural morality rises to threaten the unnatural.) Now, in a complex sentence which restates his argument (and begins "That is to say"), Strauss states that nature is a fragment unless willed as a bridge to the future: the complementary man complements nature by completing it, in a way ending its fragmentariness. Nature is provided with synonyms that stem from *Zarathustra* and that link nature and history: "the gruesome rule of non-sense and chance, nature, the fact that almost all men are fragments, cripples and gruesome accidents, the whole present and past." This catalog states what must be willed in willing suffering and inequality—the accidental past, human nature as it is, the whole present and past. This totality of present and past remains "a fragment, a riddle, a gruesome accident unless it is willed as a bridge to the future." Present and past are made whole in a future only if everything that was and is is willed; only if the fragmentary is affirmed by a piece of the fragment can it attain a kind of wholeness. And by putting the emphasis on suffering and inequality, Strauss puts the emphasis exactly where Zarathustra himself put it in "On Redemption," the crucial chapter in *Thus Spoke Zarathustra* (2.20) from which the argument is drawn: what is hardest to bear in willing the whole natural order, the whole of the natural process, is to will suffering and inequality, to will the fragmentary character of humanity, to will the absence of redemption from the natural human condition with its order of rank of the natures.

Strauss's concluding judgment unites the fundamental themes of his essay: seen as fields of study, Strauss's two great pairs of philosophy and religion, and morals and politics both come together here; seen as Nietzsche's specific teachings, will to power and eternal return, nature, history, and the complementary man all culminate in this act of willing the eternal return, an act which is understandable only on the basis of the narrative of *Thus Spoke Zarathustra*. But perhaps a clarifying perspective on this singular event can be gained by stepping outside Strauss's essay for a moment and considering the conclusion of what is perhaps Strauss's greatest book, *Thoughts on Machiavelli*. There, in his eloquent and masterful final paragraph, Strauss reflects on the immense problem bequeathed to us by modern times, and he describes just what is needed to solve the modern problem.

> It would seem that the notion of the beneficence of nature or of the primacy of the Good must be restored by being rethought through a return to the fundamental experiences from which it is derived (*TM* 299).

Nietzsche's return to those fundamental experiences is recounted in *Zarathustra*, his dance with Wisdom and Life. Out of those experiences arose his insight into will to power recounted in "On Self-Overcoming" (*Z* 2.12). As is hinted in *Beyond Good and Evil* aph. 56, and as Strauss indicated in his commentary (paragraph 14), Nietzsche presents this teaching on nature as the teaching that restores the notion of the beneficence of nature: Life is will to power ultimately means that life is lovable as it is. Because he has gained this understanding, Zarathustra can whisper to Life the words that show that he is a lover of life to the highest degree. Nature's beneficence, the goodness of nature, is affirmed in the only way now possible, as a process of becoming, as history, as a rule of non-sense and chance that necessarily generates fragments and that has no outcome in wholeness other than the complementary Yes pronounced on the process by the complementary man. "For while 'philosophy must beware of wishing to be edifying,' it is of necessity edifying." These edifying words complete Strauss's above-quoted thought and end his *Thoughts on Machiavelli*. Certainly Nietzsche avoided what philosophy "must beware of": Nietzsche never set out to be edifying; he discovered the edifying, the opposite ideal, "without really meaning to do so" (*BGE* 56), by setting out to think to its depths the least edifying—modern pessimism, modern nihilism. Strauss's essay has labored to show how Nietzsche's glimpse of the opposite ideal, the ideal of eternal return, is of necessity edifying: it does not avoid a relapse into Platonism, for the object of its pursuit becomes its worthy beloved, and it platonizes, it beautifies, the new beloved. *Nietzsche* restored the primacy of the Good: life is lovable as it is. *Nietzsche* returned to the fundamental experiences from which the primacy of the Good is derived, the experience of philosophical *eros*.

In the final two sentences of his paragraph on the complementary man's solution to the most difficult problem, Strauss names two different actions with two different actors, an act by one who paves the way for the complementary man, and an act by that "highest nature" itself. "While paving the way for the complementary man"—and just what paving the way consists of Strauss does not say—"one must at the same time say unbounded Yes to the fragments and cripples." This Yes is part of the unbounded Yes "to everything that was and is," the part that Zarathustra himself found most difficult. This affirmation leads to the act of the complementary man: "Nature, the eternity of nature, owes its being to a postulation, to an act of the will to power on the part of the highest nature." Nature complements nature in this most spiritual action, the highest individual nature willing the eternal return of nature.

"Postulation." The word invokes those most famous postulations of modern philosophy, Kant's moral postulates of God, freedom and immortality, those famous antinomies of nature that somehow, somewhere, inexplicably but necessarily, we hope, transcend nature and guarantee our unnatural morals. The postulation of the complementary man does not differ in being a postulate—"no one *knows* that," says Life when Zarathustra whispers in her ear his passionate affirmation of her, the affirmation of eternal return (Z 3.15, "The Other Dancing Song"). Nor does the postulation of the complementary man differ in being the foundation of morals—it is the highest Yes addressed to what is valuable in itself, it is the relapse into Platonism which cannot be avoided by genuine philosophy.

But this new moral postulate creates values consciously on the basis of insight into will to power; it is the postulate of the one who has glimpsed the nature of nature and been transformed by that glimpse into its lover. Zarathustra first called such acts the acts of the "gift-giving virtue" (Z 1.22), but he later retracted that virtuous name and thought it better to call it "the lust to rule," thereby rehabilitating from its customary curse the spiritual passion to rule. But even that name will not do, and Zarathustra left the highest act of spiritual philanthropy nameless (Z 3.10, "On the Three Evils"). Let us give it Strauss's Platonic name: it is the "kingship of the philosopher who, being 'a perfect man' precisely because he is an 'investigator,' lives privately as a member of an imperfect society which he tries to humanize within the limits of the possible" (*PAW* 17).

With Nietzsche's new moral postulate, 'Be what you are, be eternally what you are," with this unbounded Yes to everything that was and is, philosophy itself comes into the open. The ugly caterpillar metamorphoses; the butterfly spreads its glorious wings. With "pride, daring, courage, self-confidence," with a "will to responsibility" (*GM* 3.10), the philosophic spirit points to itself, points to its own nobility as a primary ground for gratitude for the goodness of the world.

Strauss's climactic paragraph confirms the reasoning behind his remark in a 1935 letter to Karl Löwith that "the eternal return, or more exactly the willingness to endure it, is the *conditio sine qua non* for a truly natural morality."[37] Though he avows to the respected author of an important new book on Nietzsche that he himself is "by no means a Nietzsche specialist," Strauss nevertheless demonstrates that Löwith's critique did "not do justice to Nietzsche" and that the injustice lay primarily in Löwith's failure to appreciate eternal return, the fundamental doctrine his book was written to explain. Löwith had criticized Nietzsche's teaching of eternal return as a futile attempt to recover a Greek world lost forever and with good reason to the superior perspectives of Christianity and modernity. Strauss answers on behalf of a more adequate appreciation of eternal return, doing justice to Nietzsche not only for the teaching essential to "a truly natural morality" but also for the rhetoric that Nietzsche was forced to adopt in advocating it. Strauss emphasizes that the teaching of eternal return had to be "*asserted convulsively*"—*krampfhaft*, frantically, desperately—but "only because [Nietzsche] had to wean us and himself from millennia-old pampering (softening) due to belief in creation and providence." In his subsequent letter Strauss intensifies this point, speaking now of "unbelievable *pampering*"— *unglaubliche* VERWÖHNUNG—"unbelievable" being a heavily freighted word when used in connection with the pampering caused by "the dogma of creation and providence."[38] Had his modern audience not been spoiled by such pampering, Nietzsche could have taught eternal return in the way Strauss describes: the dictates of a probity required by "loyalty to the earth," having revealed eternal return to be "the most extreme expression of world affirmation . . . innocence of becoming," would have ensured that once it was adopted because of its world-affirming character, it would be "taught calmly."

The luxury of teaching calmly was denied Nietzsche by his times. Strauss's 1935 letters make clear what he left somewhat unclear in his late essay on Nietzsche, though the historical logic is the same: the teaching of eternal return grounds a new natural morality which cannot be taught

---

37. "Correspondence of Karl Löwith and Leo Strauss" 184.
38. Ibid. 190.

calmly because the age is spoiled by an unnatural morality that is part of its blood. The doctrines of creation and providence (and their modern Baconian counterparts of the mastery and possession of nature) had taught humanity to believe that it was the crown of creation and the reason for the whole of the natural order. For any natural understanding of things, any understanding of things that recognizes and accepts the hardness of the human condition, these are ruinous doctrines because they are so easy, so welcome, so reassuring, so readily believed: just the things to spoil a child. Of course Nietzsche's teaching seemed cruel in such a setting: it forbids harmful toys whose harmful effects are only now becoming fully visible.

THE PRESERVATION OF NATURAL DIFFERENCE

Paragraph 36 Nietzsche ends chapter 7 on the theme "woman and man," the theme his advocates have thought such a regrettable lapse and his enemies have found such a handy club. Strauss puts this theme in its proper perspective, for it is in no way a fall into the ridiculous from the sublime theme of nature. Nietzsche himself said that "a thinker who has proved shallow in this dangerous place—shallow in his instinct—may be considered altogether suspicious, even more, betrayed, exposed" (aph. 238). Strauss indicates that the theme of woman and man belongs to the fundamental issue for Nietzsche, the issue of nature (see paragraph 17); here the theme provides one more focus for understanding how nature has become a problem in modern times. Nature has become a problem because of the fact that man is conquering nature and there are no assignable limits to that conquest. In one of its facets, that conquest aims at denying or abolishing the natural difference between man and woman; it aims at eradicating the suffering and inequality caused by the war between the sexes. It belongs to Nietzsche's "follies and crimes" (aph. 30) that he speak out as the advocate of nature on behalf of the preservation of natural difference here too.

Chapter 8: European Nobility

Strauss treats Nietzsche's final two chapters very selectively, choosing to mention only those few themes that best illuminate his own plan. The two paragraphs Strauss devotes to these two chapters are linked by the way he begins his second or final paragraph: "Nietzsche thus prepares the last chapter." What Strauss selects from the penultimate chapter therefore focuses on that one special item which prepares the final chapter: European *nobility*.

Strauss's substitution of a French title for Nietzsche's German chapter *Paragraph*
title anticipates the argument of the paragraph: Germany succeeds France on *37*
the one matter that counts most.[39] The paragraph deals with the Nietzschean
theme of a united Europe, the pan-Europeanism that was Nietzsche's hope
for the European future and whose achievement was one of the political aims
of his writings. But Germany dominates Strauss's paragraph. Germany has
"more of a prospect of a future" than the other two countries Strauss deals
with in the paragraph, France and England. Just what that prospect is comes
to light in the very few items that Strauss, following Nietzsche, mentions
about Germany, France, and England.[40]

Strauss finds that Nietzsche stresses the defects of contemporary Germany more than her virtues. Furthermore, those defects concern "not German philosophy but German music, i.e. Richard Wagner." The name alone
is sufficient to evoke that whole constellation of issues which Nietzsche
called *Nietzsche Contra Wagner*, the conflict which Nietzsche believed
opened an essential perspective on modern times. For Nietzsche, Wagner
was the prototype of modern humanity, the actor writ largest, genius ex-
pended in the service of modern mass humanity and of its own reputation
and fame. Nearness to such greatness "is a windfall for a philosopher,"
Nietzsche said, an irreplaceable boon for his education, and Nietzsche never
ceased expressing gratitude for nearness to Wagner (*CW* Epilogue). But
what of the unspoken virtues of contemporary Germany? They could be
found, Strauss seems to suggest, in that aspect of contemporary Germany
mentioned by Strauss as *not* targeted in Nietzsche's critique, German philosophy. The prospects for a united Europe lie in German philosophy, in the
thought of that solitary German philosopher who takes upon himself responsibility for the European future.

"More precisely"—this odd opening to the final sentence invites the
reader to treat it as a more exact statement of what has just been said, despite
the first impression that it introduces a new topic. Read as a clarification of
the rest of the paragraph, the sentence suggests that the paragraph till now
has in fact treated the theme of "European nobility": in treating the philosophers of the future and suggesting that this is where the virtue of contem-

39. Perhaps Strauss emphasizes that Europe is "still" not the united Europe of the philosophers of the future by expanding Charles de Gaulle's phrase "l'Europe des patries."

40. Strauss's Heine reference is to the end of the third letter of *Über die französische Bühne*,
where Heine speaks of what the Germans cannot understand about the French—but especially
of what the French cannot understand about the Germans, a people "with a yesterday and a
tomorrow but no today."

porary Germany lies, the penultimate paragraph suggests that European nobility must now be sought in German philosophy—a suggestion confirmed
by the final paragraph.

European nobility must now extend what had earlier been the work and
invention of France. And it must do this in continued opposition to the work
and invention of England, that commonness or plebianism—the autonomy
of the herd—which had captured modern France, according to Nietzsche's
argument in the aphorism Strauss refers to at the end of the paragraph,
aphorism 253 (and which had captured Germany as well, as evidenced by
the Wagner phenomenon). The fateful English capture of France on behalf
of the autonomy of the herd has served, Nietzsche said, to obscure the fact
that "European noblesse—of feeling, of taste, of manners, taking the word
noblesse, in short, in every higher sense—is the work and invention of
France." Nietzsche further said that "we must hang on to this proposition of
historical fairness by our very teeth." Nietzsche himself thus became the
tenacious advocate of European nobility in the face of the autonomous European herd. Thus German philosophy is heir to Montaigne and Descartes
and the French *moralistes* in the defense of European noblesse now that
France has taken England's way. And Strauss's final paragraph, like his whole
essay, argues that "European nobility" must be read in the most spiritual
sense.

This Nietzsche-centered interpretation of Strauss's paragraph on the European future is supported, to say the least, by the fact that Nietzsche viewed
himself this way and that he was almost as chary as Strauss about actually
saying so. How could he not have been? It is too ridiculous for words, too
inviting of ridicule. In order to avoid offense, the possibility of a new nobility
must be introduced with great delicacy. By dealing so courteously with
Nietzsche's role, by hardly even mentioning it out loud, Strauss allows
Nietzsche to stay somewhat masked.[41] Courteous treatment of the initially
offensive governs Strauss's last paragraph as well, and he is especially courteous about the ultimate offense that Die vornehme Natur ersetzt die göttliche Natur.

Chapter 9: Die Vornehme Natur

Paragraph "Nietzsche thus prepares"—by intimating that the staggering task of
38 founding a united Europe and preserving natural nobility falls to German

41. For some fine examples of Nietzsche's own intimations of his embarrassingly immodest
task, see *GS* 357, 362, 370.

philosophy, Nietzsche prepares "the last chapter which he entitled '*Was ist vornehm?*'" Avowing that "'Vornehm' differs from 'noble' because it is inseparable from extraction, origin, birth," Strauss refers to *Dawn of Morning* aph. 199 for support. This aphorism, entitled "Wir sind vornehmer," is a paradigm of Nietzsche's natural history of morality; but far more important than that, this aphorism has the special merit of adding one last major contribution to Strauss's essay-long contrast between Plato and Nietzsche, for here we learn the role played by Platonic morality in taming and domesticating an older Greek *Vornehmheit* and in preparing our own. Unlike Strauss, Nietzsche does not here distinguish between vornehm and some near synonym like *edel.* Instead, Nietzsche distinguishes *our* Vornehmheit from *Greek* Vornehmheit: modern, post-Christian virtue is superior to ancient Greek virtue, Nietzsche argues, because of what *our* particular "extraction, origin, birth" bequeathed to us, because of what our religion, the tyranny and discipline of our religion, bred into us. Let us not abandon this nobility of ours, Nietzsche counsels, even if we are now forced to feel that its objects have sunk in our estimation: let us instead attach "this precious inherited drive" to new objects. Our Vornehmheit may still be somewhat feudal, it may not yet have achieved its full maturity, but it can still experience quite directly just how narrow, how scarcely decent even the *vornehmsten* old Greeks were. And the Greeks to whom Nietzsche refers are the Greeks of the classical age prior to Socrates, prior to Plato's philosophy of the future. It was precisely Plato's teaching that "the virtuous man is the happiest man" that eventually cured old Greeks of their scorn for justice and taught them to repudiate the drive to tyranny that every Greek of *vornehmer* origin felt within himself, the drive to dominate, to sacrifice everyone and everything to one's own arrogance and pleasure. Nietzsche grants that the Platonic teaching of happiness through virtue could not be planted too deeply into such wild natures, but he adds that our own long schooling in Platonic virtue has now made that virtue less necessary; our Vornehmheit now permits us virtues that are different from the domesticating virtues necessary in Plato's time and place.[42]

Continuing his own argument in his final paragraph, Strauss indicates that the plan of *Beyond Good and Evil: Prelude to a Philosophy of the Fu-*

---

42. Included after Strauss's reference to *Dawn of Morning* are two references to Goethe. The first sets out the superiority of *vornehm* to *edel,* and the second (in reference to Voltaire and French literature) discusses the *vornehm* in relation to birth, rank, and capacity. These passages suggest the continuity of Nietzsche's task with Goethe's, the elaboration of a post-Christian, pan-European teaching on virtue.

ture, dictates that its last chapter turn to a specific theme: it must show "the (a) philosophy of the future as reflected in the medium of conduct, of life; thus reflected the philosophy of the future reveals itself as the philosophy of the future." The uncertainty of the article in the first part of the sentence seems to be eliminated in the second part: reflected in the medium of conduct, given expression in a new understanding of the virtues, "the (a) philosophy of the future" reveals itself as "the philosophy of the future." Every genuine philosophy of the future must exhibit the particular stamp it will give to the future; it must show how its model of the noble is worthy of drawing adherents who will make that future their present; in this way alone can a philosophy of the future actually become the philosophy of the future.

One expects a turn to the edifying at the end of a work by Strauss. Is that expectation met in this case? Strauss ends his essay on the ever-present contrast between Plato and Nietzsche, and he ends contrasting them on the theme of virtue, on "the medium of conduct." Having just drawn attention to Nietzsche's account in *Dawn of Morning* (199) of the novelty represented by Platonic virtue in Plato's historic context, Strauss ends by displaying the novelty of Nietzschean virtue in Nietzsche's context, Nietzsche's Platonic context. Nietzsche's four virtues differ from the four Platonic virtues because "Nietzsche replaces [ersetzt] temperance and justice by compassion and solitude." Temperance and justice had been the very restraints elevated by Plato as the curb on old Greek passions. They are, in certain respects, now obsolete restraints, Nietzsche suggested in *Dawn of Morning,* and he replaced them with the virtues of compassion and solitude. These virtues are hardly novel given their prominence in historic Christianity, but they are recast by Nietzsche's thought into philosophic virtues. Bred into us by two millennia of Christian practice, compassion and solitude take on an entirely different tenor with the death of the Christian God and the wiping away of his shadows. Compassion is no longer the irrational glorification of service to the low which has cost us all sense of the naturally high; compassion now sees the necessity of cruelty and suffering for the preservation of the naturally high. Solitude is no longer shared with an all-seeing God, nor is it the suspicious hideout of the cunning; it is the philosopher's pathos of distance, his separation into singularity aware of its sweetness and unafraid of flaunting it. Virtue is no longer ascetic virtue.

Strauss interprets this replacement of two Platonic virtues by two Nietzschean virtues as an illustration of what Nietzsche means "by characterizing nature by its 'Vornehmheit' (aph. 188)." To characterize nature this Nietzschean way is no longer to characterize nature in the Platonic way by *Gött-*

lichkeit, as the final, German sentence indicates. The Nietzschean virtues thus reflect the nobility of nature in the medium of human conduct. Postmodern "man as little as pre-modern man can escape imitating nature as he understands nature" (*TM* 298).

But Strauss states that "this is one illustration among many" of what Nietzsche means—perhaps the unmentioned fate of the other Platonic virtues is another illustration of what happens to human virtue under the new understanding of nature. Courage remains as a virtue in Nietzsche's list in aphorism 284, but now it stands first instead of second as it did in the *Republic.* (The *Laws,* 631c–d, with its emphasis on prudence, demotes courage to fourth place.) But Strauss himself had often intimated that philosophy as such is characterized by courage and that philosophical courage is the very opposite of the "political courage" (*CM* 107) defined in the *Republic* as the determination to stand loyal to the dyed-in opinion about which things are terrible (*Republic* iv.403b–c). Philosophical courage is the contrary, the refusal of the mind to stick fast to any loyalty bred into the heart. It was precisely Platonic political philosophy, as Strauss presented it, that succeeded in covering philosophy's courageous core, its willingness to put everything at risk for itself by abandoning opinion and pursuing knowledge. But Platonic political philosophy had hid that courageous core behind its lie of a dependable and comforting knowledge which it knew it had not attained and would not attain. Philosophy's hidden first virtue becomes its open and avowed first virtue when nature is understood in its Vornehmheit, its appalling "wasteful and indifferent magnificence."

The virtue which Platonic political philosophy paraded as first, wisdom, does not appear on Nietzsche's list; it too seems to be replaced, although Strauss does not mention it: the second virtue on Nietzsche's list is insight. How fitting for insight to replace wisdom when noble nature replaces divine nature: the gods were said to be wise by Plato's Diotima, as Strauss mentioned early—"no human being is wise, but only the god is" (paragraph 4). But when the lie of a göttliche Natur possessing wisdom is replaced, not only does divine wisdom yield first place to a human or mortal courage: second place is assigned to insight, the fruit of human courage in inquiry. The human understanding of nature having changed, the virtues must also change.

It is worth emphasizing that the "one illustration among many" that Strauss selects in order to show what Nietzsche means by nature's Vornehmheit calls attention to Nietzsche's compassion. It is most appropriate that Strauss do Nietzsche this justice in his final paragraph, given the reputation for cruelty that any novel teacher acquires and that Nietzsche in particular acquired; and given the necessity that Nietzsche reinstate cruelty in a setting of irrational glorification of compassion; and, finally, given the fact that Strauss himself had once found it necessary to indict Nietzsche publicly for preaching cruelty.

It is also worth emphasizing that for a virtue to be replaced by no means implies that it is abandoned or debased: in his account of the turn from the autonomy of the herd to the rule of the philosophers of the future, Strauss had insisted on Nietzsche's spiritualization of justice and severity.

Strauss's final English sentence refers back to Nietzsche's characterization of nature's Vornehmheit in aphorism 188—the aphorism Strauss had singled out in his seminars on *Beyond Good and Evil* as "very important." Nature had been characterized as vornehm in the central chapter, where Nietzsche had set forth the way of nature: "for here, as everywhere, 'Nature' shows itself as it is, in all its wasteful and *indifferent* magnificence, which appalls, but is noble." In this aphorism Nietzsche dealt with the history of the European spirit, specifically that long obedience and "unfreedom of spirit" which dictated that a Christian interpretation be given to all events. The European spirit owes its strength to the discipline bred into it by that long bondage; its freedom for ruthless curiosity and subtle mobility is the fruit of that long slavery. Nature's Vornehmheit is present everywhere but it is exhibited in a particularly useful way in our history. That long, wasteful history appalls us, but it has generated the thinker heir to that tradition who is equal to the challenge it bequeathed, the thinker who solves the highest, the most difficult problem, the problem presented by the fact that man is conquering nature and there are no assignable limits to that conquest.

Strauss's whole essay is a relentless pursuit comparing Nietzsche and Plato on all the major issues. It is a comprehensive display of how the thought of this philosopher of the future replaces the thought of that philosopher of the future. Nevertheless, *Plato* is not replaced, for Nietzsche platonizes; he beautifies with graceful subtlety as regards form, as regards intention, as regards the art of silence. *Plato* is not replaced, for Nietzsche cannot avoid a relapse into Platonism, a relapse that philosophy as such cannot avoid, for it is the love for the highest beloved. If Nietzsche platonizes and relapses into Platonism, if the study even of Nietzsche is a study in Platonic political philosophy, the final word must reinforce their differences while not repudiating what they share, and it must do so platonically: "Die vornehme Natur ersetzt die göttliche Natur."

Chapter Three

Nietzsche's Place in the History of Platonic Political Philosophy

The Nietzsche of Strauss's essay is the defender of the interests of philosophy in the modern setting, and the interests of philosophy are the highest interests of humanity (*PAW* 18). Nietzsche defends the interests of philosophy at the historic moment in which those interests are most threatened by modern religion with its irrational, unnatural, and vengeful belief in the mastery of nature and the end of history, and by the historicizing studies that serve these core beliefs. As philosophy's advocate Nietzsche "platonizes"; he practices an art of writing that beautifies his subject, enticing others to take it up as their own and discover in their turn the beauty of the seemingly ugly. And as philosophy's advocate, Nietzsche relapses into Platonism, the teaching that the whole is lovable in itself. Nietzsche is a Platonic political philosopher who recovers the Platonic sense of philosophy from modern oblivion.

NIETZSCHE AS ANTIMODERN

Strauss makes it apparent that Nietzsche, "the most modern of the moderns" (*KGW* VIII 2 [201]), is not a modern. Nietzsche "abhorred the modern ideas" (*WPP* 172). When Strauss defined those ideas in his "Restatement on Xenophon's *Hiero*," he assigned modernity two defining beliefs: "unlimited progress in the 'conquest of nature' which is made possible by modern science," and "the popularization or diffusion of philosophic or scientific knowledge" (*OT* 178). Nietzsche advocated neither the conquest of nature nor the Enlightenment.

Seen from the perspective of modernity's defining beliefs, Nietzsche is the enemy par excellence. He revived what moderns condemned. In the face of modern hopes for the conquest of nature, hopes or dreams of a technological Utopia based on hatred of the actual human condition as subjection to nature, Nietzsche revived cruelty and suffering and inequality as the natural prerequisites for human greatness, daring to tell frightened adherents won by more alluring aspects of his teaching: "Toughen up" (*Z* 3.12.29; *TI* end; *EH* Books *Z*, 8). In the face of the modern Enlightenment with its impossible dream of a free, equal, and wised-up humanity based on hatred of the actual human condition, Nietzsche revived an order of rank among humans as knowers and placed at their peak a "knower" marked by ambiguity and unknowing, the qualities of an ignorant Socrates.

Strauss makes clear that Nietzsche was branded a teacher of evil because he was a traitor to his times, but he also makes clear that for Nietzsche there could be no return to an earlier time.

NIETZSCHE AS ANTICLASSICAL

Strauss's Nietzsche essay does not go out of its way, to say the least, to call attention to the depth and vehemence of Nietzsche's attack on classical philosophy. When he mentions Nietzsche's primary attack on Plato as the inventor of the most dangerous of all errors, Strauss simply divorces Plato himself from that error, the basic tenet of classical or dogmatic Platonism that the pure mind, the divine mind, grasps the good in itself. And Strauss's essay on Nietzsche's *Beyond Good and Evil* omits entirely any thematic discussion of its first chapter, "On the Prejudices of Philosophers," mining it primarily for its positive assertions about will to power while leaving entirely untouched Nietzsche's dismemberment of the dogmatic "faith in opposite values" (*BGE* 2) stemming from Platonism.

Strauss is able to ignore this crucial aspect of the plan of Nietzsche's *Beyond Good and Evil*—that it begins with an extended critique of the moralism of classical philosophy—because he takes the first three chapters together and enters them from behind, from the theme of the third, religion. By beginning with the fundamental alternative of the rule of philosophy over religion or the rule of religion over philosophy, Strauss tacitly grants while seeming to ignore the two basic matters: first, that it was precisely Platonism that led to religion's actual rule over philosophy in our tradition; and second, that it is the death of Platonism that precipitated the current crisis or opportunity.

What Strauss chooses to emphasize is the different directions in which Plato and Nietzsche point. Plato points away from himself to *göttliche Natur*, whereas Nietzsche points to himself, to Mr. Nietzsche, to vornehme Natur. Nietzsche's pointing, his elevation of the human and of philosophy as the most spiritual human enterprise, is shown by Strauss to have a profound historic rationale: it occurs at that moment in human history when man is conquering nature, and there are no assignable limits to that conquest. It occurs at the decisive moment in the history of religion's rule over philosophy when philosophy itself is rendered superfluous by mass possession of the "truth"—modern fables about history and humanity that are regarded as scientific truth.

Strauss emphasizes Nietzsche's effort to surpass Plato in strength or power, and in doing so he gives Nietzsche's opposition to classical philosophy firm grounding in something other than anticlassical ire: it is grounded in the true experience of philosophy itself and in a true understanding of the present age. There is never the least suggestion in Strauss's essay that Nietzsche points to himself or aims to surpass Plato out of a love for immortal glory or out of a will to power in any crass sense of the willful exercise of power over the minds of others merely for the sake of power. Strauss elevates the rivalry between Nietzsche and Plato to the level of genuine philosophy: the philosopher's creation of values has a profound rationale in an understanding of the human place in the world and an understanding of human history.

Nietzsche as antimodern and anticlassical, as the philosophic critic of both ancient and modern, is of necessity a philosopher of the future.

NIETZSCHE AS PHILOSOPHER OF THE FUTURE

There have been philosophers of the future in the past, Strauss suggests, philosophers who took in hand responsibility for the human future. The greatest of these is Plato, whose elevation of göttliche Natur proved fundamental to the formation of Western culture and the preservation of philosophy. In other essays, Strauss had gone out of his way to argue that "the way of Plato" was a successful development of "the way of Socrates" and that its success was a political success leading to the secret spiritual rule of the philosopher king through the gradual replacement of accepted opinions.

Strauss's Nietzsche essay shows that Nietzsche as philosopher of the future breaks with the fundamental stratagem of past philosophers of the future: Nietzsche has no use for the pious fraud. He abandons classical philosophy's virtue of temperance or moderation, its manner of speaking and acting. Strauss made clear that moderation was a secondary or derivative virtue, a cover for philosophy's actual immoderation, the absolute freedom philosophy accorded rational thought and the absolute jurisdiction philosophy granted rational thought over belief. "Moderation is not a virtue of thought" (*WPP* 32; see *SA* 281–82), it is a virtue of action which set out to hide the virtues of thought because they would be taken to be vices, acts of disloyalty, crimes against society's primary virtue, steadfast adherence to what is given as true. Classical philosophy's vaunted moderation hid philosophy's actual immoderation, its mania or madness in pursuit of truth. In order to win freedom for its natural unrestraint, philosophy learned to give a restrained appearance by accommodating itself to the society on which it depended and honoring society's necessary restraints. With Plato, philosophy even learned how to provide reasons that would assist society in its necessary restraints, rational reasons for irrational fictions. Platonic philosophy succeeded in persuading society that philosophy's instruments, seemingly so ruinous to society's beliefs, could in fact be employed on their behalf; it taught society that what it most wanted to believe, what it already believed, could be proven by reason. It won over suspicious opponents and observers by persuading them that it could be an ally. The philosophical politics of classical philosophy consisted in "satisfying the city that the philosophers are not atheists, that they do not desecrate everything sacred to the city, that they reverence what the city reverences, that they are not subversives, in short, that they are not irresponsible adventurers but good citizens and even the best of citizens" (*OT* 205–6).

Classical philosophy's moderation is its noble lying, its advocacy of virtue over pleasure while pursuing the highest pleasure (*OT* 92–102). Much of Strauss's life work was centered on making this fact accessible again. In *Xenophon's Socratic Discourse*, Strauss uses Xenophon to intimate how Socrates learned what society needed from society's pillar, Ischomachus, famous husbandman and husband. Strauss alleges that Socrates set out to learn society's ways on the day after Aristophanes caught his attention, attention which had, till then, been turned immoderately and unrestrainedly in the direction of a gnat's behind. (Nietzsche, an admirer of Aristophanes living in an age more easily embarrassed, at least makes his model scientist the student of a leech's *brain*.) Socrates learned his first lessons about society's necessary restraints by attending to Ischomachus's lessons on order which Ischomachus had learned in part from a Phoenician boatswain and then taught to his wife. Ischomachus thought his wife submissive and malleable, a pliant nature subject to authoritative words; Strauss takes special pleasure in suggesting that she is anything but, "impudent hag" that she is. Socrates cemented the lessons he learned about society's necessary restraints with his own "teleotheology" of order, an account of the gods' ordering of the whole toward the good which Strauss shows to be exposed to grave difficulties (*XSD* 148–52, 153–58).[1]

With respect to Plato, Strauss allows it to be seen that the endorsement of moderation and the elaboration of a world-view on moderation's behalf masked in fact another aspect of classical philosophy's immoderation: its desire to rule, the propensity of Platonic philosophers which Epicurus captured venomously by calling them *dionysiokolakes*—"who knows: from rage and ambition against Plato perhaps?" (*BGE* 7).

Nietzsche repudiated the moderation within which Plato's philosophy of the future had sheltered itself and its ambitions, and he did so for perfectly understandable historical reasons that Strauss makes accessible and defensible. As Strauss presents matters in his Nietzsche essay, Nietzsche's famous immoderation can best be understood as his response to the immoderation of modern thought or modern religion, "the irrational glorification of compassion," with its destructive dream of an infinitely malleable nature hammered into a future utopia with the tools of a new science of nature. Nietzsche saw this dream for what it was: Christian leftovers. And he saw Christianity for what it was: Platonism for the people. Furthermore, Nietzsche knew that all gods die: the dream of a heaven on earth inhabited by humans who had become as gods was bound to die of its own excess, die of the laughter generated by its own inner ridiculousness (*GS* 1). To remedy the consequences of the death of that dream, the misology and misanthropy that is modern nihilism, Nietzsche took the fateful step of disclosing the actual immoderation of philosophy, both its unfulfillable aspiration to a complete understanding of the whole and its aspiration to rule, just as he disclosed philosophy's "moderation," its willingness to indulge in pious fraud on its own behalf and appear as an ugly caterpillar of ascetic virtue to those who thought ascetic virtue virtue itself. A whole new history of philosophy comes to light from this perspective whose novelty lies in both its candor and its perspicacity; now the history of philosophy can be recovered as what it really was: "The hidden history of the philosophers came to light for me" (*EH* Preface 3).

NIETZSCHE AND THE FUTURE HISTORY OF PHILOSOPHY

Nietzsche makes a whole new history of philosophy possible, and Strauss makes a substantial contribution to that new history. Basic to a Nietzschean history of philosophy is his distinction between genuine philosophers and

---

1. See Christopher Bruell, "Strauss on Xenophon's Socrates," for a valuable skeptical reading of Strauss's Xenophon commentaries.

philosophical laborers, genuine philosophers being those very few com-manders and legislators who set out to create values which would forge and animate whole peoples. Strauss shows how Nietzsche belongs to this small company. Nietzsche could speak "so greatly and so nobly of what a philoso-pher is" (*RCPR* 40) for one reason alone: he shared the fundamental expe-rience of the genuine philosophers and could regard them as kin. One of the most beautiful of Nietzsche's claims to such kinship begins: "I too have been to the underworld and will be there many times again" (*AOM* 408). Like Socrates at the end of the *Apology*, Nietzsche pictures his descent to the underworld as an opportunity to converse with the greatest of dead he-roes. And like Socrates, Nietzsche sees this as the occasion to judge and be judged; he measures the great philosophers of the past and allows them to measure him.

Nietzsche judges that the genuine philosophers share the fundamental Platonism, erotic attachment to the whole of which they are the rational investigators. Nietzsche too could have said with Lessing, "there is no other philosophy than that of Spinoza" (*PAW* 182). But as a judge who stands at an unprecedented turning point in the history of philosophy, Nietzsche was forced to add about Spinoza's form of Platonism, his *amor intellectualis dei:* "What is *amor,* what is *dei,* if there is not a drop of blood in them?" (*GS* 372). Nietzsche's history of philosophy is a measurement of Platonic kin from a standpoint beyond the historic necessity to compromise with popular stupidity and feign affinity with priestly asceticism.

Plato is the exemplar of the genuine philosopher, Plato that "prodigy of pride and sovereignty" (*GS* 351). For all his criticism of Plato as the inventor of the "worst, most durable, and most dangerous of all errors so far . . . a dogmatist's error" (*BGE* Preface), Nietzsche spares Plato the ultimate criti-cism which he levels against what Platonism eventually became in our dominant tradition. In an aphorism devoted to the "revenge against the spirit" endemic to such a large portion of our moral and religious tradition, Nietzsche distinguished Plato from the most powerful Christian Platonist, Augustine (*GS* 359). Both were "monsters of morality who made noise, made history," but Plato's noise-making had a philanthropic motive, tender regard for disciples who had to be "defended against themselves by means of faith in a person (by means of an error)." Plato permitted his followers to believe that their teacher was a knower, that his pure mind had grasped the good in itself. The inventor of the most dangerous dogmatism was himself no dogmatist. On the question of knowledge, the philosopher Nietzsche dares to speak for all his kin, explicitly including in their number Plato him-self: "they simply do not believe in any men of knowledge" (*GS* 351).

When summing up his great debt to the ancients, Nietzsche criticized Plato for lacking "*courage* in the face of reality," and fleeing to the ideal (*TI* Ancients 2). But Nietzsche also held that Plato was the most beautiful growth of antiquity and the philosopher with the greatest strength at his disposal (*BGE* Preface, 191). Plato's lack of courage in the face of reality was therefore not fear for himself; it was fear for others. Plato feared for civility and humanity, and his fears led him to make the fateful compromises with stupidity that turned him pre-existently Christian and led him to invent a dogmatism that eventually gave heart to fierce dogmatists. Nietzsche's complete skepticism about Plato is coupled with the highest regard for Plato's strength; this combination of skepticism and regard opened the door to the dialogues as in part exercises in salutary education that did not blush to employ inventions that were, as Montaigne said, "as useful for persuading the common herd as they are ridiculous for persuading [Plato] himself."[2]

But when the history of philosophy turns to the Christian Platonist Augustine, Nietzsche's regard falls away. Not philosophic eros but revenge is fundamental to Augustine in Nietzsche's view (*GS* 359); not philanthropy but misanthropy lay behind Augustine's noise-making. Revenge on a world-historical scale transformed the Platonic lie of a moral universe into a malevolent system of cosmic revenge employing an all-powerful cosmic spider lurking at the center of its web with a retinue of regents to bind on earth what would be bound in heaven. Nietzsche's blame of Plato is based on two and a half millennia of subsequent European experience: Plato's philanthropy, Plato's lack of courage, unwittingly opened the door to the most fateful subsequent event in the history of philosophy, Christianity's capture of philosophy and science. The Christian rule of religion over philosophy rendered "the whole labor of the ancient world *in vain*," for that Greek and Roman labor was "preliminary labor" which laid the foundations of a scholarly culture based on science (*A* 59) and was ready to *begin*. Plato's salutary lie facilitated Jerusalem's capture of Athens and the destruction of the very science Plutarch once credited Plato with saving.[3]

With Strauss's help, it is possible to see that the eros which signals philosophy's true Platonism was not exclusive to Plato. In his commentaries on Xenophon, Strauss makes it evident that philosophy knows itself to be the highest pleasure and that it prudently masked its own pursuit of pleasure by elevating virtue. In the spirit of Xenophon, Strauss made somewhat more prominent Xenophon's quiet notice that Socrates danced alone when he

---

2. Montaigne, *Essays* ii.12, "Apology for Raymond Sebond" 379.

3. Plutarch *Nicias* ch 23. The reference stems from *OT* 206; for Strauss's reason for citing it see n. 20 to chap. 4.

thought no one was looking, and that Socrates was evidently right to hide his dance for when Charmides caught him in the act he feared that Socrates had gone mad (*XS* 147–48). Strauss showed how Xenophon helped Socrates hide a dance that could look criminal behind an almost perfect sobriety that the gentlemen could think worthy of emulating as mere sobriety.

But Strauss is of special use to a Nietzschean history of philosophy in the effort to understand the place of philosophy in modern times, to recover the revolution effected by early modern philosophers. They were as profoundly opposed to Christianity as Nietzsche was, but they lived within a Christian social order that made it necessary for them to hide their hostility in careful speech. Strauss shows that the hideout they chose for their hostility was actually subtly marked with signs and arrows for it was meant to be discovered and entered by those whose toil of discovery and entry would turn them into accomplices and coconspirators. Strauss makes available to a Nietzschean history of philosophy the breathtaking enterprise of thinkers as diverse as Machiavelli, Montaigne, Bacon, Descartes, Hobbes, Spinoza, Locke. For all its variety, it is one enterprise (*TM* 231), and although it did not advertise itself as such it could nevertheless bear the title Francis Bacon gave to one of its finest documents: "Advertisement Touching a Holy War"— a war against Christianity. Strauss makes it possible to view and appreciate the hostility between Athens and Jerusalem that moved all the genuine philosophers of early modern Europe.[4]

In addition to his study of individual thinkers, Strauss makes an essential contribution to a Nietzschean history of philosophy through his studies in esotericism. Nietzsche himself rediscovered the fact that all philosophers prior to the Enlightenment knew the difference between the exoteric and the esoteric (*BGE* 30), that they made use of the pious fraud to work their "improvements" in human morals (*TI* Improvers 5), that "the emergency conditions" surrounding philosophy's first appearance in the world required that it adopt the cloak of ascetic ideals inimical to its own world-affirming spirit (*GM* 3.10): a Nietzschean history of philosophy finds rich resources within Nietzsche's writings for appreciating the depth and extent of philosophical esotericism.

And Strauss adds immensely to those resources. His boldness in exhibiting the lying ways of the philosophers provides great gains for a Nietzschean history of philosophy: neither Plato, nor Alfarabi, nor Maimonides, nor Bacon, nor Descartes need be weighed down by their pieties any more. Nearly

---

4. I have argued for this viewpoint with special reference to Bacon and Descartes in *Nietzsche and Modern Times*.

two centuries of post-Hegelian scholarship have viewed philosophy as essentially impossible: even the greatest thinker is a child of his time. But Nietzsche and Strauss recover philosophy: the genuine philosopher is a step-child of his time who, having transcended it in thought, often found it necessary to mask that transcendence in an appearance of conformity. The genuine philosophers were not victims of their times, half rational half superstitious. They were rational masters of the superstitions of their times who knew both the dangers of the rational and the uses of superstition.

Strauss's studies in esotericism have shocked an academy whose innocence and naiveté led it to believe that such practices demean or embarrass philosophy. Scholarly reaction to Strauss's studies in esotericism confirms Nietzsche's humbling claim that modern scholarship degenerated into good-natured credulity based on faith in modern democracy and modern science: "lack of reverence, shame, and depth," a "plebianism of the spirit," cost scholarship the mistrustful spirit, the cold suspicion that marked its achievements in premodern times (GS 358). What Pietro Redondi, in his study of Galileo, called "the intellectual virtue of honest dissimulation" has fallen into neglect and disgrace in contemporary scholarship, where the very mention of it is thought a vice.[5] But Strauss's studies in esotericism are in fact contributions to a recognition of philosophy's greatness. And if Nietzsche says with respect to esotericism of this historic sort, "That's all over now," a Nietzschean history of philosophy is in a position to recover the history of philosophy as it really was, with its virtue intact.

For all its necessity, however, appreciation of esotericism is a sub-theme in the history of philosophy, a mere means to the recovery of the core issues. But it is so entertaining in its intricacies, so intoxicating in its audacity that it threatens to overwhelm the more basic matters. How could a lone writer like Descartes presume to take on the powers of the age and, by feigning loyalty to what he loathed, actually defeat those powers on behalf of the posterity for which he wrote? Being entertained by the sheer magnitude and mastery of Descartes's undertaking must not be allowed to deflect attention from the basic matter: Descartes belongs among the few genuine philosophers who created values that accord with a philosophic Platonism and that were meant to legislate a new people. In the midst of powers that understood divinity differently, Descartes advocated a love of "divine providence" that was a love of natural necessity, a love of God or nature, *amor fati*.

A Nietzschean history of philosophy, aided by Strauss's appreciation of the genuine philosopher and his necessary esotericism, can recover our spiri-

---

5. Redondi, *Galileo: Heretic* 283; see 24, 146, 293, 323.

tual history in its highest moments. Nietzsche's place in the history of Platonic political philosophy is clear: he stands as a genuine philosopher at the end of a history of pious fraud offering the necessary philological and psychological tools for a complete survey of that history and for the recovery of its basic Platonism.

NIETZSCHE AND RULE OF PHILOSOPHY OVER RELIGION

But Nietzsche was more than a historian of philosophy. As a philosopher of the future, Nietzsche embodied philosophy's immoderation in himself while pointing to himself. What is noble? The highest nobility is a human aristocracy of mind and heart. Saint, statesman, scientist, gentleman—all occupy a lower spiritual rank than the genuine philosopher because all live within worlds created for them by others, worlds of values not of their own making. Nietzsche's immoderation is his public disclosure of philosophy's rank and his pointing to Mr. Nietzsche: Mr. Nietzsche is a creator of values who commands and legislates natural values true to the earth and to humanity's order of rank.

With Nietzsche, philosophy sheds its ascetic mask and comes forth— How? Unmasked? "Everything profound loves masks" (*BGE* 40), which means in part that everything profound is unavoidably masked because it cannot help being taken superficially and being understood as something other than what it is. The philosophy of the future can no more escape this fate than the philosophy of the past; nor would it want to escape this fate. What is the Nietzschean mask loved by Nietzschean profundity? Nietzschean secrets seek display; they want to overcome their natural obscurity while knowing that they can never surface as they are. Nietzschean secrets admit display only through new poetry—new songs of becoming and new epiphanies of philosophizing gods. Nietzschean profundity generates Nietzschean masks, Nietzschean philosophy generates Nietzschean religion. Nietzsche's talk of masks is not traffic in pious fraud; he opens his hand on all the "deadly" truths, knowing full well that it is beyond his or anyone else's power to close them up as secrets again. If in the portrayal of these deadly truths Nietzsche platonizes, his beautification is not a cosmetic smeared over the deadly or ugly, for "without really meaning to do so," without setting out to be edifying, Nietzsche's gaze into the deadly led him to see its beauty, and to glimpse a new ideal—for the sovereignty of becoming, the fluidity of all concepts, types, and kinds, and the lack of any cardinal difference between man and animal (*UD* 9) are the moving foundation of the new poetry. Nietzsche's platonizing beautifies, but it beautifies the already lovable, the whole seen in its "intelligible character," its " 'necessary' and 'calculable' course" as will to power (*BGE* 36, 22).

The platonizing of this philosophy of the future is decisively different from Plato's platonizing because its surface accords with its depth, its songs accord with its secrets. It does not falsify the hidden profundity but displays it in beautifying poetry. It does not regard its secret core as poison to every viable social order, however much it poisons existing social orders to which it must seem folly or crime (*BGE* 30); its secret core aspires to be the foundation of a new social order, the thousand and first people envisioned by Zarathustra whose goal, whose good and bad, is a tablet of values true to the earth. Nietzschean philosophy comes forth masked in a poetry that exhibits its inwardness or that is true to its inwardness. The relationship between philosophy and poetry is no longer a quarrel, because philosophy itself has become Homeric. The Nietzschean mask, like the Homeric mask, allows what is seen to accord with what is not seen, it "lies" by augmenting and supplementing; it "lies" willfully with poetry that enhances the already beautiful beloved, life itself. The mask is complementary to the masked; its highest parables are parables of becoming; its gods philosophize because they too are charmed by the unknown; and its gods are well-disposed toward humanity because they are not the enforcers of a moral order called into existence to certify and police a fragile social harmony. Nietzsche's philosophy of the future allows the forbidden Homeric poetry back in to the Platonic city which tried to keep itself pure by banishing all poets except those who were the valets of its civic morality. It welcomes back the once banished poetry that sings the virtues of warriors and voyagers, not those of gentlemen farmers, poetry that celebrates the spirited over the stolid, questioners over answerers, butterflies over caterpillars.

If the gods too philosophize, if Dionysos is a philosophizing god, *Socratism* or zetetic openness to the fundamental problems is elevated to the place of divinity. The apologies for Socrates invented by the great Socratics Plato and Xenophon were built on the noble lie that *really* he got his commission from Apollo, *really* he knew that just gods ruled our affairs, *really* he knew of ideas and an ontotheological order and could talk so persuasively about them that he could charm young Glaucon and Adeimantus, or old Spartan and Cretan legislators, into believing what he said he knew. Nietzsche buries this lying Socrates. More than that, he shows that such moralism is now immoral, a crime against mortals and the earth that generated them. The philosophy of the future says with respect to this once successful philosophy of the past: "That's all over now" (*GS* 357).

What was Nietzsche's intent? To rule the world. Nietzsche had the same intent as Plato. To ascend to a secret spiritual kingship that could no longer be as secret as Plato's spiritual kingship. To be an "investigator" living privately as a member of an imperfect society trying to humanize it within the limits of the possible (*PAW* 17), where "humanize" meant to bring society into accord with the highest human achievements, to make society friendly to philosophy.

What was Strauss's intent in making Nietzsche's intent accessible?

Chapter Four

Strauss's Place in the History of Platonic Political Philosophy

WHAT WAS STRAUSS'S INTENT?

Strauss's intent cannot have been fundamentally different from Nietzsche's intent: Strauss too is the defender of the cause of philosophy, the cause of reason in the world. He is an advocate of enlightenment and rationalism, to use the words Strauss himself occasionally employed for what political philosophy advances.

But Leo Strauss, as great as he is, is not a Nietzsche or a Plato. If we use Nietzsche's standard of measure, Strauss must be seen as a "philosophical laborer." And we must add immediately what Nietzsche added immediately: this is not an insult. Philosophical labor can be something truly great; it can reach as high as the noble models of Kant or Hegel; it can be "an enormous and wonderful task in whose service every subtle pride, every tough will can certainly find satisfaction" (*BGE* 211). On this elevated scale, the enormous and wonderful task Strauss took up was to discover and then to indicate what Platonic political philosophy is, or, in Nietzschean terms, what the "genuine philosopher" is. As one aspect of this great task, Strauss indicates how the genuine philosophers Nietzsche and Plato are akin, and what these kin share as aspirants to the highest achievement: secret spiritual kingship that defends the interests of philosophy and of nothing else. Strauss himself did not aspire to such kingship: "We cannot be philosophers but we can love philosophy" (*LAM* 7). Strauss was not belittling himself when he said he was not a philosopher, nor was he being ironic; he recognized that he was not himself a maker of worlds, however much he made himself an indispensable guide to world-making philosophers.

If "philosophy as such is nothing but genuine awareness of the problems, i.e., of the fundamental and comprehensive problems," and if "it is impossible to think about these problems without becoming inclined toward a solution, toward one or the other of the very few typical solutions" (*OT* 196), toward what solution did Strauss incline? Regarding philosophy proper, Strauss surely remained a "zetetic," a skeptic in the original Socratic sense. But with respect to a politics for philosophy, toward what solution did Strauss incline? We can disregard, I think, any suggestion that Strauss became a "sectarian," whose "subjective certainty" of a solution became stronger than his awareness of the problematic character of that solution.

If Strauss did not become a sectarian, he did not become a Straussian. This much at least seems evident of that elusive master of other men's elusiveness. He did not hold as timelessly true those twin pillars of a popular Straussianism alleged of him by both friends and enemies: he was not ultimately a loyalist to God and nation because he was not ultimately a loyalist at all; philosophy required, as Nietzsche said, that he learn never to stick fast (*BGE* 41), in particular never to stick fast to a fatherland, whether a victorious or a beaten one (*SPPP* 190). Had Strauss wanted to leave an unambiguous legacy, had he wanted to declare the beliefs to which he was simply loyal, nothing would have been easier for him than to write a little essay at the end of his career with some such title as this: "Hear me! For I am this and this and this. Above all, do not mistake me for someone else" (*EH* Preface 1). The absence of any such essay pointing to himself and his real beliefs suggests on its own that Strauss had no intention of making himself clear in the way that popular or political Straussianism is clear. And if the very teacher of the uses of ambiguity himself remains resolutely ambiguous on this matter, the presumption must be that he knows what he's doing and that ambiguity here is of use to him. After all, "provisional acceptance of the accepted opinions" was a practice with a very high authority, as Strauss pointed out; Alfarabi learned from Plato's correction of Socrates that "conformity with the opinions of the religious community in which one is brought up, is a necessary qualification for the future philosopher" (*PAW* 17).

Nevertheless, Strauss did go out of his way, from time to time, to indicate just where he stood and just what had primacy for him. And on those occasions he let it be known that he too stood where philosophy stood: beyond good and evil and not within some moral view, some revelation, some poetry passed down from generation to generation. An amusing example occurred on a personal occasion, "a giving of accounts" in which Strauss talked about himself in public and explained the difference between himself and his old friend Jacob Klein. At the end of this exchange, Strauss simply insisted on forcing into the open their difference regarding the primacy of morality: Klein, taking himself to be following Plato, measured all things morally; Strauss, also basing his conclusion on Plato, did not.[1]

A still finer example occurred at the end of a public lecture on liberal education. There Strauss spoke explicitly in his own name, having just shown the historic necessity of such speech where all authoritative traditions have been destroyed. Human thought—the life of thought and the gains of thought—provides the sole justification of the world, and it is a sufficient justification. The "act of understanding may be accompanied by the awareness of our understanding, by the understanding of understanding . . . and this is so high, so pure, so noble an experience that Aristotle could ascribe it to his God." Having given this experience such a singular pedigree, Strauss spelled out its radical implications: "This experience is entirely independent of whether what we understand primarily is pleasing or displeasing, fair or ugly. It leads us to realize that all evils are in a sense necessary if there is to be understanding. It enables us to accept all evils which befall us and which may well break our hearts in the spirit of good citizens of the city of God." This is theodicy become cosmodicy, justifying the ways of the world to man. "By becoming aware of the dignity of the mind, we realize the true ground of the dignity of man and therewith the goodness of the world, whether we understand it as created or as uncreated, which is the home of man because it is the home of the human mind" (*LAM* 8).[2] This is Platonism, insight into the goodness of the world even where the world offers the citizen only tragedy, tragedy masked perhaps by an impossible, a pampering comedy.

More characteristically, Strauss provided guidance to his own thinking through the access he provided to the true thoughts of the authoritative thinkers on whom he commented. Strauss showed that Maimonides, for instance, held that the philosophical life is beyond good and evil,[3] and that the moral virtues can only be understood with a view to their political function (*WPP* 166–67). A similar kind of evidence can be found in the very last essay Strauss wrote, "Xenophon's *Anabasis*." What looks like an emphasis on Xenophon's piety and justice is an emphasis on the *peculiarities* of that piety and justice, the ways in which Xenophon was willing to accede to gods while following his own counsel, and to accede to the Spartans out of realistic

1. "A Giving of Accounts" 2, 4–5.
2. For a lucid commentary on the implications of this statement see Udoff, "On Leo Strauss: An Introductory Account."
3. Strauss, "How to Begin to Study the *Guide*" xxvii.

self-interest. Xenophon's piety and justice was calculated to serve an end higher than piety or justice because Xenophon viewed the height of piety and justice from above.[4]

Still, if Strauss was not a Straussian, he was responsible for Straussianism. He evidently believed that it was in the interests of philosophy here and now to encourage the appearance of shared loyalties with believers in God and nation—and the appearance of complete opposition to Nietzsche. Strauss's chosen rhetoric for philosophy, his Xenophontic lip-service, made it seem at first glance as if the interests of philosophy itself were permanently aligned with the God of our religion, the now dead God (according to Nietzsche), the God "with the hellish fear of *science*" (*A* 48) who stood opposed to the chief intellectual achievements of the past three and a half centuries in the West. And Strauss's chosen rhetoric for philosophy gave heart to a school of patriots in a land that took itself to be founded on what is almost literally an updated version of the lie of noble origins, even while it was committed to the pursuit of comfortable self-preservation in the best modern way. Strauss's view of philosophy, plus his synoptic view of philosophy's politic alliances across the breaks and tears of philosophy's history, make it apparent that for Strauss himself these allegiances were dictated by philosophy and not by the intrinsic merits of two dying localisms.[5]

4. It has been said with respect to Strauss's reading of Xenophon that "Strauss . . . studied Xenophon with a care and seriousness that have not been seen before and will not likely be seen again" (Clay, "On a Forgotten Kind of Reading" 255). But if in fact one of Socrates's auditors wrote books interpreting his master's place in the Greek enlightenment that would first be studied with the attention due them by a University of Chicago professor, then the whole effort of recovery is absurd. The only way to save Strauss's enterprise of reading from such absurdity is to recognize a tradition of reading of which Strauss is a late clear member. There is obvious evidence for such a tradition within Western philosophy, attested as it is by great contributors to it such as Montaigne, Bacon, Descartes, and Lessing, the latter a particular inspiration for Strauss. At least once, a handbook of guidelines for such reading had been made public by a reader who judged that the time had come at last to make the whole necessary game public: it has not been adequately appreciated that Strauss had a precursor who wrote his version of *Persecution and the Art of Writing* in 1720—John Toland, who called his version *Clidophorus*, bearer of the key. For a valuable study of the history of esotericism see Cantor, "Leo Strauss and Contemporary Hermeneutics." In addition to Cantor's examples, useful discussions are found in Grotius, *The Rights of War and Peace* Bk. 3, ch. 1, 7–17, and Newman, *Apologia pro vita sua* 253, 317–19, note F, where biblical and ecclesiastical precedents are discussed under the title "The Economy," an aspect of prudence.

5. Shadia Drury's *The Political Ideas of Leo Strauss* has been aggressively excoriated by some of Strauss's followers partly because it showed that Strauss was not simply the loyalist he seemed—"bizarre splenetic" is one of the more inventive outbursts against Drury's work (Emberley and Cooper, *Faith and Political Philosophy*, xv n. 2). Such mindless dismissals excuse their authors from facing the fact that Drury's book contains many fine skeptical readings of Strauss's texts and acute insights into Strauss's real intentions. Still, Drury's work is less effec-

Strauss's chosen rhetoric for philosophy placed him in public opposition to Nietzsche. How can this public stance be reconciled with Strauss's private elevation of Nietzsche? An answer to this question can be approached by looking back over Strauss's writings from the perspective won in his essay on Nietzsche.

Strauss's writings bear the character of a return, one that at first seems both impossible and undesirable. But Strauss's movement of return betrays no trace of nostalgia, no sense of longing for the revival of some lost, earlier world. It is a philosophical and not a sentimental voyage. It is given its impetus by discontent with the present and prospective future of philosophy, discontent with the modern Enlightenment and its consequences. Strauss's move backward focused first on the Medieval enlightenment, on Maimonides and his Islamic predecessors. But it could not come to rest there because those teachers pointed further backward—to Plato, the one they regarded as the teacher of enlightenment and of the necessary politics of enlightenment.

What did Strauss find in Plato, in Platonic political philosophy, that made it possible for him to believe that a return to Plato was viable after all, and that it was the only adequate response to the crisis of our time, the breakdown of the Enlightenment or the loss of faith in the goals of the Enlightenment? What was it in Plato that Strauss came to regard as timelessly true? Once the answer to the question of the Platonic enlightenment became clear to Strauss, the whole sweep of the history of philosophy opened itself to him in a new way. And the history of Platonic political philosophy could eventually encompass even Nietzsche; eventually even the anti-Platonist par excellence could be seen to have platonized and to have relapsed unavoidably into Platonism.

A brief consideration of Strauss's way from the modern Enlightenment back to the Medieval enlightenment and from there back to the paradigmatic enlightenment may help to show how Strauss came to understand that para-

---

tive than it might have been because of its own missionary tone, for Drury never seems to have recovered from the shock of discovering a diabolical teaching. Herself a believer in the rationality of moral values and loyal to the modern ideas, Drury ends in mere censure of Strauss for *dis*loyalty to modern traditions and for being less than candid about his intentions. But the chief shortcoming of her book is its explicit refusal to examine the question of the truth or falsity of Strauss's thesis of esotericism; she chooses to treat Strauss's readings simply as willful manipulations of past philosophers. This makes it too easy to condemn Strauss without addressing the essential claim that justifies his position. If Strauss is in fact one of a long line of philosophical dissemblers who had reasoned grounds for dissembling, then Drury's umbrage is undone. A useful if somewhat exasperated retort to the issues raised by Drury is found in Clifford Orwin, "Leo Strauss, Moralist or Machiavellian." See also Schaefer, "Shadia Drury's Critique of Leo Strauss."

digm and how he could finally put Nietzsche himself at the center of his studies in Platonic political philosophy.

THE MODERN ENLIGHTENMENT

Dominated and charmed by Nietzsche from 1921 to 1929, Strauss came to hold a view during those years which he never abandoned, a view also held by Nietzsche: the modern Enlightenment had demonstrably failed, and its failure made imperative what it also made possible: the reassessment of earlier periods of philosophy. Strauss described his state of mind during those years more than thirty years later, in the 1962 Preface to the English translation of *Spinoza's Critique of Religion*, which sets forth the intellectual prehistory of his book on Spinoza.[6] At the culmination of this dense autobiographical essay, Strauss summarized the essential components of the modern Enlightenment: it was an unprecedented form of liberation from the religious delusion in that it set out to make that delusion superfluous by making humanity the master and owner of nature. But the new faith that human effort could realize this great goal began to wither, and what was left standing was only the new kind of fortitude, "intellectual probity," the new atheism which revealed itself after all "as a descendent of Biblical morality." Strauss's passage (*SCR* 29–31) sets forth tersely Nietzsche's analysis of modern philosophy and its culmination in a proud probity which Nietzsche called the youngest virtue.[7] Nietzsche was explicit about his reasons for setting forth his provocative analysis of this contemporary, comfortless atheism of the "free minds": he wanted to clarify it to its own adherents in order to move them further along the path he himself had traversed to its end, the path which led to the insight into will to power, to the affirmation of eternal return, and to discipleship to Dionysos. *Beyond Good and Evil* exists for that purpose, Nietzsche said; it turns to the near in order to entice to the far, to the Yes-saying opposite ideal of *Zarathustra* (*EH* Books *BGE* 1).

Strauss's own path did not lead directly along the forward path the tempter Nietzsche set out. It led backward first, to a reconsideration of the orthodoxy which the modern Enlightenment claimed to have refuted. Nevertheless, the extremely careful way in which Strauss, in 1962, ended his

6. Given the dates of Strauss's dominance by Nietzsche, it is perhaps important to note that Strauss admitted in a private letter that his autobiographical essay "omitted in a way everything which comes after 1928" (cited in Green, *Jew and Philosopher* 148).

7. Victor Gourevitch remarked in an important essay in 1968 that "Strauss's explicit rejection of Nietzsche . . . must not be allowed to obscure the unstated but important affinities between his own and Nietzsche's critique of modernity" ("Philosophy and Politics" 306 n. 156).

account of his early pathway shows that Nietzsche's analysis was crucial for his own setting forth. More importantly perhaps, it shows that Strauss knew even then that Nietzsche himself did not fall victim to the suicide of reason that was the full outcome of the modern Enlightenment. He spares Nietzsche the indictment due Heidegger, but he does so only after he has made the indictment clear by translating one of his own luminous and complex sentences written twenty-seven years earlier for the Introduction to *Philosophie und Gesetz* (1935):[8]

> This atheism, the heir and the judge of the belief in revelation, of the secular struggle between belief and unbelief, and finally of the short-lived but by no means therefore inconsequential romantic longing for the lost belief, confronting orthodoxy in complex sophistication formed out of gratitude, rebellion, longing and indifference, and in simple probity, is according to its claim as capable of an original understanding of the human roots of the belief in God, as no earlier, no less complex-simple philosophy ever was. (*SCR* 30)

Despite this high claim that it makes on its own behalf, however, Strauss maintains that the new atheism "can not deceive one about the fact that its basis is an act of will, of belief, and, being based on belief, is fatal to any philosophy (*SCR* 30)."

But Strauss immediately adds qualifications to this conclusion regarding "the victory of orthodoxy," and the second qualification states the essential response on behalf of Nietzsche's own position, the response elaborated later in Strauss's essay on Nietzsche but stated here simply as a claim that may perhaps be worthy of investigation some day:

> The hierarchy of moralities and wills to which the final atheism referred could not but be claimed to be intrinsically true, theoretically true: "the will to power" of the strong or of the weak may be the ground of every other doctrine; it is not the ground of the doctrine of the will to power: the will to power was said to be a fact. (*SCR* 30)

Nietzsche's own view was not founded on a belief. Nietzsche's own view was never a radical historicism, for it claimed to be founded on insight into the fundamental fact. Furthermore, as Strauss later made clear, it belongs to the fundamental fact that it opens the eyes of its discoverer to the highest value. Like Socrates, Nietzsche became guilty of introducing new divinities. What

---

8. There are many echoes of the Introduction to *Philosophie und Gesetz* in the final pages of the 1962 Preface to Strauss's Spinoza book. See Adler, "Leo Strauss's *Philosophie und Gesetz*."

looked like the final atheism turned out to be a vindication of God. But this is an explication of the way of Nietzsche that Strauss gives only decades later after following his own way of return. Still, Nietzsche helped give him his start.

THE MEDIEVAL ENLIGHTENMENT

Did Strauss come to think that the Medieval enlightenment represented the permanent solution to the problem of philosophy's politics? Strauss set forth the core of the Medieval enlightenment in his writings on Maimonides and Maimonides' essential predecessor Alfarabi. That core was a Platonic solution to the political problem of philosophy which had been carried forward by Platonists of the Hellenistic age such as Cicero and Philo. In Alfarabi and Maimonides, that core consisted of an apology for philosophy that took its bearings from the sacred texts of their peoples. Their apology for philosophy set out the legal grounding for philosophy in the divine law; in return, as it were, their apology provided a philosophical grounding for the law. The key item in their apology was what Strauss came to call "prophetology."[9] Applying the logos to the prophet meant understanding the prophet via Plato's notion of the philosopher king; the prophet was the fundamental lawgiver or legislator, the wise giver of precepts whose rule made the good city possible. Comparing their own situations with that of their pagan master, Alfarabi and Maimonides could maintain that fundamental progress had occurred: the social conditions that Plato himself could only wish for or pray for, they found already actualized thanks to Mohammed or Moses. Philosophy, always in jeopardy according to Strauss's general view, always at odds with the fundamentals of social order because it must question those fundamentals and conclude that they are less than fundamental or fundamental only to the well-being of this particular society—philosophy found a way to finesse its danger even in the new setting of revealed religion. In that setting it could seem to be not only dangerous but utterly superfluous: who needs inquiry with its frail methods and dubious results when we've been told the essential truth on the highest possible authority and commanded to be loyal to it?

Strauss's fresh turn to the Medieval enlightenment, unencumbered by convictions of the superiority of the modern Enlightenment, led him gradually to the view that esotericism was essential to the Medieval enlightenment, that the Medieval solution to the perpetual political problem of phi-

9. Kenneth Green concludes that "prophetology" was Strauss's own coinage; see *Jew and Philosopher* 205.

losophy depended upon a highly refined art of veiled writing. It seems that Strauss rediscovered philosophical esotericism and its full range of uses through his deepening study of Medieval philosophy.[10]

In the accounts he gave of the Medieval enlightenment, Strauss seems to have been more candid about the skeptical implications of Alfarabi's esotericism than about the skeptical implications of Maimonides'. Moreover, Strauss seems to have been most candid about Alfarabi in an essay which he chose never to reprint in the later books of essays that he assembled.[11] In this 1945 essay, "Farabi's Plato," Strauss exhibits Alfarabi's skepticism about such pieties of Plato as the immortality of the soul and the existence of God. Strauss also exhibits Alfarabi's understanding of the great caution Plato exercised in conveying the truths uncovered by philosophy, most especially the hard truth about the possibility of human happiness, namely, that it was possible only for the few philosophers. The deadliness of that truth required the encouragement of false beliefs about happiness which dictated that happiness be viewed as attainable only by the moral. Strauss assigns Alfarabi an importance second only to Plato in the history of philosophy: Alfarabi is the precursor of the philosophers of the future, such as Maimonides, who learned from him how philosophy could best survive in the hostile climate of revealed religion. Alfarabi learned how to transmit "the most precious knowledge" (377) in the guise of the commentator. That guise provided him his essential freedom, and Strauss indicates how Alfarabi exercised that freedom when he applies to Alfarabi the fitting variant of Phaedrus's jest to the Platonic Socrates: "With what ease dost thou, o Farabi, invent Platonic speeches" (376; *Phaedrus* 275b). That is to say: I have discovered you and your diabolical techniques and hold them in the highest honor; therefore, I will make them known only in a way which does not betray you.

Strauss "made free use of" this seminal essay in the two published studies of Alfarabi that assumed prominent places in his books: the Introduction to *Persecution and the Art of Writing,* and one of two central essays in *What is Political Philosophy?* The former sets Alfarabi at the beginning of Strauss's indispensable account of esotericism and exhibits his relation to Plato. The latter, "How Farabi read Plato's *Laws,*" is a virtual manual on the philosophic art of writing, the art practiced by men of judgment. Such men set

---

10. See the detailed chronological study of Strauss's return to Maimonides in Green, *Jew and Philosopher.*

11. Bruell notes a similar growing reticence in Strauss's treatment of Xenophon, beginning with greatest openness in "The Spirit of Sparta or the Taste of Xenophon" (1939), another uncollected essay; see "Strauss on Xenophon's Socrates" 270.

about first to establish their character in order then to be free to speak the truth, the then unbelievable truth that would no longer endanger either themselves or others. Implied throughout Strauss's studies of Alfarabi is a basic interpretive lesson: Alfarabi's careful skepticism about Plato demands a corresponding skepticism on the reader's part about Alfarabi. Such skepticism is the very opposite of debunking; it sees and appreciates the reasons Alfarabi wrote as he did. Skepticism of Strauss's sort about the writings of the great philosophers provides the guidelines for understanding the practice of the Platonic art in non-Greek settings—most particularly, in the setting altered by the appearance of the God of revealed religion.

Schooled in skepticism by his discovery of the essential esotericism of the Medieval enlightenment, Strauss let it be known that Alfarabi and his successors could not possibly have believed the primary concession which they seemed to make in order to win philosophy its freedom. They could not possibly have believed that the law under whose commandments they were required to live had its source in God.

Nevertheless, the question of Strauss's view of the timeless worth of the Medieval enlightenment does not hinge on what the greatest Medieval philosophers actually believed about their God and their prophets. They could be as skeptical of revelation as Strauss suggests they were and still believe that *belief* in such revelation is the ideal setting for philosophy. Did the Medieval enlightenment in its highest advocates believe that belief in a timeless God whose laws were given by our prophet provided the best possible setting for the survival of philosophy, the best possible setting for enlightenment? Did Strauss believe they believed it?

In my view the answer to both questions has to be No. It seems highly improbable to me that these offspring of Plato could have believed in permanent solutions any more than they seem to have believed in timeless gods. The Medieval enlightenment, as Strauss described it, is irrevocably tied to a God who claims timelessness; it is located within actual theocracies and prophetocracies where conceding authority to God or the prophet was the obvious precondition for philosophizing. The well-being of philosophy dictated that philosophy apparently concede authority to existing authority which believed its authority divine. Did the offspring of Plato who made this concession really believe what they *had to say* they believed, namely that they lived in the actualized best political order which their pagan master could only pray for? Did they really believe that the rhetoric which their times *compelled* them to adopt also happened to be true? Did they really believe that in their case "best" and "ours" actually *did* coincide? When one considers Alfarabi's account of philosophy's rule over religion, of the way in

which the ideas perceived by the intellect and assented to by certain demonstrations come to rule over the similitudes that imitate the ideas and that
are known by imagining them and assented to by persuasion—and when
one considers his account of the responsibilities of the prudent legislator as
the inventor of the images and of the persuasive arguments as a religion for
others—and when one considers his skeptical reading of Plato, it is extremely difficult to believe that he believed what he said he believed, what
his place and time said he *had* to believe.[12]

If Strauss believed that the Medieval enlightenment was the timeless
solution to the problem of philosophy's politics, then his task was clear: he
had to encourage not only the subtle skeptical reading of the few old philosophers; he had to encourage as well the return of the world in which their
subtle writings found their rationale. If Strauss believed that the Medieval
enlightenment achieved the true and final politics for philosophy, its advance
into the actually "perfect society" (*PL* 100), then the defense of philosophy
required of him a prephilosophic politics of massive dimensions: the revival
of the social conditions that had made it possible in the first place. But there
is no evidence that Strauss sought the reestablishment of theocracies or prophetocracies or that he believed that such reestablishment was possible—
that it was possible now to overcome "the true doctrine," as he called it,
"that God is dead" (*SPPP* 177). And the evidence that he in fact aimed at
such a reestablishment would have to be evidence of a quite different sort
from quiet implications left to be drawn by his most patient and most acute
readers: it would have to be evidence of open advocacy of the public beliefs
that best conduce to philosophy, the old beliefs in God and his prophet. Such
advocacy would have required that Strauss train—or at least encourage others to train—emphatic public orators of Orthodoxy and not only quiet, private readers with a skeptical bent. There is no evidence that return had this
meaning for Strauss, which constitutes clear evidence that it did *not* have
this meaning.

There is a further, related difficulty in asserting that Strauss believed
the Medieval enlightenment to be the timelessly true solution to philosophy's politics: the Medieval enlightenment was an event in Islamic and Jewish history; it was *not* an event in Christian history. Christianity's stance
toward philosophy was essentially different from that of Islam or Judaism,
because Christianity understood itself not to be fundamentally law, but to
be fundamentally faith. As such, it understood itself to be the true philosophy, the philosophy revealed by revelation. Christianity therefore stood to

12. *Alfarabi's Philosophy of Plato and Aristotle*, pp. 44–47.

philosophy in a friendly if condescending position: philosophy as the exercise of mere reason required the supplement of Christian truth to complete its endeavor; philosophy could begin on its own, proceed a modest distance on its own, but never end successfully on its own with possession of the full truth. Christianity therefore could and did co-opt philosophy as Islam and Judaism never could. Christianity represented a danger to philosophy very different from the mere prohibition that was the ultimate threat of Islam or Judaism: Christianity could parade itself as the true philosophy, the indispensable extension of the best efforts of ancient pagans to grasp the mystery of things with unaided reason (*PAW* 21). To tyrannize philosophy as the True Philosophy is far more dangerous than banishment, as Strauss suggests when he speaks of Plato's "success" (*PAW* 21), of his "resounding success" (*OT* 206), which led him to wonder "whether it has not been too successful"—this is Nietzsche's view that "Christianity is Platonism for the people" put Straussianly.

Strauss exercised extreme reserve in his indictment of Christianity.[13] Nevertheless, it is not all that difficult to read between Strauss's lines, those devoted to Aquinas in *Natural Right and History* for instance (157–64), to see that in Strauss's view Christianity trapped philosophy within a dogmatism that left no room for doubt about the immutable character of its fundamental beliefs and that subjected philosophy to a higher authority. Strauss argues that it was precisely *this* capture of philosophy by religion, *this* form of religion's rule over philosophy, that forced a return to the classics by early modern European philosophy (*NRH* 164). Given this profound difference between Judaism and Christianity with respect to philosophy, any suggestion that the West, that Europe, return to the conditions that made the Medieval enlightenment possible implies the reestablishment—not of the conditions of Medieval Europe or the "age of faith" eulogized by some—but of the conditions of the earlier Islamic empire, for it was within Islam and the Jewish Diaspora of the Islamic empire that the Medieval enlightenment as Strauss understood it took place. Did Strauss believe that a return to that world was possible or desirable for modern Europe, which, as Strauss himself emphasized, had Europeanized the globe?

Strauss's elevation of the Medieval enlightenment has to be understood

---

13. George Grant makes an issue of this reticence in "Tyranny and Wisdom" 108–9. Himself an advocate of the ultimate superiority of faith over philosophy, Grant appeals to Strauss to make his own standpoint clear. But Grant was himself a student of reticence, and he knew very well what Strauss's reticence implied: see page 108 middle. Other Christian commentators are more direct and more impatient with Strauss's "Averroism." See Wilhelmsen, *Christianity and Political Philosophy* 194, 209–25; Sokolowski, *The God of Faith and Reason* 156–64.

in a way that relieves him of absurdity or naiveté. Willingness to be seen as an innocent is not innocence. Strauss can be spared absurdity and naiveté by noting two general features of his elevation of the Medieval enlightenment in his 1935 book *Philosophy and Law*. These features show that Strauss's elevation of the Medieval enlightenment is something quite different from a desire for a return to its preconditions.

First: the Medieval enlightenment shows the way to an intelligent repudiation of the Enlightenment, of that politics for philosophy which had shaped the modern world since Machiavelli. The philosophers of the Medieval enlightenment were not enlighteners: "They constantly impress upon the philosophers the duty to keep rationally recognized truth secret from the unchosen many" (*PL* 82). With respect to the relative superiority of the Medieval enlightenment to the modern Enlightenment, it is noteworthy that the silent partner in Strauss's argument against the Enlightenment in the Introduction to *Philosophy and Law* is Nietzsche. Nietzsche is present as the historic outcome of the Enlightenment, an outcome Strauss described as the new bravery or probity, the intellectual conscience, the choiceworthiness of atheism because it is comfortless (*PL* 18–19).[14] The Enlightenment radicalized, Nietzscheanized, forces one to question the adequacy of the Enlightenment's criticism of its historic opponent, Orthodoxy. It is not plausible that the radicalized Enlightenment with its extreme probity respecting the truth could ever surrender its intellect to Orthodoxy as simply true. On the other hand, it is completely plausible that that very probity could conclude that Orthodoxy was, with respect to enlightenment itself, preferable or superior to the Enlightenment's alleged enlightenment, and that it could conclude that esotericism of a kind was unavoidable or that philosophy was so rare and so supreme that it always needed a defense. Nietzsche himself had made these very points in his own argument for the superior sophistication of premodern scholarship and the superior depth of the premodern Church (see e.g. *GS* 358), and in his argument that the modern Enlightenment had allowed science to eclipse philosophy, made scholars the loyal valets of science, and pressed both science and scholarship into the service of modern politics (see e.g. *BGE* 22).

Second: the Medieval enlightenment, deeper, wiser, more skeptical than the modern Enlightenment, itself points backward to roots that are not its

---

14. Nietzsche's role in *Philosophy and Law* has been noted with acuteness and insight by Rémi Brague, "Leo Strauss and Maimonides," especially 104–6. "One may ask oneself whether Strauss is not basically Nietzschean" in this work (104)—Brague asks this question and then provides a page and a half of considerations that answer it in the affirmative.

own, to Platonic political philosophy. Therefore, Strauss's case for the superiority of the Medieval enlightenment to the modern Enlightenment in *Philosophy and Law* must be considered from the perspective supplied at its
end: Strauss ended his account of the Medieval enlightenment with Plato,
with a statement of "the unbelieving philosophical foundation" of the philosophical politics generated within a believing world (*PL* 56, 109–10). What
Strauss chose to emphasize of the unbelieving Plato is that Plato no longer
permitted what had been permitted: "You must go down," says the Platonic
Socrates to the philosopher inclined to remain outside the cave (*Republic*
vii.520c). Alfarabi and Maimonides are Platonic political philosophers: they
went down, they followed Plato's injunction to act on behalf of philosophy.
Their actions on philosophy's behalf retroactively conferred the crown of
philosophy on Mohammed or Moses. Epicurus's venomous joke against
Plato applies to them too, for they too are *dionysiokolakes*. Because Plato is
their prophet, they pay obeisance to everyone else's prophet; they flatter the
tyrant who rules absolutely and win his permission to philosophize. They
do even more, they procure his commandment to philosophize.[15]

Despite the overwhelming evidence that he did not regard the Medieval
enlightenment as the timelessly true solution to philosophy's political problem, and despite the evidence that he did not hold revelation to be true,
Strauss continued to set out the alternatives of reason and revelation as if
philosophy always came to ruin as a reasonable choice because of its inability
to refute religion if religion simply insisted that it got it all from God (see
e.g. *SCR* 29–30; "Progress or Return" 305–10; *NRH* 75). An excellent remark by David Lowenthal makes clear why Strauss did this: "By settling the
argument in favor of religion, Strauss seems to have given his support to
the cause of human consolation. He has certainly placed a huge obstacle in
the way of those seeking to enter philosophy."[16] Strauss's way of settling the
argument amounts to a large "Keep Out" sign placed over the path leading
off to philosophy, a sign to which Strauss appended a little "unless" in quite
small print. It is Strauss's variation, let us say, on "wide is the gate and broad
is the way" (Matthew 7:13) that leads to human consolation, the way of
religion, whereas "strait is the gate and narrow is the way" that leads to the
comfortless conclusions of philosophy and the deep pleasures of the philoso-

15. The difference between Maimonides' political science and that of Plato and Aristotle is
beautifully presented in "Maimonides' Statement on Political Science," *WPP* 155–69.

16. Lowenthal, "Comment on Colmo" 162. See also Lowenthal, "Leo Strauss's *Studies in
Platonic Political Philosophy*" 313–20, a penetrating and appreciative weighing of Strauss's
statements on the relationship of reason and revelation.

pher. Like Rousseau, Strauss holds that it is unwise to remove "the difficulties that blocked access to the temple of the muses and that nature put there as a test of strength for those who might be tempted to learn."[17] Regarding the exclusivity of philosophy, Strauss did not differ from Nietzsche; regarding saying out loud the truth about revelation, he did.[18]

Strauss's stance toward the Medieval enlightenment is definitively illuminated, it seems to me, by his most authoritative book on the shift from the medieval to the modern, *Thoughts on Machiavelli*. In that great book, Strauss does not speak explicitly on behalf of the Medieval enlightenment whose termination Machiavelli successfully masterminded. On behalf of what does he speak? If we turn to the last magnificent paragraph of *Thoughts on Machiavelli* schooled by the book itself, we are in a position to see that Strauss's conclusion is written in a kind of code, a code which can be unlocked only by the argument of the book itself. For the last paragraph is no place to introduce new themes, and if we are sufficiently puzzled by the introduction of the apparently new themes of technology, science, and mastery of nature to ask about their sudden appearance at the end, a little reflection makes it apparent that these themes are to be understood in the senses illuminated by the whole book. The "essential defect of classical political philosophy," its unavoidable defect which belongs to its very nature, is its necessary accommodation to competing regimes not themselves subject to the restraints which it placed on itself and its own regime: "technological inventions" in the pursuit of warfare is a phrase that stands for far more important inventions than the phalanx or the legion, the stirrup or gunpowder. The phrase

---

17. Rousseau, *First Discourse* 62.

18. The 138 pages of text in Kenneth Hart Green's valuable study of Strauss, *Jew and Philosopher*, present the view that Strauss himself, like his master Maimonides, held to the dual primacy of philosophy and Judaism; reason and faith or inquiry and loyalty were, Green alleges, equally fundamental. "Cognitive theist" is the label Green affixes to Strauss at the end of his first chapter (27) But the 98 pages of notes, set in smaller print with apparently more text than the text, temper the assurances of the text. Was Strauss a cognitive theist? Maybe not: one of the last things Green explains (in a note to his final chapter) is what he meant by his earlier bare announcement that Strauss was a cognitive theist (237): he meant that Strauss may be called a "theologizing philosopher." And Green further explains that he had made "this point so emphatically only in order to differentiate" Strauss from Kojève with respect to Kojève's "announced atheism" as "philosophically necessary." Strauss certainly does not hold that announced atheism is philosophically necessary. So call him a cognitive theist.

Evidently, one of the problems Strauss bequeathed to his followers was a problem of candor: how far should they go in helping Strauss preserve his cover once they concluded that he had labored to provide himself with one? Does loyalty require it? Does philosophy require it? Stanley Rosen is refreshingly direct: Strauss is an atheist (*Hermeneutics as Politics* 17); Strauss is a pagan ("Politics or Transcendence" 265).

stands instead for the ways of thought which competing regimes and whole populations took up and fought for. The arts of war practiced between these competing regimes included, above all, spiritual warfare whose peculiar weaponry Strauss had demonstrated throughout his book. Strauss's final paragraph therefore considers the one theme most befitting a book on a Renaissance thinker: warfare, spiritual warfare caused by philosophy's historic compromise with religion, classical political philosophy's accommodation to, its eventual capture by, a most dangerous form of the competing regime, the Christian religion.

And if the great adversary of Machiavelli and his successors is no longer powerful in our time, if Christianity, the kingdom of darkness Machiavelli and all his successors fought, no longer forces on us the necessity it forced on them, we realize gradually and retrospectively the intransigence that has governed Strauss's whole presentation in this book, the disciplined silence he forced on himself: from beginning to end and not only in the final paragraph, Strauss has judged Machiavelli's effort "entirely on its intrinsic merits" (p. 298) and not on its relative merits, not on its superiority to its once powerful adversary. Strauss has not judged Machiavelli's effort by its historic desirability and necessity as the movement to crush Christianity's spiritual tyranny; he has judged it only on its intrinsic merits, how it in fact served the long-term interests of philosophy as those interests look to us now. This perspective forces one to reflect on the great invention that tamed Christianity, the comprehensive spiritual enterprise set in motion by Machiavelli and his successors, namely, "the use of science for such inventions," the inventions of warfare. This particular invention of spiritual warfare—the employment of science on behalf of philosophy to overthrow the tyranny of an ostensibly philosophical religion—broke with classical philosophy's understanding of science and resulted in the highest, the most difficult problem, "the fact that man is conquering nature and there are no assignable limits to that conquest" (SPPP 190). This and this alone is the necessity that now spurs philosophy on; this and this alone is the necessity that now renders impossible the good city in the classical sense; this is the unrestraint of a competing regime which now threatens to engulf the regime friendly to philosophy. The Machiavellian strategy succeeded in its one great aim; but by adopting its enemy's means and conscripting science into the service of propaganda, it caused philosophy to fall prey to a new tyranny, the tyranny of supposed enlightenment via science. Founding is continuous: that great Machiavellian lesson is carried forward by Strauss. Defense of what was well founded requires subsequent foundings, introductions of great novelties in the service of the original founding.

And how does the continuous founding now display its necessities? We can no longer believe in the beneficence of nature in one of the ways appealed to by the classics, namely, those natural cataclysms which ensure that humanity will not fall final prey to human inventions, those beneficent cataclysms, cataclysms of grace, whose goodness toward humanity consists in their annihilation of civilized human life and the enforced return of humanity to its natural primitive conditions from which the earth can again be repopulated and recivilized. If the experiences of the last centuries have rendered the hope of annihilation and rebirth incredible and forced on us the recognition that humanity could in fact fall prey to its latest inventions, namely, modern ideas about humanity's nature and destiny, then the notion of the beneficence of nature must be restored by being rethought through a return to the fundamental experiences from which it is derived. A relapse into Platonism is called for. This paragraph too is an acknowledgement of the necessity which spurred Nietzsche on.

Strauss's thoughts on Machiavelli, then, do not point back to the Medieval enlightenment as the timeless solution to philosophy's political problem. On the contrary, they transcend it in both directions, backward to Plato, forward to Nietzsche.

Strauss's concern with enlightenment, the concern of a lifetime triggered first by the failure of the modern Enlightenment, caused a movement of return which passed through the Medieval enlightenment and came to rest on Plato. What was the Platonic response to the Greek enlightenment, the first enlightenment ever to examine rationally the whole of nature and humanity? What was the Platonic enlightenment?

THE PLATONIC ENLIGHTENMENT

What did Strauss take to be paradigmatic about Plato? Was it the ideas? Was it the teaching on God and the soul? Was it the argument on behalf of justice and the other virtues? Strauss's writings on Plato show that none of these topics is truly fundamental. Instead, the Platonic paradigm is the Platonic response to the Greek enlightenment, Plato's means of preserving and furthering enlightenment.

Strauss did more than point out that the philosophers of the Medieval enlightenment took their inspiration from Plato: his own approach to Plato was guided by theirs. Strauss's writings on Plato resemble Alfarabi's in that they too make fundamental to Plato the two matters Alfarabi had isolated as the differences between Plato and Socrates. First, that Plato's investigations were not confined to "the scientific investigation of justice and the virtues" but became comprehensive, for they were meant to supply "'the science of the essence of every being' and hence especially the science of the divine and of the natural things" (PAW 16). Second, that "the way of Plato" corrected the intransigent way of Socrates and became a way of compromise, a politic way that enabled philosophy to avoid the suspicion of the non-philosophical permanently symbolized by the fate of Socrates.

There is an additional similarity between Strauss and Alfarabi in their study of Plato, namely, the shelter each affords himself in what Strauss called "the specific immunity of the commentator" (PAW 14). This immunity allows the commentator to avoid overt pronouncement of his own views. The way of the commentator thus wins for itself the gains of Plato's own chosen way, the dialogue: it too is a way in which a speaker can avoid speaking in his own name. Strauss's commentaries on Plato show that Strauss too "established for himself the character of a man who never explicitly and unambiguously says what he thinks about the highest themes" (WPP 137). But that means that Strauss too "thus enabled himself sometimes to say explicitly and unambiguously what he thought about the highest themes." Did Strauss ever say explicitly and unambiguously what he found to be paradigmatic in Plato, the timeless basis of the Platonic enlightenment? Perhaps "explicitly and unambiguously" are not quite the right words here, but as a commentator on Plato Strauss does, I believe, make clear what is paradigmatic and timeless in Plato. Strauss's understanding of the essence of the Platonic enlightenment can be found in his essay "On Plato's Republic," the central essay of The City and Man. What comes to light in Strauss's account of the Republic is the central importance of one of Socrates' interlocutors, Thrasymachus.

By exhibiting the crucial role of Thrasymachus, Strauss makes explicit what he found implicit in Alfarabi. On three different occasions, Strauss noted what Alfarabi held to be fundamental in Plato's correction of the way of Socrates: Plato added "the way of Thrasymachus" to the way of Socrates ("Farabi's Plato" 382–84; PAW 16–17; WPP 153). Plato's adoption of the way of Thrasymachus constitutes the invention of political philosophy. By making the way of Thrasymachus his own, Plato found the means to shelter philosophy's comprehensive rational investigation of nature and man, rational enlightenment, within a public teaching on virtue that blunted popular suspicion about philosophy. What is timeless in Plato turns out not to be any timeless entities at all, but a timeless strategy that recognizes the fundamental and permanent problem faced by philosophy. A close look at Strauss's Thrasymachus will make clear just what is timeless in Plato. It will also make clear just how Strauss and Strauss's Nietzsche belong to Platonic political philosophy.

Strauss introduces the Thrasymachus section of the first book of the *Republic* in an arresting way, for he says that "in a sense . . . it forms the center of the *Republic* as a whole" (*CM* 73). But this is a very odd center, given that it is completed within the first book of a ten-book dialogue. This center is found by dividing the *Republic* "in accordance with the change of Socrates' interlocutors," the change from a father and son combination to Thrasymachus alone to a brother combination. Strauss means what he says about the centrality of Thrasymachus, for he reasserts his claim at a crucial point later and adds a fitting modifier: "Thrasymachus justly occupies the central place among the interlocutors of the *Republic*" (123–24). If we watch Strauss's treatment of Thrasymachus throughout his commentary, it will become clear why Thrasymachus and not Glaucon or Adeimantus is justly central to Socrates' defense of justice in the *Republic*.

i. Thrasymachus Tamed.   In his lengthy account of the Thrasymachus section of the first book, Strauss places the emphasis on Socrates' taming of Thrasymachus. Thrasymachus tamed is a beaten opponent, Strauss emphasizes, but he is in no way a poisoned or resentful opponent harboring revenge against his victor. For Thrasymachus tames himself when he comes to recognize that Socrates is his superior. Tamed by his own self-control, Thrasymachus disciplines himself into careful attention and learns something from Socrates' talk with Glaucon and Adeimantus that is essential to his own advantage.

Strauss makes this point clear by emphasizing that Thrasymachus is an *actor*; his initial anger at Socrates is calculated, he *plays* at anger to create anger, to anger others against the object of his own feigned anger—In this case, Socrates. Strauss, of course, is not tempted by Thrasymachus into anger at Socrates; he is no more disposed to fall for Thrasymachus's act than any other reader of the *Republic*. The obvious reason for this, as Strauss emphasizes, is Plato's art, for Plato exploits the advantages of a narrated dialogue to kindle anger at the very one who plays at kindling anger. Plato kindles anger at Thrasymachus particularly through Socrates' characterization of him: Thrasymachus is a "wild beast" whose threat to destroy the civility of their conversation is averted only by Socrates' foresight and care.

But Strauss goes out of his way to state that he himself will not be angry at Thrasymachus, that he will not fall prey to this part of Plato's charm, Plato's altogether fitting effort to engender a salutary loathing of Thrasymachus (74). Instead, Strauss will observe Plato's charm, Plato's manipulation of his readers; he will not himself be so charmed as to fail to notice Plato's own acting. Strauss gives the highest significance to his observer's stance: "It is *most important* for the understanding of the *Republic* and *generally* that we should not behave toward Thrasymachus as Thrasymachus behaves" (emphasis added). Strauss thus looks "without indignation at Thrasymachus' indignation" (75) and he learns Plato's lesson on the uses of indignation.

By play-acting anger at Socrates, Thrasymachus exhibits the city's real anger at Socrates (78). But he play-acts the city as one who truly holds the city's view of justice: "the just is identical with the lawful or legal"; this is "the most obvious, the most natural, thesis regarding justice" (75). But if Thrasymachus shares the city's natural view of justice, he shares it as a cynic, one who sees through it to its core of advantage and disadvantage; he shares it as one who is "greedy for money and prestige" (74), greedy for his own advantage as he perceives advantage. Furthermore, he shares it as an artist, a famous teacher of rhetoric. As Strauss's reference to the *Republic* vi.492a ff. indicates (78), Thrasymachus is a sophist who knows how to manage the great sophist; he is the individual whose art can direct the city, the animal trainer who knows "the angers and desires" of "the great strong beast" and how to manipulate them.[19]

Thrasymachus's art is "concerned with both arousing and appeasing the angry passions of the multitude." His own passions are placed in the service of his art of manipulating passions; his anger "is subordinate to his art" (78). As a consummate artist, Thrasymachus is shameless; he can be tamed but he cannot be shamed: Strauss even interprets Thrasymachus's famous blush (350d) as a result of the *heat* and not of the shame consequent on defeat (74). Because Strauss is not blinded by indignation at Thrasymachus's indignation, he can interpret Thrasymachus as himself not blinded by indignation. Strauss's Thrasymachus acts on the basis of knowledge and acts for his own advantage: coming to see that Socrates is his unbeatable superior in the persuasive art of dialectic and seeing that others will see it too, Thrasymachus learns that he will have to change his behavior toward Socrates.

Thrasymachus lacks competence precisely where Socrates most pos-

19. There seem to be two textual errors in the discussion of Thrasymachus in *CM:* page 76 line 13 requires *dis*advantage in place of advantage (see the parallel passage in Strauss's "Plato" article in *HPP* 38); page 78 2 lines up requires *facility* in place of felicity.

sesses it; even though Thrasymachus's art of speech has made him famous (80), he is no match for Socrates in the art of dialectic. This is a result, Strauss says, of "his slow comprehension" (78); he makes a fatal mistake in saying rulers make no mistakes. The mistake was made "with a view to his own advantage" (80) as a teacher of rulers, but it turns quickly to his decided disadvantage because Socrates' superior skill in dialectic enables him to prove on Thrasymachus's chosen premise that rulers rule to the advantage of the ruled (342e–343a). Strauss's conclusion to this first dialectical victory of Socrates is very illuminating, for it shows how the way of Plato will have to include the persuasive way of Thrasymachus, the way of persuading the multitude: "Even the rulers themselves need the art of persuasion in order to persuade their subjects that the laws which are framed with exclusive regard to the benefit of the rulers serve the benefits of the subjects" (80). This is the persuasive art Socrates lacked and Thrasymachus possessed. Socrates can easily best Thrasymachus in dialectic, but dialectic is an art for an intellectual "elite," an art that is not appropriate for dealing with the "vulgar," to use Strauss's two words for these complementary arts from *Persecution and the Art of Writing* (16).

Thrasymachus's art of dealing with the multitude, the art of which he is an acknowledged master, requires of him that he know very well what Strauss says next: "Thrasymachus' own art stands and falls by the view that prudence is of the utmost importance for ruling" (*CM* 80). Thrasymachus's prudence will enable him to learn new uses for his anger from his encounter with Socrates: having made him submissive and attentive to the one who rules him in dialectic, his prudence will eventually make him Socrates' friend. For Thrasymachus is prudent enough to know the place of his art or where his art places him: the shepherd of the sheep is not the owner of the sheep; the shepherd serves the owner as one of the owner's stewards or ministers. "Thrasymachus can derive benefit from his art, from the assistance which he gives to the rulers (regardless of whether they are tyrants, the common people, or the men of excellence), only if he is loyal to them, if he does his job for them well, if he keeps his part of the bargain, if he is just" (81–82). Strauss will show that the central part of the *Republic* displays Thrasymachus's shift to an alliance with the men of excellence: rather than kindle anger against Socrates, Thrasymachus will prudently employ his persuasive art on philosophy's behalf to soothe the city's anger against philosophy (501e–502a).

What Socrates' argument in Book One allows the prudent actor Thrasymachus to see—what Strauss's extended account of Thrasymachus's "downfall" (80–83) allows his reader to see—is that Socrates himself has a view of justice not unlike Thrasymachus's and that Socrates is prudent enough not to flaunt it. Strauss himself refuses to simply announce Socrates' view, but he allows it to be seen through the salutary cover of what he calls the "terrible result" of Socrates' conversation with Thrasymachus: "The difference between Thrasymachus and Socrates is then merely this: according to Thrasymachus, justice is an unnecessary evil whereas according to Socrates it is a necessary evil" (83). This terrible result is never retracted. On the contrary, it is confirmed by the central argument of the Thrasymachus section, the only one of the three arguments that is not "defective" in the sense that it is based on mere agreement (83; cf. 53), the argument that "no society however unjust can last if it does not practice justice among its members" (83). There will arise, in time, the appropriate justice between the members of that little society composed of Socrates and Thrasymachus, a society that began with feigned savagery and ends with friendship between unequals. Thrasymachus transformed into a "willing listener" (84) will learn to do justice to Socrates; he will concede Socrates' superiority, his right to rule him; and his concession will serve his own private advantage. Thrasymachus's reasoning proved to be poor, but his principle remained victorious—this, as Strauss concludes, "goes far toward explaining Thrasymachus' taming" (84).

ii. Thrasymachus Converted and Employed.   Strauss emphasizes that the beginning of the fifth book of the *Republic* represents "a new beginning" in the conversation as "the repetition of a scene which had occurred at the very beginning" (115), and he uses this repetition to make a key point about Thrasymachus. Once again Socrates' companions act like a city, they make a decision and take a vote; and Socrates once again obeys. But there is a "decisive difference" between the second city and the first: Thrasymachus "has become a member of the city in the second scene" (116). Strauss draws a conclusion which applies this narrative event to the whole economy of the *Republic:* "It would seem that the foundation of the good city requires that Thrasymachus be converted into one of its citizens" (116). Converted Thrasymachus is exhibited in the essential feature of his conversion when he next appears in Strauss's account.

The rule of the philosopher has meanwhile become the theme. In treating this theme, Strauss never departs from the setting Socrates gave it: the question of whether it is possible and for the best to actualize the just city built in the conversation of the *Republic*. Socrates reduced the first of these questions "to the question of the possibility of the coincidence of philosophy and political power" (123). Strauss comments: "That such a coincidence should be possible is to begin with most incredible." But it becomes apparent that this incredible coincidence is possible in a certain way after all, through the employment of Thrasymachus. By ruling Thrasymachus, the philosopher can successfully rule the city.

How can the philosopher rule Thrasymachus? By showing that his advantage is best served by making his art ministerial to philosophy. The key, according to Strauss, is to understand the context in which "Socrates declares that he and Thrasymachus have just become friends, having not been enemies before either" (123). The context is the change required in cities to make them willing to be ruled by philosophers whom they naturally regard as vicious or useless. "To bring about the needed change on the part of the city, of the non-philosophers or the multitude, the right kind of persuasion is necessary and sufficient." In this part of the conversation, Socrates is speaking with Adeimantus; and he acts as if his goal were to persuade the dubious Adeimantus that philosophy is not vicious, not corrupting. Once Adeimantus is charmed into agreement, Socrates acts as if Adeimantus were the one to persuade the multitude; he even gives Adeimantus a commission to soothe the multitude (449e–500a), to make them less angry at philosophy, to gentle and persuade them "from shame, if nothing else" (501e–502a).

But the shaming and angering art is not Adeimantus's, it is Thrasymachus's; "that mighty man of Chalcedon" has a genius for rousing the multitude to anger and soothing it again with his charms (*Phaedrus* 267c–d). Socrates may be conversing with Adeimantus, but his real addressee is Thrasymachus, that silent wolf capable through his speech of turning his quarry speechless (336d), the most powerful man at both inventing and answering slanders and accusations (*Phaedrus* 267d). Socrates speaks to Adeimantus about Thrasymachus's particular genius with a view to converting Thrasymachus into his friend. And Strauss makes it emphatic that Socrates succeeds. "The right kind of persuasion is supplied by the art of persuasion, the art of Thrasymachus, directed by the philosopher and in the service of philosophy" (123). Strauss ignores Adeimantus entirely; he places the whole focus on "the only man professing an art who speaks in the *Republic*" (80). "Without 'Thrasymachus' there will never be a just city" (123). "Thrasymachus" will go by many names, as Strauss makes clear in the culmination of his essay, for it will turn out that "Thrasymachus" is the key to understanding philosophy's victory in its ancient quarrel with poetry. Strauss anticipates that culmination here: "We are compelled to expel Homer and Sophocles but we must invite Thrasymachus" (123). Tragedy and the father of tragedy must be expelled if the just city is to be achieved. This is by no means the banishment of poetry as such; it is the banishment of Homeric poetry, whose lies have been shown to be unsalutary because they tell of crimes at the origin of order, and of wars among the gods, and because they put a curse on the human afterlife. Strauss will make it clear that the name "Thrasymachus" stands for a new poetry directed by the philosopher and designed to persuade the multitude.

After emphasizing Thrasymachus's role as Socrates' friend, Strauss repeats his claim that "Thrasymachus justly occupies the central place among the interlocutors of the *Republic*" (123–24). Strauss implies by his language that a new pair has been formed or a new alliance forged between men who, till now, stood alone: in his first reference to the centrality of Thrasymachus, Strauss noted that he "stands alone as Socrates does," and he likens his aloneness to "that of the impious Cyclops" (74); in his second reference, Strauss notes that Thrasymachus "justly occupies the central place among the interlocutors of the *Republic*, the place between the pair consisting of the father and the son and the pair consisting of the brothers" (123–24). The central place is justly occupied by the new pair, the friends Socrates and Thrasymachus.

Strauss then gives the reasons why Socrates and Thrasymachus "have just become friends." In a long, complex sentence he intimates the real significance of Socrates' conversation with Adeimantus by showing why Adeimantus's misunderstanding of it is irrelevant: Thrasymachus has understood. "Socrates had just said that in order to escape destruction, the city must not permit philosophizing, and especially that philosophizing which is concerned with 'speeches,' to the young, i.e. the gravest kind of 'corrupting the young'" (124). Socrates has just proposed a ban on the public practice of philosophy and in particular a ban on exposing the young to philosophy. What is the effect of that proposed ban? Adeimantus thinks he knows: "Adeimantus believes that Thrasymachus will be passionately opposed to this proposal." Adeimantus makes no distinction between Socrates and Thrasymachus with respect to philosophy and supposes that the ban applies to Thrasymachus, who needs the young in order to further his advantage as a "philosopher." Adeimantus has no idea that Thrasymachus "is or plays the city," that Thrasymachus has viewed the philosopher Socrates from the perspective of the city, seeing him as a useless talker, and that he is now being educated in the philosopher's true role. What looks like the education of Adeimantus (and Glaucon) is, as Strauss presents it, the education of Thrasymachus.

Adeimantus has created a dramatic moment by inviting Thrasymachus to object, to rekindle the fight on which Book One turned between the angry Thrasymachus and his foe Socrates. Adeimantus has no understanding of the drama Strauss has opened for our inspection; but Adeimantus's misunderstanding is both expected and welcomed by Socrates, who counts on the understanding of the silent Thrasymachus: "Socrates who knows better [than Adeimantus] holds that by making that proposal he has become the friend of Thrasymachus who is or plays the city." As the one who plays the city, Thrasymachus must welcome Socrates' proposal as a most attractive offer: for his part of the bargain, Socrates permits the city not to permit the public practice of philosophy. The ban he proposes is a ban on himself; he will cease to "corrupt" the young. For his part of the bargain, Thrasymachus turns his art of persuasion to a new end: he will persuade the multitude that philosophy is not vicious; he will do what Socrates plays at imagining Adeimantus doing; and he will succeed, for the multitude is "of an ungrudging and gentle character" (500a). "Socrates' friend Thrasymachus" (129) will serve as minister to the ruler, the philosopher ruler, now retired from public corrupting into a defensible private life of philosophy.

Socrates' offer of friendship to Thrasymachus is made over the heads of the passionate young men who are present. The young men are incapable of the feigned passions of the prudent actor; alternately angry and mollified, dismayed and edified, they see only anger where Socrates, master of irony, sees feigned anger. The two older masters of their passions make themselves understood to one another in the very presence of the boys whose opinions define the opinions of the city and whose subjection to their passions defines the city's manipulability. The boys are always transparent; they lack self-control or prudence. As for the two older men, they possess the cap of Hades, they possess the ring of Gyges. There are two such rings in the version invented by Glaucon, one each for the unjust man and the just man. As far as Glaucon knows, the ring of invisibility leads each to the same actions—but "Glaucon could not have known what a genuinely just man is" (137). Socrates knows what the younger men don't: the ring of invisibility for the unjust man enables him to kill the king, possess the queen, and rule the kingdom with her; the ring of invisibility for the just man enables him to retire to the private life he has always most desired, the life of inquiry which puts everything into question but now puts nothing at risk because he has covered his retirement with the rhetoric of innocence pronounced by the master of rhetoric.

This is the core of Platonic political philosophy. Here the way of Plato replaces the intransigent way of Socrates. Plato achieves the retirement of philosophy into privacy, the sheltering of philosophy from the impassioned Yes and No of the young who lack, as Nietzsche said, that art of nuances which is the best gain of life (*BGE* 31). Plato shows how philosophy draws up an agreement with the city not to corrupt its young. The Platonic Socrates makes an irresistible offer to the one who plays the city and plays it knowingly, plays it capable himself of corrupting the young into cynicism and the pursuit of private advantage. The Platonic Socrates wins the friendship of Thrasymachus by offering him the highest office to which he could reasonably aspire. Philosophy will curb itself in its own interests, and it has found the means to curb Thrasymachus through his own interests: the rule of the wise will be a secret spiritual kingship mediated by the art of persuasion and its famous practitioner. No wonder Thrasymachus remains silent. He is a speaker for whom everything relevant has just been said by another. He must be listening in amazement as Socrates conducts their fundamental business within the hearing but out of the understanding of those whom it most concerns. By silently refusing to take up Adeimantus's invitation to oppose Socrates, he accepts in the fitting manner Socrates' offer of friendship. In the bargain for these boys, in the bargain for the city whose future they represent, he and Socrates both "know better" than they do. Strauss makes it possible for us to know better as well, for us to watch as Platonic political philosophy places "Thrasymachus" in its employ.

After making his essential point about the newly achieved friendship between Socrates and Thrasymachus, Strauss turns to Socrates' efforts to tame the many (124). He asserts that Socrates cannot succeed in this effort because he lacks the art of Thrasymachus. But the cause of philosophy is not lost, for "the many will have to be addressed by Thrasymachus and he who has listened to Socrates will succeed" (124). This confident assertion of success by Socrates' new friend seems to be qualified by the next four paragraphs (124–27), which deal with the conditions Socrates adds to the achievement of rule by the philosophers. These paragraphs place a necessary limitation on the success achievable by the new rhetoric which speaks on philosophy's behalf: not even that rhetoric can bring the philosophers to rule in the cities. Strauss therefore concludes that the actualization of the just city is impossible (127). And he explicitly retracts his earlier assertion of success: "the multitude is not as persuadable by the philosophers as we san-guinely assumed in an earlier part of the argument" (125); "it is against nature that rhetoric should have the power ascribed to it" (127). Why bother to ascribe it that power, then? The answer seems to be given in the same sentence: "the *Republic* repeats, in order to overcome it, the error of the sophists regarding the power of speech" (127). Rhetoric lacks the power sophists like Thrasymachus ascribe to it. But it is not therefore powerless on behalf of philosophy. Thrasymachus the rhetorician remains a believer in his art; and he remains converted to citizenship and a friend of Socrates. His efforts to persuade the multitude that philosophy is not vicious remain a necessary effort even if it falls short of the ultimate success of bringing the just city into being; it brings into being a city whose suspicions about phi-losophy have been tempered by a belief in philosophy's salutary character. It is precisely the inculcation of this belief that motivates Socrates' return to the theme of poetry in Book Ten and Strauss's return to the theme of Thrasymachus.[20]

iii. "Thrasymachus" and Philosophy's Quarrel with Poetry.   Thrasyma-chus makes his next prominent return to Strauss's narrative in a context in which the *Republic* itself does not even mention him, Socrates' sudden re-

---

20. With respect to the issue of the success of philosophy's new Platonic rhetoric, Strauss leaves no doubt elsewhere that in some sense "Thrasymachus" succeeded. "This defense of philosophy before the tribunal of the city was achieved by Plato with a resounding success" (*OT* 206; see also *PAW* 21). Strauss's reference in *OT* to Plutarch's *Nicias* chapter 23 is to Plutarch's argument that it was because of Plato that the reputation of natural philosophy was rescued from its earlier suspicions and natural philosophers freed from persecution and enabled to pursue their studies in the open. The two reasons Plutarch gives for Plato's success in per-forming this essential service for natural philosophy or for enlightenment are these: first, the life he led (its difference from Socrates', perhaps? his acting on the promise to retire from teaching philosophy to the young?); second, the case he made for the physical world being ultimately subject to divine principles.

But Strauss goes further than the attribution of success to Plato; he wonders whether "Thra-symachus" has been "too successful." *Too* successful would mean that philosophy's very suc-cess in winning over the multitude jeopardized what is essential to it, its freedom to investigate the whole of things without restraint of any kind except what it imposed on itself. What it means historically to be "too successful" is suggested by the list Strauss gives in *OT* of success-ful Platonisms for the people (206): prominently absent from that list is Christian Platonism, the form of Platonism that co-opted philosophy, turning it into a public enterprise (*OT* 206). Strauss is explicit about this particular danger of success at the end of the Introduction to *PAW*: "The official recognition of philosophy in the Christian world made philosophy subject to ecclesiastical supervision" (21). On "the distinctively timely character of [Plato's] religious defense" of philosophy and its "brilliant success," see Ahrensdorf, "The Question of Historical Context," especially pp. 127–35.

turn to the subject of poetry in Book Ten. "We must try to understand this apparently unmotivated return" (*CM* 133), Strauss says, and his means of understanding it is the role of Thrasymachus. "The fate of Thrasymachus in the *Republic*" becomes "a key to the truth about poetry" (134). Once again becoming friends is the main issue: "The poets . . . foster injustice. So does Thrasymachus. Therefore, just as in spite of this Socrates could become a friend of Thrasymachus, there is no reason why he could not be a friend of the poets and especially of Homer" (133–34). Becoming friends with the poets also occurs on Socrates' terms: the poets must stand to Socrates as Thrasymachus now stands to Socrates; they must become the valets of a Socratic morality. In Strauss's definitive word, poets must become "ministerial" to the philosopher king. The philosopher king, as Strauss explains, is the "user" par excellence; in the second of the two hierarchies set out in Book Ten to exhibit poetry's place in the philosopher's vision of things, the philosopher king replaces the god.

Strauss introduces Nietzsche into his discussion of poetry, and he does so because Nietzsche expressed most clearly Socrates' suggestion of the relationship between the legislator and the poet. Nietzsche's presence continues in a decisive way throughout Strauss's account of philosophy and poetry, for "the genuine 'quarrel between philosophy and poetry' (607b5–6) concerns, from the philosopher's point of view, not the worth of poetry as such, but the order of rank of philosophy and poetry" (136). "Order of rank"—this Nietzschean phrase indicates that for Plato too the rule of philosophy over religion was a fundamental issue. The one Strauss calls the "prudent legislator" will have learned that poetry in its "autonomous" form—poetry free of restraints in its dual pursuit of pleasing imitations and incitements to the passions—undermines the civil order built by the legislator. The prudent legislator, the philosophic legislator, will curb poetry's autonomy and bring it under his legislative sway; he will make poetry "ministerial" to philosophy. "According to Socrates, poetry is legitimate only as ministerial to the 'user' *par excellence*, to the king (597e) who is the philosopher, and not as autonomous."

"Using the fate of Thrasymachus in the *Republic* as a key to the truth about poetry" enables Strauss to cast essential light on one of his fundamental themes, Athens and Jerusalem, philosophy and religion. And he almost says the fundamental point directly; he almost brings the philosophic legislator Plato out into the open. For after having shown how Socrates secures friendship with the poets as his ministers, his valets, he says: "The greatest example of ministerial poetry is the Platonic dialogue" (137). And he then closes as Plato closed, presenting three things: a proof of the immortality of the soul, a picture of attentive gods who reward justice and punish injustice, and a myth of the rewards for justice and the punishments for injustice. That is, Strauss closes displaying the new ministerial poetry, the Platonic poetry that ministers to Platonic philosophy. The kind of poetry that will be admitted into the just city can make an argument for itself (607c–608a) because it submits to the two standards set down by the prudent legislator: it sings hymns to the gods and celebrates good men (607a). Plato's poetry ministerial to philosophy is innocent of the primary charge hurled against philosophers by the poets themselves, namely, that they were "howling bitches" who turned on their masters the gods (*Republic* 607b; see *AAPL* 183). Platonic political philosophy civilizes the mad dog philosophy and effects its reconciliation with poetry while charging that unsupervised poetry, autonomous poetry, poetry not ministerial to the prudent legislator, itself undermines civic order.

In the midst of his edifying conclusion, Strauss emphasizes the need for edification: he goes out of his way to lecture his reader on the appropriateness of edifying poetry for Glaucon—for Glaucon, of course, and not for Thrasymachus, that artful man viewing the effects of these charms "conjured" by "the genuinely just man," Socrates (137). Platonic rhetoric had already established the proper rank order of philosophy and sophistry in the *Republic*. Using this, using the fate of Thrasymachus in the *Republic* as the key to understanding Socrates' return to the theme of poetry, Strauss shows clearly that Platonic poetry established the proper rank order of philosophy and poetry. Platonic poetry conjured a moral view of the world order; it conjured immortal souls and just gods, outfitting them with shiny new arguments and fables to fit. It charmed vulnerable youths into a new loyalty to the virtues which had been bred into them by their training in decency but which were now threatened by the death of the gods and by rash speakers like autonomous, unbridled Thrasymachus.[21]

Strauss shows how Plato responded to the death of the gods or to the great dangers of public enlightenment: banish Homer and Sophocles, banish tragedy and the father of tragedy; banish their gods and make unspeakable their "biggest lie about the biggest things," that order proceeds out of chaos and crime and perishes back into them (*Republic* 377e); and banish heroes

---

21. To confirm just how much Strauss's interventionist and revolutionary Plato conforms to Alfarabi's Plato, see especially the final pages of Alfarabi's *The Philosophy of Plato:* "One ought to devise a plan for moving them [the multitude] away from their ways of life and opinions to truth and to the virtuous ways of life, or closer to them" (67).

who speak ill of the underworld, counting mortal life above immortal life. Invite in new poets who sing hymns to reconstituted gods, gods responsible only for the good, gods who never change their shape and never lie; invite in new poets who sing the praises of reconstituted heroes, just men whose justice is reinforced by belief in the now moral gods and belief in an afterlife prepared for their reward and punishment, just men who no longer count Achilles among their number because they cannot tolerate Achilles' curse on Hades, his elevation of mortal life above immortal life.

Banished Achilles is banished even from the tale which the poet of the just city tells of the underworld: Er reports on the choice made "twentieth" by Ajax and the choice made next by Agamemnon—by mentioning "twentieth" and the order of choice between Ajax and Agamemnon, Er indicates just how resolute his silence on Achilles in the underworld is and will remain; for in Homer's underworld, Achilles had appeared nineteenth, after Agamemnon and before Ajax, and Ajax had there too appeared twentieth.[22] Banish Achilles but invite back Odysseus to make the last and wisest choice, the choice Odysseus would have made even had he chosen first. "The wisest of men" (*Republic* 390a) can be invited back because he too has been reconstituted by Platonic poetry: Plato's Odysseus has recovered from his love of honor (620c). Recovered from that high love, the wisest of men pursues the highest love, he seeks and finds a private life in which to pursue wisdom.

Odysseus, present in so many of Plato's dialogues as Homer's nearest counterpart to Socrates, Socrates' prephilosophic precursor, is given his definitive Platonic endorsement in *Hippias Minor:* polytropic Odysseus, Odysseus of the many guiles, is the best man in Homer because "he hides one thing in his mind but says something else." The conflict between Hippias and Socrates is a paradigm of Plato's response to the sophistic enlightenment. Straight Hippias, representative of the sophistic enlightenment, condemns Odysseus because Odysseus balked at public enlightenment, because he did not trust, as straight Achilles trusted, that gods or a moral order guaranteed the victory of the good and the true. In *Hippias Minor* Socrates elevates Odysseus for the very reason the sophist condemned him: unable to trust that gods or a moral order enforce the good and the true, Odysseus preserved the good and the true by taking matters into his own hands and saying whatever was necessary to preserve them, lying even to Athena. Platonic Odysseus has inherited the arms of a fully dead and forcibly forgotten Achilles and added them to his innate cunning; in addition he has taken the funda-

---

22. See Plutarch, *Table Talk* ix. Question 5, on why Ajax chose twentieth in the myth of Er.

mental step of surrendering his love of honor. The *Republic* shows how the wisest of men, having searched among the available lives, chose the life of a private man who could successfully pursue the highest goal. Reformed Odysseus is not irresponsibly private, shunning involvement in the wars that seem to others the greatest events; he is no Epicurean. Reformed Odysseus is responsibly private, having himself gone down to rule through those useful ministers whose artifacts cast the shadows that rule the hearts of men.

"On Plato's Republic" exhibits the core of Platonic political philosophy. There Strauss shows how Plato set out to make all high human functions ministerial to the highest, ministerial to philosophy. Platonic political philosophy found the means to successfully preserve the Greek enlightenment, the first appearance in the world of the passion to understand the whole rationally.[23]

PLATONIC POLITICAL PHILOSOPHY

Strauss's movement of return came to rest in the Platonic enlightenment, the principles of which are conveyed in the *Republic*. The *Republic* presents the timelessly true politics for philosophy. That timelessness is not found in the ideas or the gods or the immortal soul or the moral order of the gentleman, for all these are timely matters called forth by a particular setting. The timelessness of Platonic political philosophy is found on the one hand in its understanding of the order of rank in the human and natural things,

---

23. It is unfortunate that Allan Bloom's Interpretive Essay on the *Republic* is bound up with his translation: given Bloom's association with Strauss, it is all too easily thought that Bloom's Plato is Strauss's Plato. But Bloom's essay, for all its merits, contains little trace of the daring radicalism of Strauss's interpretation; it contains virtually nothing of Strauss's expansion of Alfarabi's insight into Plato's use of the way of Thrasymachus, his account of how the philosopher actually rules through his friend Thrasymachus and through poetry. Bloom's Plato seems to have no higher ambition than to temper the folly of revolutionary political hopes and to further the way of life Bloom himself seems to present as most philosophical, quiet perpetuation of little cells of readers of Plato where reading masters train the puppies of their race to become like themselves. Bloom's Plato lacks the willingness to take in hand the education of a whole age. Followers of Strauss like Bloom are more than willing to view modern times as the consequence of a massive project undertaken by philosophers, but they are entirely unwilling to view Plato himself as the paradigm of philosophic ambition. For an illuminating account of Plato's political ambitions see Rosen, *The Question of Being* 137–75, 187–91, a discussion encapsulated by the following statement: "Nietzsche . . . retains the general Platonist understanding of the nature of the philosopher and, correlatively, of the conception of philosophical *paideia*: of the political task of the philosopher as the attempt to produce a new human type" (141).

Strauss would have made it a lot easier for us if he had provided a few public comments about the work of Bloom, Jaffa, White, Dannhauser, Cropsey, and the rest. But it seems that Strauss had no intention of making it easy.

and on the other hand in its successful practice of the kingly art, its conscription of high autonomous human achievements into its ministerial service. This marriage of philosophy and politics, insight and action, *is* Platonic political philosophy.

Plato provides the permanent model of enlightenment, for he devised the successful means of preserving the first ever rational enlightenment. That pre-Platonic Greek enlightenment had been jeopardized by its very discoverers and practitioners because their zeal for their achievement had made them inattentive to the human world in which their work was unavoidably set and on which it depended. The folly of such inattention, such rash flaunting of enlightenment by natural science and sophism, appeared on stage in that laughable combination of scientific care and personal neglect, of sophistic speech and civic irresponsibility called "Socrates" by the wise poet of the *Clouds;* for, as Strauss frequently indicated, Aristophanes showed where the careless atheism of the "howling bitches" could actually lead. The Socrates made younger and more beautiful on Plato's stage has learned the lesson that Aristophanes addressed to the wise (*Clouds* lines 518–27): he has learned "fear of the gods" (line 1461). He has learned, that is to say, that new and strange gods can be introduced only with the permission of the old. Clouds, those philosophical divinities so ephemeral in their appearance, so open to interpretation in the multiplicity of their changing shapes, so indiscriminate in their favor as to rain on the just and the unjust alike, so high as to float higher than any city's gods—Clouds are divinities visible at first only to Socrates as divine. Such novel divinities can be admitted into the city only after they have properly acknowledged the city's Zeus and the city's Hermes. Strauss's commentary on the *Clouds* shows that the Clouds knew this from the beginning: silently observing while their lone worshiper Socrates gives a demonstration to Strepsiades that Zeus does not exist, the Clouds wait till Socrates and Strepsiades have gone offstage before singing their Ode: "Lofty guardian, great Zeus, king of gods" (563–64). The Clouds, universal if vague divinities destined to exercise sway over all cities, wisely prepare their apotheosis in Athens by paying due respect to the local gods. And as Strauss makes clear, if the *Clouds* turns out badly for Socrates, it turns out well for the Clouds (*SA* 46–48).

Plato's Socrates has learned as well a second, more general lesson of the *Clouds*, a lesson to be drawn from what Strauss calls "Strepsiades' principle," namely, that "knowers have no obligation toward the ignorant" (*SA* 36–37). Strepsiades quite naturally learned that principle from a Socrates who seemed its very embodiment. A Strepsiades made "wise" by Socrates was more than content to reap his personal gains from this liberating principle, right up to the moment in which he was forced to discover just how far that principle could carry a superior product of Socratic education, his own Pheidippides. Only when he is touched by that extremity in the deepest loyalties of his own being does Strepsiades at last become civic-minded and destroy its cause.

Strauss presents Plato as the philosopher who learned these two fundamental lessons that Aristophanes addressed to the wise—and who moved beyond even Aristophanes. For Plato stands to Aristophanes as "Socrates" stands to "Aristophanes" in Plato's *Symposium*. Socrates' divinities, revealed to him by Diotima, are suitably civilized or given an Olympian pedigree, but they surpass, they may even ultimately suppress, Aristophanes' Zeus and Apollo because they provide a place for a human eros higher even than the eros for a severed and lost half; they provide a place for an eros that transcends mate and family and city while honoring and encouraging those other loves. Plato's new ladder of loves places philosophy at the top and introduces gods who certify it; these gods do not themselves philosophize, but only because they don't need to: they already possess wisdom as the highest possible possession. No civic-minded citizen could burn down a thinkery, an Academy, whose members acknowledge the city's gods, encourage the city's loves, and seek to emulate the highest activity of the gods themselves by striving to acquire what the gods already possess.

But Plato's gods are not only as civic-minded as Aristophanes' gods; they wield far more powerful instruments in their enforcement of personal and civic justice. Though he is far too urbane to mention it to the sophisticated few like Aristophanes who assemble to celebrate Agathon's victory, Plato's Socrates will not blush to allege, when the audience is right, that we possess immortal souls that are at the gods' disposal. The obligation of the knowers toward the ignorant is fulfilled with a vengeance by the civic-minded philosopher Plato. No wonder Montaigne could marvel at Plato, quoting the ancient opinion that he was "the great forger of miracles," for Plato and his teacher Socrates were "marvelous and bold workmen at bringing in divine operations . . . everywhere that human power failed."[24] Strauss lets it be seen that Plato could not possibly have believed in such gods and such souls, but that he had learned the uses of such belief. Plato had learned to tie the permanence of enlightenment to what passes for enlightenment.

Strauss's commentary on Plato's *Laws* allows us to watch this new Platonic legislation on behalf of enlightenment in the very process of its enactment. Civic-minded philosophy is given its place in the city by the Athenian

24. Montaigne, *Essays* ii.16, "Of Glory" 477.

Stranger, whose "philanthropy" (*WPP* 31) consists in opening a place for the highest interests of humanity within a decent social order now being established by law-abiding patriots who can, after sufficient exposure to him, have no doubt about the piety of their Athenian master. Philosophy, the study of the soul and the stars, of the things under the earth and the things aloft, is introduced only very late and in a way that will guarantee that what once happened will no longer happen: "There was . . . a time when the study of the stars was not guided by the awareness of the priority of the soul and hence of intellect to body, and thus led to atheism; at that time the poets abused those who philosophized by comparing them to howling bitches. (The terrible error of those men does not deprive them of the title or honor due to men who philosophize)" (*AAPL* 183).

Cicero's much-quoted saying about Socrates captures exactly the core of Platonic political philosophy: "Socrates was the first to bring philosophy down from the heavens into the homes of men." This does not say that Socrates changed the subject; it says that Socrates was the first to provide the divine activity of philosophy with a human home, the first to take it upon himself to give the new gods a human habitation. Strauss's whole recovery of Socrates in Aristophanes, Xenophon, and Plato can be seen as a commentary on Cicero's sentence.[25]

The Platonic Socrates is a revolutionary theologian—it is not only the *word* "theology" that makes its first appearance in his reasoning about the gods; rational gods themselves appear there for the first time. But in the very act of generating the lie that the gods do not lie and the lie that they are responsible only for the good, Plato seems to acknowledge that "the biggest lie about the biggest things" is a truth, if a deadly truth. That our allegedly high and sacred origins in fact hide a crime is a truth so dangerous that, if it must be told at all, let it be told to as few as possible; and let even them hear it as an unspeakable secret after they have made a very great sacrifice in order to be permitted to hear it at all (*Republic* ii.378a)—presumably the sacrifice of all other loves to that one great love, the love of the truth.

By what right does Plato undertake his great venture on behalf of enlightenment, his transformation of the very gods? To use the language Strauss takes from Nietzsche: By what right is he "commissioned to maintain in the world the order of rank, even among the things and not only among men"? (*SPPP* 187). The only possible answer is: natural right. Plato's preservation of enlightenment, his defense of the highest interests of hu-

---

25. Cicero, *Tusc. disput.* v.10; *Brutus* 31; see *CM* 13–14.

manity, is based on the natural right of the wise to rule, a natural right that conventional right (or "natural" law) always resists. This natural right is, as the great practitioners who dared to exercise it have recognized, always lawless. Machiavelli acknowledged this awe-inspiring fact by stating that those who put themselves at the head of introducing new orders arouse the opposition of "adversaries who have the laws on their side."[26] Francis Bacon acknowledged it by varying an Aristotelian theme and speaking cryptically of the "speculative platform, that reason and nature would that the best should govern; but not in any wise to create a right."[27] Nietzsche dared to bring this lawlessness into the open by flaunting the "criminal" character of the great lawgivers and explaining quite openly why they, why he, would be regarded as teachers of evil, as nihilists—they whose love of the true and the good so outstrips that of their opponents as to seem its opposite to them. As Nietzsche puts it, Plato is the very embodiment of the evil principle (*D* 496).

Platonic political philosophy is the permanent solution to philosophy's political problem, a permanent solution characterized by its capacity for change, its ability to adapt its defenses to the world in which it finds itself. Its permanence is the steadiness of its defense of philosophy as the highest way of life. Its steadiness discloses itself as a willingness to let go of gods to which it once professed loyalty, or even to bring down those gods if they usurp the highest authority; but the highest audacity of this steadiness is seen in its willingness to introduce new divinities which certify or command its practice. Strauss announced the philosophical legislator's timeless principle of timely change by quoting Plato's *Laws* (xii.948d): "Human opinions about the gods having changed, the laws also must change" (*AAPL* 172). The great shifts which mask the timeless permanence of the Platonic solution always involve dying and rising gods, some twilight of idols and some dawn of gods. A keen critic of Strauss's way of elevating the Medieval enlightenment cast his recognition of this aspect of Strauss's insight into the form of a complaint: "'Maimonideanism' in this odd [Straussian] sense would be devoid of any Jewish content."[28] Precisely. The very model of this approach, Platonic political philosophy in Strauss's odd sense, is devoid of

---

26. *Prince* chapter 6.

27. See *Advertisement Touching A Holy War, Works* VII.29; and Lampert, *Nietzsche and Modern Times* 99–101.

28. Harvey, "The Return of Maimonideanism" 265. A similar observation is made by Brague, who seems more sympathetic to it and who extends it in the fitting way: "Strauss's Maimonides wanted to maintain religion's political role, to favor in religion that which aims more or less toward philosophy. . . . This operation . . . can be applied to other, more or less religious traditions—for example, the American civil religion" ("Leo Strauss and Maimonides" 103).

any Platonic content insofar as that content is identified with the ideas, say, as anything other than the permanent problems.

By reading Plato this way, Strauss shows that he himself, like Nietzsche, is a complete skeptic about Plato. And he shows at the same time that complete skepticism is consonant with complete piety: Plato's teaching can be seen to be the true teaching when one discovers what that teaching is via an appropriate skepticism about its crafted appearance. The ministerial poetry which necessarily accompanies Plato's teaching gives the appearance to almost all readers of being its very core. This appearance masks the continuity of Platonic political philosophy throughout our tradition because it covers up what the genuine or Platonic philosophers have shared, hiding what they shared in quarrels that appeared fundamental, that appeared, falsely, to occupy the same degree of radical difference that separated Plato from a rival like Epicurus. Platonic political philosophy's core never changes; it defends the highest interests of humanity against the ever-threatening high interests of humanity. Platonic philosophy's ministerial poetry changes as the gods change, and poets, always the valets of some morality, conduct their allegedly fundamental battles on a surface spread over, spread almost impenetrably over the fundamental core.

Strauss's history of Platonic political philosophy opens a new way to read the history of philosophy, a new way to read our whole spiritual tradition. It was Nietzsche's fundamental critique of the Enlightenment that helped give Strauss his beginning, that helped set him on his movement of return that took him back to the Medieval enlightenment whose presuppositions the Enlightenment had destroyed. From there, Strauss followed the Medieval enlightenment back to its model, the Platonic enlightenment whose presuppositions had been supplanted by the rise of the God of revealed religion. Strauss discovered in Plato what Nietzsche had already discovered: the one teacher who set all philosophers (and theologians) on the same track (*BGE* 191). Like Nietzsche, Strauss found in Plato, the most beautiful growth of antiquity, a philosopher who knew the difference between the exoteric and the esoteric and who gave himself the right to employ the pious fraud (*BGE* 30; *TI* Ancients 5). Like Nietzsche, Strauss found in Platonic poetry the true, the genuine antagonism, Plato versus Homer, the moral view versus the tragic view (*GM* 3.25).

It was Strauss's Plato that enabled him to look differently on Nietzsche than anyone else has. For Strauss's Plato is the paradigm of philosophic, philanthropic ambition. When Strauss returned from his rediscovered Plato to Nietzsche himself, he found in Nietzsche Plato's fundamental philosophical rival, the philosophic poet of a revived Homeric celebration of life, fully aware of where he stood, fully aware of what he was attempting. Nietzsche is a thinker and actor on the scale of a Plato, the heretofore unrivaled scale. Strauss's summary of the clash between these two thinkers states the fundamental reality of our time from the perspective of Nietzsche's moral aspiration: Die vornehme Natur ersetzt die göttliche Natur.

Chapter Five

The Nietzschean Enlightenment

> The trumpet of morning blows in the clouds and through
> The sky. It is the visible announced,
> It is the more than visible, the more
> Than sharp, illustrious scene. The trumpet cries
> This is the successor of the invisible.
>
> This is its substitute in stratagems
> Of the spirit. This, in sight and memory,
> Must take its place, as what is possible
> Replaces what is not. The resounding cry
> Is like ten thousand tumblers tumbling down
>
> To share the day. The trumpet supposes that
> A mind exists, aware of division, aware
> Of its cry as clarion, its diction's way
> As that of a personage in a multitude:
> Man's mind grown venerable in the unreal.
>
> Wallace Stevens
> *Credences of Summer* VIII

Strauss went a long way with Nietzsche. But did he go far enough?

Strauss's elevation of Nietzsche is subterranean, almost invisible, thoroughly un-Nietzschean. From a Nietzschean perspective, Strauss can be faulted for his reticence, for attempting to make philosophy shy again just when boldness and courage had come to characterize its public task as they always had its private task.

However grateful the friends of Nietzsche must be for the services Strauss performed—and what services they are! revealing Nietzsche's true greatness and providing the context within which that greatness could be understood, the history of Platonic political philosophy—gratitude must be tempered with reservation. If Strauss ended with a whispered elevation of Nietzsche to the highest rank, he publicly and powerfully contributed to the already existing prejudice against Nietzsche and permitted the development of a school of interpretation, diverse in its ways, but almost uniform in its opposition to Nietzsche as the enemy of true philosophy and decent religion.

As regrettable as that public vilification of Nietzsche is, the primary reservation must lie precisely where Strauss placed the greatest emphasis, on the proper politics for philosophy today. This, it seems to me, is the fundamental difference between Nietzsche and Strauss. Nietzsche can say with respect to the conditions that endangered philosophy in its first appearance and that forced upon it the ascetic mask it has worn ever since: All that has really altered. Strauss implicitly denies that anything essential has really altered that could end philosophy's need to be furtive.

Even in the last words of his key study, *The City and Man*, Strauss finds it desirable to put the crucial issue as a question and to put even that question in a foreign language: *quid sit deus*, he asks, as if he were still in Cicero's world and had to be less bold even than Cicero—what might god be, or what might a god be? To treat this still as a question is to pretend that his book had not in fact provided the answer by its demonstration of the uses to which the thinkers, especially Plato, put the gods. No Dionysos versus the Crucified stands at the end of Strauss's books. Even at the end stand little opacities which pretend that the very things the book exists to make clear were still completely puzzling. "Mistake me for someone else," Strauss says at the end.

Strauss stated with great simplicity his basic argument for the unchanging character of philosophy's strategic imperative, and though it is derivative from Nietzsche, its conclusion contrasts sharply with Nietzsche's (*WPP* 221–22; see *OT* 27). Society's element is, unalterably, opinion (a viewpoint Nietzsche held from beginning to end), and philosophy attempts to dissolve the element in which society breathes, thus endangering society (a premise Nietzsche advanced as early as *The Uses and Disadvantages of History for Life*). From these two premises Strauss drew the conclusion that philosophy must preserve itself and society by exoteric allegiance to society's false opinions while esoterically pursuing its betrayal of them, and that it must do so always and do so in the old ways. Nietzsche denied the timeless necessity of this conclusion drawn from his timelessly true premises, and he did so for one primary reason: modern opinion necessitates what it also makes possible, the attempt to bring society's opinions into accord with philosophy's character, not by making society wise but by making its opinions reflect rather than contradict the truth.

Who read the needs of our age with greater acuteness, Strauss or Nietzsche? Do the times call for old caution or new boldness on philosophy's behalf?[1]

NIETZSCHE'S POLITICS OF ENLIGHTENMENT

What does the eclipse of the Enlightenment dictate for the politics of enlightenment? It dictates a radical break with past strategies, Nietzsche maintains, and his argument is essentially historical and diagnostic. Nietzsche's argument depends upon the art of reading well, where the text is human history and the reader's conclusions are interpretations of where we now stand and what we can reasonably aspire to. Because his argument appropriately rests upon interpretations of present reality, past trajectory, and future possibility, reasonable inquirers may disagree over its merits. Nevertheless, it seems to me that Nietzsche's case is entirely persuasive. Viewed from a long historical perspective, Nietzsche is Strauss's superior as a strategist for philosophy.

i. The Present.   "The greatest recent event—that 'God is dead'" (GS 343) makes our times so singular that unprecedented, unexampled actions must be risked by the most far-ranging philosophy. For Nietzsche, the death of

---

1. Stanley Rosen's challenging and instructive critiques of Strauss focus on the issue of Strauss's politics for philosophy. Rosen judges those politics not only to be inappropriate in a postmodern age but also to have "bad political consequences for philosophy" (*Hermeneutics* 136). As fitting as this judgment is, it seems to me that Rosen provides too narrow a base for it by emphasizing Strauss's allegedly unshakable preference for a regime of rural aristocrats. The broad and fitting base for the criticism of Strauss's politics for philosophy is, in my view, the untimeliness of his apparent loyalty to God and nation, issues far more prominent in Straussianism than rural aristocracy (ibid. 133–38, and "Leo Strauss" 158, 162–63, 165). Besides, it can be doubted whether Strauss really thought that the classical alliance of philosophy with an aristocracy of rural gentlemen was the timelessly true politics for philosophy: the political alliances forged for philosophy by Alfarabi and Maimonides do not have that character. Rosen's other main focus concerns philosophy proper, and here he finds that Strauss surrenders to a skepticism that brought him "dangerously close to Nietzsche" ("Leo Strauss" 162): "I suspect that Strauss did not take seriously the doctrine of the noetic perception of pure form," a suspicion which, if confirmed, would mean for Rosen that "Strauss regarded philosophy as finally impossible." Therefore, Rosen judges that Strauss "is almost a Nietzschean but not quite: he comes closer to Kant in the roots of his thought," where Kantianism is defined as the view that "nature understood as the Greek *physis* is not accessible to us" (*Hermeneutics* 125–26).

God was the public sign of something still greater though less noticeable: the death of Platonism, where Platonism is understood Nietzscheanly as the worst and most dangerous dogmatism, the invention of the pure mind and the good in itself. Strauss teaches skepticism about Platonic dogmatism; Nietzsche teaches convalescence and surmounting. Attack seemed hardly necessary, for Platonism lay on the ground, already dying. But even the momentous event of the death of Platonism was the sign of something still greater, for in the long perspective gained by Nietzsche, the death of Platonism portends the death of the still older, still more pervasive view for which Plato dared to provide a philosophical defense, the moral view of the world order. The moral view is ancient Zarathustrianism, in Nietzsche's historical imagery, and he allowed that ancient prophet to return as the harbinger of his own new and contrary teaching that the "immorality" of nature, its fecundity and indifference, are grounds for human gratitude.

The strategic conflict between Strauss and Nietzsche can be put this way: Why force philosophy to make concessions to a moral world view at the very moment in which that world view is becoming publicly discredited? Did Strauss take this event seriously enough? Nietzsche himself continued and advanced the spiritual warfare, both ancient and modern, that was partially responsible for the greatest recent event: "Hooray for physics!" Nietzsche says (GS 335). Physics—open inquiry into the natural order and public display of the results—assists in the triumph over the historic moralism with which Platonism made its compromises. Did Strauss take modern science seriously enough as a public presence contributing to the greatest recent event?

Strauss did not publicly endorse the public advancement of science, and Nietzsche did. Nietzsche praised Descartes for the first proper physio-psychology (A 14). He praised Copernicus and Boscovich for their opposition to "the visual evidence" which had made the earth and the material order seem to stand fast and which had therefore seemed to give heart to a view according to which all the truly valuable things stood fast (BGE 12). He praised Democritus and Pyrrho and Epicurus (KGW VIII 14 [99–100] = WP 437) over "the philosophers of virtue" who sprang from Socrates and his moralizing (KGW VIII 14 [129] = WP 434). He spent years composing a natural history of morals, a natural history of religion, a natural history of the priestly function—natural histories of the anti-natural or unnatural views very much alive in our tradition. Even his fabulous Zarathustra is a modern man standing within modern cosmology and evolutionary biology: the sun is our star and humanity sprang from the apes and any new teaching on nature and humanity must stand within these gains.

Strauss, for his part, acknowledges that modern natural science destroys the foundation of the moral view of the world order. He acknowledges that old dreams of nature's benevolence (that nature will favor us by annihilating human corruption and letting us start over) have "been rendered incredible by the experiences of the last centuries" (*TM* 299). Nevertheless, he does not openly endorse natural science as Nietzsche does, and he does not openly take the additional step with Nietzsche of allowing natural science to ground judgments against the old morality.

Nietzsche's natural histories ground a fundamental condemnation of the old dreams of a moral order, for his histories showed that the so-called moral view of the world order was worse than false: it had very suspicious foundations in human passion, in hatred of the actual conditions of human life and dreams of escape from them and revenge on them. The moral view that dominated human society for ten millennia (*BGE* 32) harbored twin passions of *ressentiment* (it's all your fault) and bad conscience (it's all my fault): the moral view begins with the judgment that something is seriously wrong with the world and moves to the conclusion that someone must be blamed. Platonic lies once thought salutary, lies of moral gods dishing out reward and punishment and immortal souls taking it, are judged from a Nietzschean perspective to be base teachings, detrimental to what life actually is on earth, what life on earth can be shown to be with a high probability by an honest public science. For Nietzsche, the Platonic lies are both false and base. And both judgments claim a scientific foundation; intellectual probity employing the tools of rational investigation of natural phenomena shows them to be false and base.

For all his praise of science, Nietzsche was by no means a servant of modern natural science, and by no means an admirer of its independence and presumption, its dominance of philosophy. He could say "Hooray for physics!" even though the prevailing public form of physics in his own time, Cartesian positivism, advanced a materialist world-view and a method of mere counting that he regarded as perhaps the dumbest yet (*GS* 373); and he could say it despite the *hubris* of its "whole attitude toward nature," its "rape of nature with the help of machines and the ever so heedless inventiveness of technicians and engineers" (*GM* 3.9). Physics, the science of *physis* or nature, was reformable into a philological science of subtle interpretation of nature (*BGE* 22); its end was not the technological mastery of nature, but the understanding of nature and the human place in nature. Yet even in its unreformed state, physics could curb the loyalty or obstinacy with which one clung to world-views contrary to the world-view opened by both ancient and modern physics. Ancient rumor thus had it that Plato "ignored Democritus out of envy," never once mentioning him in his writings; and the rumor went on to allege something still stronger: Plato wanted all of Democritus's books burned.[2] One would like to believe that the rumor could not be true, but it attests in any case to the salutary character of physics: it is fatal to the Platonic lies.

One looks in vain for any "Hooray for physics!" in Strauss. Instead of a cheer for honesty about the natural order, one finds in Strauss an almost submerged acknowledgment of the almost submerged acknowledgment in Plato and Xenophon that Socrates continued to study the cosmos and that he did so privately with his good friends behind the curtain woven of piety and irony. The carefully guarded privacy of that study attests to its heterodoxy, its non-teleological, non-theistic character (*AAPL* 183, *XS* 29–30). Strauss stands with his Socrates: privately, philosophy allows no limits on its open inquiry into nature; but publicly, it sells the belief that it has discovered something it calls natural right which dictates society's limits and grounds society's morals.

One also finds in Strauss a more specific reason why he forbids himself any "Hooray for physics!": physics posed a still greater danger to the revealed religions than it could ever pose to Greek religion. "The public discussion of 'the account of creation,' i.e., of physics, did not harm the pagans in the way in which it might harm the adherents of revealed laws" (*WPP* 164). Physics imperiled the authority of the deity who claimed that *he* created heaven and earth. Strauss's philosophical accounts of the first chapters of Genesis isolate the basic conflict between physics and biblical piety. For Strauss maintains that "all philosophy is cosmology ultimately," and he shows that the Bible begins by depreciating cosmology or the study of the heavens and by announcing a prohibition on inquiry into the human good: the Bible opens forbidding both natural and human philosophy and commanding obedience to its own dictates.[3] Strauss's acknowledgment that physics poses a special danger to revealed religion is a polite translation of a nice Nietzschean phrase: the God of Genesis, Nietzsche says, is the God "with the hellish fear of science" (*A* 48).[4]

It seems to me that there can be little doubt that Strauss held that the

---

2. Diogenes Laertius, *The Lives of the Philosophers* 9.36, "Democritus."

3. Strauss, "On the Interpretation of Genesis" 15–19.

4. On the significance of modern natural science for Strauss's understanding of the crisis of natural right see Masters, "Evolutionary Biology and Natural Right." In addition to clarifying the theme stated in its title, this essay provides another example of the presence of Nietzsche in Strauss's text even when the explicit discussion does not name him. Masters offers persuasive reasons for regarding the phrase "the victory of modern natural science" in a crucial passage of *NRH* as a stand-in for what is really meant: Nietzsche.

human species was mortal and the whole natural order subject to perpetual change—that he agreed with Nietzsche on these ultimate matters. For where in Strauss is there an argument on behalf of the contrary view, an *argument* as opposed to the occasional expression of alignment with traditional beliefs in the contrary view? Strauss knew the implications of the absence of argument on this crucial issue, for he never tired of pointing out what such silence implied in other thinkers. To omit the essential argument, to omit any attempt to make such an argument, is itself the decisive argument in a writer like Strauss. Besides, he is not completely silent, for he knew the implications of a statement like this which placed him wholly with the philosophers: "By becoming aware of the dignity of the mind, we realize the true ground of the dignity of man and therewith the goodness of the world" (*LAM* 8).[5]

Still, Strauss could not follow Nietzsche in his radical, open, and intransigent endorsement of the advancement of science, his exposure of the truth about nature. For Nietzsche, the intellectual conscience basic to science needed to become more and more a publicly valued conscience (*GS* 2; see *D* 146); in the historic conflict between the true and the good, the true and the edifying, we can countenance only that form of the edifying which is based on the true. Nietzsche states his intransigence in a manner that anticipates Strauss's hesitation: to insist on the intellectual conscience by forcing its demands on everyone is, he says, "my form of injustice." Nietzsche is unjust, he does not give people their due, he acts as if everyone had an intellectual conscience. In this way Nietzsche fueled the trajectory of the modern enlightenment without believing in the Enlightenment fictions of a wise, free, and equal posterity.

This is the point, it seems to me, at which Strauss cannot avoid embarrassment. There can be no question about Strauss's inward intransigence. But there must be more than a question about his willingness for outward compromise, his willingness to countenance pious fraud. The issue is more strategic than moral. Nietzsche attempted to forge an alliance between philosophy and science and scholarship; he aimed to bring science and scholarship into the care of the new philosophy while providing a new poetry of gratitude and praise for the world as it is. By spurning such an alliance and sticking fast to the old poetry, Strauss opened himself to the most serious strategic challenge: Strauss misjudged the power of modern virtue—honesty or intellectual probity—and made himself vulnerable to its attack.

5. See also *HPP* 77: "Philosophy is the highest human activity, and man is an excellent, perhaps the most excellent, part of the whole."

The post-Enlightenment intellectual world of science and scholarship has no place for a defense of noble lying; it questions both lying and the nobility of the lied-for. In this respect Nietzsche seems a more acute reader than Strauss of the power of modern virtue.

Strauss seemed to see no opportunity in the present except a return to "the Platonic notion of the noble delusion" (*NRH* 26). But Plato's own use of the noble delusion was extremely radical; he chose "judicious conformity," but he did so in order to advance a revolutionary program that replaced dying Homeric gods with new Socratic ones. Strauss makes Plato's strategy visible to an age experiencing the death of God, but he himself can offer only an old God. From a Nietzschean perspective, Strauss could be thought a strategist guilty of injudicious nonconformity: he unwisely held on to two great Platonic delusions just as their time was passing. First: Does the public good always depend upon public belief in just gods and immortal souls? When a public science has discredited such beliefs, and when the history of such beliefs, including contemporary history, testifies to their principled inhumanity, can it serve the interests of philosophy to make it seem that philosophy itself is tied to such beliefs, or even that philosophy's reasoned opposition to them leaves them standing in proud obstinacy, dumb with certainty? Second: Does the public good always depend upon public identification of one's own with one's people or nation? When a public science has discredited the grounds of such localism and provided a new basis for appreciating the unity of our species across space and time and within the whole staggering array of species, and when history continues to testify to the dangers of such local loves and hates, can it serve the interests of philosophy to make it seem that philosophy itself is tied to such beliefs?

Strauss could not show his followers any way toward political responsibility except perpetuating a supposedly noble lying on behalf of views rendered both incredible and unpalatable by modern experience.

From a Nietzschean perspective on modern times, the question is less "Does humanity need Platonic fictions?" than it is "What is to be done now that humanity must live without Platonic fictions?" In answering the question, What is to be done, Nietzsche took his guidance from a very long view backward and forward, a view of past actuality and future possibility not wholly shared by Strauss.

ii. The Past.   Nietzsche's argument for a radical strategy on behalf of philosophy grounds itself on historical precedent. His reading of the Western past sees its essential struggle as Athens versus Jerusalem, a struggle for rule through the transvaluation of all values. Strauss maintains that "the secret of the vitality of Western civilization" is the unresolved conflict between the biblical point of view and the philosophic point of view,[6] a conflict that remains unresolved only as long as philosophy remains reticent in speaking about the degree and character of the conflict. Nietzsche is not reticent about the conflict because he regarded "the biblical point of view" as a tyranny, especially the contemporary secular form of the biblical point of view, "modern ideas" which threaten the very existence of philosophy.

Nietzsche's historical argument begins where it must begin: How is ancient Greek philosophy related to the Greek enlightenment? The high point of the Greek enlightenment was achieved by the tragic poets, by Aristophanes, by Thucydides, and by the philosophers of the tragic age of the Greeks. "The height attained in the disposition of a Democritus, Hippocrates, and Thucydides was not attained a second time" (KGW VII 36 [11] = WP 443). If Greek philosophy peaked with Greek classical culture in the age of tragedy, then Socrates marks a decline, a turn from tragedy to moralism that corrupted even the most beautiful growth of antiquity. Platonic philosophy was a failure of nerve that betrayed the Greek enlightenment; its concessions to popular religion through the invention of new moral gods unwittingly helped prepare philosophy's subjection to religion.[7]

Traces of Nietzsche's interpretation of the history of Greek philosophy appear in Strauss: in admiration for Thucydides expressed in the highest terms (WPP 260), in insistence on Socrates' friendly disposition to the enlightenment and especially to sophism (see e.g. "On the Euthydemus," SPPP 67–88), in cautiously expressed wondering whether Plato has not been too successful (OT 206). Still, Strauss offers no strategy except Plato's even for the contemporary crisis.

Nietzsche, however, offers Epicurus as the great example of philosophy's more appropriate response to the crisis facing the Greek enlightenment. And Nietzsche emphasizes what is too often forgotten: Epicurus succeeded, for "every respectable mind in the Roman Empire was an Epicurean" (A 58). And Epicurus's success would have been more permanent, Nietzsche argues, but for one thing: Christianity, or the apostle Paul's reformulation of a sectarian Jewish peace movement into a salvation religion for the masses. Christianity ruined the Roman preservation of the Greek enlightenment, and Christianity's way had been smoothed by Platonism's willingness to

6. Strauss, "Progress or Return?" 289; RCPR 270.
7. Nietzsche's reading of the history of Greek philosophy has a powerful precursor in Francis Bacon; see Lampert, Nietzsche and Modern Times 118–23.

compromise philosophy with religion. Nietzsche's reading of the politics of philosophy in the ancient world thus elevates Epicurus above Plato even though Plato's success made it extremely difficult to recover Epicurus: Plato's successors had God's permission to burn his books. But as valuable as Epicurus is for understanding philosophy's past, Epicurus does not serve Nietzsche as a timeless example, as Plato serves Strauss: "We must overcome even the Greeks" (GS 340), Nietzsche said; and although he was speaking of Socrates, Epicurus is included as well. In particular, we must overcome Epicurus's willingness to be primarily an observer, which made him content to experience a private happiness while watching the sun set on antiquity (GS 45, BGE 62); and we must overcome Epicurus's romanticism, which made his teaching "the pagan doctrine of redemption" (GS 370).

We must overcome even the greatest Greeks and Romans because of the difference between their times and our times, a difference caused in large measure by the victory of Christianity. For if the Roman enlightenment provided Nietzsche with a model for the preservation of enlightenment, the ultimate lesson was to be drawn from its demise, not from its Epicurean success.[8]

The great blame which Nietzsche levels against Platonism is that the Platonic compromise made possible the victory of Christianity. And the vehemence of Nietzsche's late attack on Christianity is partly explained by the historical judgment that Christianity cost humanity the Greek enlightenment preserved by Rome. "All the presuppositions for a scholarly culture, all scientific *methods* were already there" (A 59) in the Roman world prior to the Christian revaluation of all its values. At the foundation of the Roman preservation and advancement of the Greek enlightenment lay the fundamental art, the art of interpretation, Nietzsche's art of philology: "The great, the incomparable art of reading well had already been established—that presupposition for the tradition of culture, for the unity of science." This liberating art did not oppose the natural sciences but encouraged them and was employed by them: "Natural science, allied with mathematics and mechanics, was well along on the best way—the *sense for facts*, the last and most valuable of all the senses, had its schools and its already centuries-old tradition." With all this in place in a great civilization, "everything *essential* had been found, so that the work could be begun." *Begun* because this is the work of millennia, scholarly and scientific work investigating nature and the

8. Strauss emphasized the Medieval and not the Roman enlightenment, but his discussions of Alfarabi's successful strategy have very little to say about "the eventual collapse of philosophical inquiry in the Islamic . . . world" merely a few centuries later (PAW 19).

human place in nature, carrying forward the Greek enlightenment within a settled civic order friendly toward enlightenment though hardly an enlightened society. Christian cunning destroyed those foundations and thwarted that work in its very beginnings: "The whole labor of the ancient world *in vain:* I have no words to express my feelings about something so tremendous" (*A* 59).

But the Christian victory was not complete. Renaissances occurred, events of spiritual warfare in which fresh incursions of Greek and Roman vitality were countered by a victorious Christian Rome with inquisitions, crusades, and religious revivalism aimed at stamping them out, whatever the cost. The renaissances provided Nietzsche with another model. Regarding the renaissance of the twelfth century, Nietzsche could speak of "the Provençal knight-poets" as "those magnificent and inventive human beings of the '*gai saber*' to whom Europe owes so many things and almost itself" (*BGE* 260). These were the human beings crushed, as Nietzsche well knew, by the Albigensian Crusade and St. Dominic's Inquisition; their inventions on behalf of the gay science were likewise hunted down and destroyed. Nietzsche's celebration of the Renaissance of the fifteenth and sixteenth centuries focused on its classical spirit as a total opposition to Christianity: "Does one understand at last, does one *want* to understand what the Renaissance was? The *transvaluation of Christian values,* the attempt, undertaken with every means, with every instinct, with all genius, to bring the *counter* values, the *noble* values to victory" (*A* 61). With respect to the Renaissance too, Nietzsche drew his ultimate lesson from its demise and not from its temporary success in reviving the classical spirit. Its demise was caused by the religious revival of Luther, that "calamity of a monk" who restored Christianity at the "very moment *when it was vanquished*" (*EH* Books *CW* 2) and prepared the way for modern ideas.

Nietzsche's politics for philosophy aimed to ground a successful renaissance. In his own way, Nietzsche sought a return. But unlike Strauss, Nietzsche returned to the pre-Platonic, to the Greek enlightenment for which Platonism was itself a preserving strategy. What Nietzsche saw as permanently valuable was the spirit of the Greek enlightenment; he did not see as permanently valuable or viable one of the strategies for its preservation, the Platonic. On the contrary, in viewing that strategy historically, he judged it a failure, a compromise with the enemy of enlightenment bound to fail because its strategy was to lend its enemy all the weapons in its own armory. It puffed up the enemy as itself rational and loaned it rational-looking arguments. It said that claims contradictory to reason were invulnerable to reason. And it surrendered one of the great uses of philosophy, to deprive stupidity of its good conscience (*GS* 328). And it failed to flaunt the advantage of having the laugh on its side (*GS* 1).

Nietzsche refused to accept the failure of all past renaissances as proof of the necessity of failure. The novelty of present conditions, the successful modern fight against Platonism and Christianity, presented a historic opportunity. Furthermore, Christianity's modern heir, the global society pursuing individual self-preservation and easy contentment, raised the stakes by presenting a novel threat, the interminable reign of the last man or the autonomy of the herd.

Nietzsche aimed to establish, through the philosophic leadership of science, a cultural renaissance that would begin again what the long interregnum of Christianity had extinguished. From a Nietzschean point of view, return in Strauss's sense is a return to the very aspects of dogmatic Platonism which allowed philosophy to be captured and ruled by religion in the first place. In *Beyond Good and Evil* (10), Nietzsche spoke approvingly of the passion that had impelled some moderns to desire return: "their instinct, which repels them from *modern* reality, is unrefuted." But he recognized that mere return was not only undesirable but impossible; it was a "wish to get *away*" which lacked the essential energy called for by revulsion against the modern ideas: "A little *more* strength, flight, courage, and artistic power, and they would want *up and out*—not return!" If "no one is free to be a crab," as Nietzsche whispered to conservatives (*TI* Skirmishes 43), if there is no going backward, what could "up and out" mean? It meant that "one *must* go forward," and that meant, at first, "step by step further into decadence."

iii. The Future.   To go step by step further into decadence is to think pessimism through to its depths. It is to write the history of the next two centuries. It is to recognize the fatedness of European nihilism as the spasms of a dying Platonic culture terrorized by the death of its dream. Nothing could halt or deflect the accumulated velocity of a culture in decline because it had refuted its own highest values. The arresting novelty and vividness of Nietzsche's descriptions of the coming nihilism, plus his apparent surrender to it as our fate, have led many to the ridiculous conclusion that Nietzsche was nihilism's advocate. But to think pessimism through to its depths, Nietzsche reported, is to glimpse a new ideal opposite to the old ideal of world-denial. To write the history of European nihilism presupposes having sighted land on the farther side.

If not our future nihilism, or our present pursuit of comfortable well-being, or a return to past orders, what *did* Nietzsche advocate? He advocated what Strauss presents as his Platonism and his platonizing, philosophy's open love of the whole, of the earth and mortal life, and the beautification of the beloved in a novel poetry. In Strauss's language, Nietzsche's Platonism entailed his platonizing; his advocacy of the philosophy of the future entailed his advocacy of the religion of the future.

Our ability to appreciate Nietzsche's philosophy of the future and religion of the future has been hampered, even crippled, by the unfinished character of his work. *Ecce Homo, How One Becomes What One Is* would perhaps have made things clear except for two things: it came too late, for it was first published in 1908, and what it was written to introduce never came at all. *Ecce Homo* provides the essential clarification of the whole of Nietzsche's task, for its review of his writings puts on display the entire trajectory of his career as Nietzsche came to understand it after he had glimpsed its proper completion. *Thus Spoke Zarathustra*, Nietzsche says, *solved* the affirmative part of his task; Zarathustra's flight into the European future unveiled the new highest ideal, the ideal belonging to the most world-affirming human being who had glimpsed that the world in its "intelligible character" was will to power and nothing besides—and seen that it was good. Having solved the affirmative part of his task, Nietzsche returned to the present, to the critique of modern times, and wrote a series of "No-saying" books aimed at winning to his view those few who were related to him. These books now have a prominence and a character which Nietzsche could never have expected or desired for them: now they are his *last* books and therefore seem the best books in which to find his last, his deepest thoughts. In fact, however, they are all polemics, No-saying fishhooks for free minds discontented with the modern ideas but knowing nowhere to turn. The polemics are meant to turn them to Nietzsche, whose critique of modern times was not only more thoroughgoing than theirs but knew a way out: "We are Hyperboreans, we know the road, we have found the exit out of millennia of labyrinth" (*A* 1).

But why write *Ecce Homo* after these polemics, why point in that astounding way to Mr. Nietzsche, reversing the instinctive cunning which till then suppressed the little word "I" (*EH* Books *HH* 6)? For one reason alone (*EH* Preface): *Ecce Homo* was needed as the calling card introducing the author of a book then in the process of being written, *The Transvaluation of All Values*, a book so ambitious in its undertaking that its reader had to be assured in advance that its author had a right to its audacity. His calling card told how he became what he was, how he gradually grew into himself and came to possess what he had never aspired to, how he fit himself, without really meaning to do so, to found the philosophy of the future and to prepare the religion of the future.

In the absence of that promised and perhaps indispensable book, and in the presence of its author's credentials and prehistory, we must piece together on our own, from *Zarathustra* and the hints dropped in the polemics, Nietzsche's most audacious or affirmative teachings for a European future beyond nihilism. Two audacities stand out above all others, for they touch the basic matters, philosophy and religion—in the language favored by Strauss, a teaching on fact and a teaching on the ideal. Just here, Nietzsche's language had to be least ardent and most playful; just here, the hammer was the least fitting of writing instruments. Those attuned to the hammer would have great difficulty hearing the subtle tones of Nietzsche's most important teachings.

Nietzsche was acutely aware of his predicament: the free minds, the most advanced European spirits, were his only possible audience, but philosophy and religion were the two themes they least wanted to hear and were least capable of hearing. Any talk of "knowledge" of the intelligible character of the whole inevitably sounded like the old dogmatism, annoying especially to free minds who took their skepticism to be the highest possible state of mind. And any talk of religion or divinity naturally sounded far worse, for how could there be religion that was not superstition or bondage, the surrender of the newly freed mind? "The strict habits" of the ears of the free-minded (*BGE* 295) were bound to be offended by the untimely things that Nietzsche had to say and that he had barely begun to force his audience to hear, namely, why "will to power," though a weak and attenuating metaphor, can serve as an initial naming for the "intelligible character" of the world seen from the inside; why eternal return must be the highest ideal for a nonascetic philosophy in love with the world viewed as will to power; and why Ariadne and Dionysos were part of a fitting new poetry that could perhaps outfit the new sensibility with festivals of recognition and celebration.

Nietzsche was fated to speak his thoughts about the deepest matters of philosophy and religion in the midst of a dying Platonism and a rising nihilism, and to speak them to skeptics who knew above anything else that philosophy was impossible and religion contemptible. And at just that moment when he was poised to offer Europe his calling card and then to offer it humanity's "most independent" book (*TI* Skirmishes 51), he lost his voice to a malfunction of his body; and his chief work, the main work by the destiny who had become what he was, did not get written—yet another impediment to *amor fati*, but above all an impediment to understanding the teacher of *amor fati*.

Strauss made accessible the Platonic core of Nietzsche's philosophy of the future, its continuity with philosophy's inexpungeable paganism, its love of the world. And Strauss made clear how the religion of the future followed from the philosophy of the future. But he resolutely refused to lend the advocacy of the religion of the future any of his assistance. Yet what is that new religion? In the fragmentary form in which it exists in Nietzsche's writings, it is the material for festivals offered by one who is not a prophet consumed by belief but a thinker who knows the rationale for world-affirming beliefs. Those materials maintain that:

—the intelligible character of the whole shows itself to our best penetration as a process of relentless, surging energy in which every power draws its ultimate consequences at every moment—blind, meaningless, wasteful abundance that consumes whatever it generates and is lovable as it is;

—the highest ideal is a post-Platonic, post-modern loyalty to the earth that can learn how to assign limits to the human conquest of nature and human nature out of love of the natural order of which we are dependent parts;

—the only possible world-affirming divinities are pre-biblical and post-biblical, earthly gods who are male and female and are neither otherworldly nor moral but who philosophize and are well disposed toward humanity;

—both the gains of knowledge and the tenets of belief must submit to the test of an intellectual conscience embued with a distaste for pious fraud and a gratitude for the possibility of science;

—the always partial knowledge of our natural history made possible by the subtle historical sense can assign the future a past of struggle for enlightenment and renaissance without clutching to any particular element of the past as if it were timeless;

—a proper physio-psychology can become aware of the unity of our species amid the whole array of species, and aware that all species share the common fate on our planet of appearing, flourishing, and falling extinct.

Out of such materials alone can come the new imperatives, the new tablet of good and bad which Nietzsche's Zarathustra anticipated as the thousand and first goal for humanity (Z 1.15). Out of such materials alone can come "the poems of our climate," to quote Wallace Stevens, whose poem of that title gives a fitting image to both the Nietzschean ideal and its mode of expression:

> The imperfect is our paradise.
> Note that, in this bitterness, delight,
> Since the imperfect is so hot in us,
> Lies in flawed words and stubborn sounds.

In no one was the imperfect so hot as in Nietzsche. And if his delight in the imperfect "lies" in flawed words and stubborn sounds, those "lies" are effulgences of delight which transfigure reality without changing it and without wishing it were other than it is. In Nietzsche's words and sounds lie the materials for a religion of the future, a paradise of the imperfect. Wallace Stevens captures the movement toward that paradise perfectly in the Nietzschean stanzas quoted as the epigraph to this chapter. It is a natural movement, a movement of growth, of maturing into a vast historic replacement in which the visible comes to replace the long-cultivated invisible; but the visible is transfigured now by the absence of the invisible and by the presence of the human mind grown venerable in service to the invisible, the human mind deepened and sharpened, grown more spirited, more playful, more grateful, through the long discipline of service to the unreal.

Nietzsche as the poet of a transfigured reality is necessarily very far from the fictional Nietzsche of contemporary scholarship who supposedly taught a strain of modern individualism, of universal free-mindedness. In fact, Nietzsche taught regard for philosophy, for the highest human undertaking in pursuit of truth and beauty. To the ultimate truth-seeker there falls a responsibility for community, for establishing the preconditions of community. That responsibility entails respect for religion. Nietzsche knew that such respect must necessarily be recovered very slowly by those so soured on religion by their struggle against their own that "they no longer even know what religions are good for" (BGE 58). What they are good for, what they are simply indispensable for, is the structuring poetry of everyday life, that web of beliefs and values lived spontaneously by any and every human community as its testament of the useful, the good, and the holy. From Plato to Nietzsche, philosophers have regarded religion, without invidious intent, as the poetry of the multitude, group persuasions dyed into the community as almost involuntary beliefs lived out, more or less loyally, by all except the very few for whom life is thought.

Nietzsche did not oppose religion, a universal and necessary phenomenon; he opposed *our* religion both sacred and secular, biblical religion and the modern ideas that preserve its spirit. In his opposition to our religion, Nietzsche felt free to say out loud that God is dead and we're glad. He felt free to say out loud that in the fight between Athens and Jerusalem, we stand wholly with a tragic wisdom against a slave morality, while gratefully acknowledging that the long and severe discipline of our religion deepened our inwardness, trained us in virtue, and broadened our fascination: we're a spectacle fit for gods.

The vehemence of Nietzsche's denunciation of our religion (and the absence of *The Transvaluation of All Values*) has made almost invisible those quieter passages in which Nietzsche invites the free-minded to the consideration of new religious possibilities. But Nietzsche expressed himself with complete clarity about the need for a religion of the future and described some of its contours even before he had discerned its particular focuses on eternal return and Dionysos:

> The individual must be consecrated to something higher than himself—that is the meaning of tragedy; he must be free of the terrible anxiety which death and time evoke in the individual: for at any moment, in the briefest atom of his life's course, he may encounter something holy that endlessly outweighs all his struggle and all his distress—this is what it means to have a *sense for the tragic*. And if the whole of humanity is destined to die out—and who dares doubt that?—so the goal is set for it that is its supreme task, so to grow together in one and in common that it sets out as a whole to meet its coming demise with a sense for the tragic.[9] All the ennoblement of humanity is enclosed in this supreme task; the definite rejection of this task would be the saddest picture imaginable to a friend of humanity. That is my view of things! (*RWB* 4 end)

"So to grow together in one and in common that it sets out as a whole to meet its coming demise with a sense for the tragic." The human species lives an interpretation of life; it lives in the medium of religion. The religion of the future which Nietzsche envisioned as the celebration of mortal life would live communally the fundamental truths of human existence as glimpsed by those rare achievements of the community, the complementary human beings whose high spirituality commissions them to maintain in the world the order of rank even among the things and not only among humans.

What Nietzsche once viewed from a still Platonic perspective and there-

---

9. Unfortunately, this key sentence is omitted in the Hollingdale translation—just as its meaning is omitted in the customary interpretations of Nietzsche.

fore judged deadly—that the greatest danger of science is its eradication of all horizons, its removal of the protective atmosphere in which alone humanity had been able to thrive—he eventually came to see as a gift: our science, our inquiry shows us that we dwell within an unfathomable whole as its unriddlers and celebrants. Nietzsche seemed to think that the conscious inhabitants of this enigmatic marvel of a cosmos could experience once again what he found most worthy of wonder in ancient Greek religion: "the enormous abundance of gratitude it exudes" (*BGE* 49). The human expression of gratitude for what is infinitely greater than ourselves reaches its peak in the new ideal of eternal return, "the highest formula of affirmation that is at all attainable" (*EH* Books Z 1). In the songs that close part 3 of *Thus Spoke Zarathustra*, Nietzsche showed how Zarathustra arrived at and expressed the highest affirmation; love for life as it is becomes the desire that life be eternally what it is, that our paradise of the imperfect eternally return just as it is.

The god-forming instinct that shares this grateful disposition knows that the gods too philosophize, for the highest form of the godly is to seek to know; and what it seeks is elusive and mysterious, sheltered in enigma but luring and giving. Unlike Platonic gods, philosophizing gods do not guard an already established dogma; they do not know the truth about the origins of things, nor do they need to cloud their unknowing in a lie. That the highest beings philosophize means that being itself is to be understood as the innocence of becoming: there is no eternal order from which it has fallen away. In Nietzsche's language, the gods take the names Dionysos and Ariadne again, Greek names that oppose any ideal of an abstract personhood untainted by gender, or any suggestion that the gods fathered us and that we owe them everything. Instead, Dionysos and Ariadne give religious expression to the most primordial affirmative instinct of life, the instinct that hallows procreation and the sexual function, that hallows life itself which reproduces through sexual generation. "What I Owe to the Ancients," Nietzsche says at the end of his work, is ultimately the artistic and religious expression of an affirmative sensibility toward life that our religion attempts to assassinate. Eternal return and Dionysos and Ariadne belong together as mysterious elements of a religion grounded in philosophy's affirmation of the world. They are reasonable expressions of mystery and desire. They are as opposed to Platonic gods as Yahweh and his offspring were once opposed to them, though they employ different means than the jealous god.

Nietzsche takes a very long view forward into what is worth fighting for, a millennia-long view; and he bases his sense of the fight on a very long view backward into what has been accomplished in our culture and against what odds; and he measures his speech with an acute sense of where we now stand as heirs to Athens and heirs to Jerusalem.

The most severe criticism of Strauss from a Nietzschean perspective must be that he understood the Nietzschean moment in our history but failed to flaunt it, to become its reasoned advocate. Nietzsche claimed the Persian virtue, "to speak the truth and shoot well with arrows" (*EH* Destiny 3), the virtue of "the strongest most evil spirits" who have so far done the most to advance humanity (*GS* 4), the virtue most essential if the present is to be a moment of advance beyond the merely modern. Strauss's virtue cast his lot with "those who cultivate the old thoughts, the farmers of the spirit" (*GS* 4), Ischomachus and his like, blind masters praying for grace while presuming to teach lessons to nature. By writing as he did, Strauss endorsed a premodern Platonic politics that encouraged obfuscation, gave heart to the irrational, and was not ashamed of intellectual uncleanliness. An odd combination, this late in the day, of Epicurean and Platonist, Strauss dwelt within a carefully walled garden cultivating an observer's naturalistic understanding of the whole while encouraging a public Platonism outside the garden wall as the only possible preservation of both the public and the garden. Perhaps Strauss saw still less reason than did Nietzsche for any hope and therefore prepared as he thought best for the coming night, the eventual collapse of philosophical inquiry in the modern world.

Strauss's great legacy, it seems to me, is compromised by his lack of boldness on behalf of philosophy at a decisive moment in its history. No one could reasonably accuse Strauss of cowardice, given what he was willing to bear on behalf of his undertaking for philosophy. Nevertheless, to have come so near to Nietzsche, to have penetrated Plato to his radical core, to have seen the history of genuine philosophy in all its breathtaking ambition, to have understood so clearly the inward intransigence of philosophy's opposition to the idiocies of revealed religion—and then to have whispered the results of these intrepid voyages of the mind in a way that makes them accessible only to such a small number of readers blinded neither by contemporary intellectual fashion nor by excessive loyalty to the piety of his own texts—that, it seems to me, is a failure of the historical sense.

STRAUSS'S POLITICS OF ENLIGHTENMENT

Strauss's studies in Platonic political philosophy defined for him what had to be endured on behalf of philosophy. Its defense and advancement in the present, Strauss apparently concluded, required that philosophy endure an alignment with one of the forms of modernity itself, the form in whose midst Strauss happened to find himself and which encouraged the native piety toward God and nation. Strauss, always so subtle and cunning, chose to endure being thought an innocent. In greater measure than Nietzsche himself, Strauss chose to adopt that impish and cheerful vice, courtesy, and willingly endure being thought more stupid than he was (*BGE* 284, 288). Thus Strauss perfected his own form of what he called "irony in the highest sense . . . the dissimulation of one's wisdom, i.e. the dissimulation of one's wise thoughts" (*CM* 51). His feats of endurance preserved for him the radical freedom of zetetic inquiry, a freedom which from the beginning took part of its inspiration from Nietzsche.

Strauss reflected on the Nietzschean solution to philosophy's political problem educated by Aristophanes and Plato and Maimonides. His viewpoint required that he decline membership in the confederacy to introduce new divine things once visible only to Nietzsche as divine. That will to power is the fundamental fact, that eternal return is consequently the new highest ideal, that the complementary man stands at a decisive point in human spiritual history facing the problem of nature in an unparalleled way—all this Strauss makes clear without assenting to it. Strauss's service to this possible philosophy of the future was confined to introducing the new Nietzschean divine things from the standpoint of a still skeptical admirer who recognized the arguments in their favor without being persuaded that they could be made persuasive. Having established his character as something of a pious ascetic, Strauss could tell the truth about the new view of things and never be believed except by those very few he had trained to skepticism about pious masks, his own included. The character he had labored to establish dictated that he tell the truth non-Nietzscheanly, that he introduce the new gods Aristophanically, dressed up as Maimonides, poet of the old order enchanted with these new clouds.

This is the view of Strauss's intent to which I incline. This, it seems to me, is the Strauss who finally peers out at us from those seventeen matchless pages elevating Nietzsche—a zetetic thinker marveling at the attempted birth of new highest things, aware of their profound likeness to their only historic rival, aware too of the arguments favoring them in the only struggle that really mattered, the struggle between philosophy and religion for rule. And yet zetetic to the end, a watcher clothed in garments that fit him for the watch.

Both Strauss and Nietzsche take the religion of "modern ideas" with its global tyranny to be philosophy's greatest threat. Did Nietzsche tie his case for philosophy to a public teaching on the earth and earthly divinities that is at all possible for modern humanity? This seems to be the question that Strauss held open while making it appear that he sided against Nietzsche in favor of the classical philosophers. And this is precisely the kind of question that one can imagine a zetetic thinker holding open for himself in the first generations after Plato, or in the first generations after Alfarabi, or in the first generations after Machiavelli: who can know whether the new gods will triumph over the old? And who can know whether their rule will be more benign?

Therefore, in the end—if we are permitted to view Strauss's end somewhat whimsically, recognizing that the Champion Wiremaster spiral notebook in which Strauss copied out his last essays could never have a public presence and that Strauss himself could not have been sure that they *were* the end—in the end it seems altogether fitting that in his final months Leo Strauss should turn from Nietzsche and Plato, those two greatest, most sublime, most commanding philosophers, that he should turn from the clangor of these great clashing armies, and take up Thucydides again, and take up Xenophon again, and compose his final quiet and beautiful essays on their politic speech, their observations on the gods and on what the gods they no longer believed in required of them. These two men were, perhaps, his cure too for the excesses of Plato and Nietzsche, men more to his bearing and taste, men whose temperament and sense for strategy were more akin to his own, however much the spectacle of Plato and Nietzsche swam within his contemplative ken.

Appendix

Note on the Plan of Nietzsche's *Beyond Good and Evil*
by Leo Strauss

Reproduced from *Studies in Platonic Political Philosophy* (Chicago: University of Chicago Press, pp. 174–91. Copyright © 1983 by The University of Chicago.

Note on the Plan of Nietzsche's
Beyond Good and Evil

[1]   *Beyond Good and Evil* always seemed to me to be the most beautiful of Nietzsche's books. This impression could be thought to be contradicted by his judgement, for he was inclined to believe that his *Zarathustra* is the most profound book that exists in German as well as the most perfect in regard to language. But "most beautiful" is not the same as "most profound" and even as "most perfect in regard to language." To illustrate this partly by an example which is perhaps not too far-fetched, there seems to be general agreement to the effect that Plato's *Republic*, his *Phaedrus* and his *Banquet* are his most beautiful writings without their being necessarily his most profound writings. Yet Plato makes no distinction among his writings in regard to profundity or beauty or perfection in regard to language; he is not concerned with Plato—with his "ipsissimosity"—and hence with Plato's writings, but points away from himself whereas Nietzsche points most emphatically to himself, to "Mr. Nietzsche." Now Nietzsche "personally" preferred, not *Beyond Good and Evil* but his *Dawn of Morning* and his *Gay Science* to all his other books precisely because these two books are his "most personal" books (letter to Karl Knortz of June 21, 1888). As the very term "personal," ultimately derivative from the Greek word for "face," indicates, being "personal" has nothing to do with being "profound" or with being "perfect in regard to language."

[2]   What is dimly perceived and inadequately expressed through our judgement on *Beyond Good and Evil*, is stated clearly by Nietzsche in his account of that book which he has given in *Ecce Homo*: *Beyond Good and Evil* is the very opposite of the "inspired" and "dithyrambic" *Zarathustra* in as much as

Reprinted from *Interpretation: A Journal of Political Philosophy* 3, nos. 2 and 3 (1973).

Zarathustra is most far-sighted, whereas in *Beyond Good and Evil* the eye is compelled to grasp clearly the nearest, the timely (the present), the around-us. This change of concern required in every respect, "above all also in the form," the same arbitrary turning away from the instincts out of which a Zarathustra had become possible: the graceful subtlety as regards form, as regards intention, as regards the art of silence are in the foreground in *Beyond Good and Evil* which amounts to saying that these qualities are not in the foreground in the *Zarathustra*, to say nothing of Nietzsche's other books.

[3]   In other words, in *Beyond Good and Evil*, in the only book published by Nietzsche, in the contemporary preface to which he presents himself as the antagonist of Plato, he "platonizes" as regards the "form" more than anywhere else.

[4]   According to the preface to *Beyond Good and Evil* Plato's fundamental error was his invention of the pure mind and of the good in itself. From this premise one can easily be led to Diotima's conclusion that no human being is wise, but only the god is; human beings can only strive for wisdom or philosophize; gods do not philosophize (*Banquet* 203e–204a). In the penultimate aphorism of *Beyond Good and Evil* in which Nietzsche delineates "the genius of the heart"—a super-Socrates who is in fact the god Dionysos—Nietzsche divulges after the proper preparation the novelty, suspect perhaps especially among philosophers, that gods too philosophize. Yet Diotima is not Socrates nor Plato, and Plato could well have thought that gods philosophize (cf. *Sophist* 216b5–6, *Theaetetus* 151d 1–2). And when in the ultimate aphorism of *Beyond Good and Evil* Nietzsche underlines the fundamental difference between "written and painted thoughts" and thoughts in their original form, we cannot help being reminded of what Plato says or intimates regarding the "weakness of the *logos*" and regarding the unsayable and a fortiori unwritable character of the truth (*Ep.* VII 341c–d, 342e–343a): the purity of the mind as Plato conceives of it, does not necessarily establish the strength of the *logos*.

[5]   *Beyond Good and Evil* has the subtitle "Prelude to a philosophy of the future." The book is meant to prepare, not indeed the philosophy of the future, the true philosophy, but a new kind of philosophy by liberating the mind from "the prejudice of the philosophers," i.e. of the philosophers of the past (and the present). At the same time or by this very fact the book is meant to be a specimen of the philosophy of the future. The first chapter ("Of the prejudices of the philosophers") is followed by a chapter entitled "The free mind." The free minds in Nietzsche's sense are free from the prejudice of the philosophy of the past but they are not yet philosophers of the future; they are the heralds and precursors of the philosophy of the future (aph. 44). It is hard to say how the distinction between the free minds and the philosophers of the future is to be understood: are the free minds by

any chance freer than the philosophers of the future? do they possess an openness which is possible only during the transitional period between the philosophy of the past and the philosophy of the future? Be this as it may, philosophy is surely the primary theme of *Beyond Good and Evil*, the obvious theme of the first two chapters.

[6]   The book consists of nine chapters. The third chapter is devoted to religion. The heading of the fourth chapter ("Sayings and Interludes") does not indicate a subject matter; that chapter is distinguished from all other chapters by the fact that it consists exclusively of short aphorisms. The last five chapters are devoted to morals and politics. The book as a whole consists then of two main parts which are separated from one another by about 123 "Sayings and Interludes"; the first of the two parts is devoted chiefly to philosophy and religion and the second chiefly to morals and politics. Philosophy and religion, it seems, belong together—belong more closely together than philosophy and the city. (Cf. Hegel's distinction between the absolute and the objective mind.) The fundamental alternative is that of the rule of philosophy over religion or the rule of religion over philosophy; it is not, as it was for Plato or Aristotle, that of the philosophic and the political life; for Nietzsche, as distinguished from the classics, politics belongs from the outset to a lower plane than either philosophy or religion. In the preface he intimates that his precursor par excellence is not a statesman nor even a philosopher but the *homo religiosus* Pascal (cf. aph. 45).

[7]   Nietzsche says very little about religion in the first two chapters. One could say that he speaks there on religion only in a single aphorism which happens to be the shortest (37). That aphorism is a kind of corollary to the immediately preceding one in which he sets forth in the most straightforward and unambiguous manner that is compatible with his intention, the particular character of his fundamental proposition according to which life is will to power or seen from within the world is will to power and nothing else. The will to power takes the place which the *eros*—the striving for "the good in itself"—occupies in Plato's thought. But the *eros* is not "the pure mind" (*der reine Geist*). Whatever may be the relation between the *eros* and the pure mind according to Plato, in Nietzsche's thought the will to power takes the place of both *eros* and the pure mind. Accordingly philosophizing becomes a mode or modification of the will to power: it is the most spiritual (*der geistigste*) will to power; it consists in prescribing to nature what or how it ought to be (aph. 9); it is not love of the true that is independent of will or decision. Whereas according to Plato the pure mind grasps the truth, according to Nietzsche the impure mind, or a certain kind of impure mind, is the sole source of truth. Nietzsche begins therefore *Beyond Good and Evil* with the questioning of love of truth and of truth. If we may make a somewhat free use of an expression occurring in Nietzsche's *Second Medita-*

tion Out of Season, the truth is not attractive, lovable, life-giving, but deadly, as is shown by the true doctrines of the sovereignty of Becoming, of the fluidity of all concepts, types and species, and of the lack of any cardinal difference between man and beast *(Werke*, ed Schlechta, I 272); it is shown most simply by the true doctrine that God is dead. The world in itself, the "thing-in-itself," "nature" (aph. 9) is wholly chaotic and meaningless. Hence all meaning, all order originates in man, in man's creative acts, in his will to power. Nietzsche's statements or suggestions are deliberately enigmatic (aph. 40). By suggesting or saying that the truth is deadly, he does his best to break the power of the deadly truth; he suggests that the most important, the most comprehensive truth—the truth regarding all truths—is life-giving. In other words, by suggesting that the truth is human creation, he suggests that this truth at any rate is not a human creation. One is tempted to say that Nietzsche's pure mind grasps the fact that the impure mind creates perishable truths. Resisting that temptation we state Nietzsche's suggestion following him in this manner: the philosophers tried to get hold of the "text" as distinguished from "interpretations"; they tried to "discover" and not to "invent." What Nietzsche claims to have realized is that the text in its pure, unfalsified form is inaccessible (like the Kantian Thing-in-itself); everything thought by anyone—philosopher or man of the people—is in the last analysis interpretation. But for this very reason the text, the world in itself, the true world cannot be of any concern to us; the world of any concern to us is necessarily a fiction, for it is necessarily anthropocentric; man is necessarily in a manner the measure of all things (aph. 3 end, 12 end, 17, 22, 24, 34, 38; cf. Plato, *Laws* 716c 4–6). As is indicated sufficiently by the title of the book, the anthropocentrism for which Nietzsche opts is transmoral (cf. aph. 34 and 35 with 32). At first glance there does not seem to be a connection between the grave aphorism 34 and the lighthearted aphorism 35 and this seems to agree with the general impression according to which a book of aphorisms docs not have or need not have a lucid and necessary order or may consist of disconnected pieces. The connection between aphorism 34 and 35 is a particularly striking example of the lucid, if somewhat hidden, order governing the sequence of the aphorisms: the desultory character of Nietzsche's argument is more pretended than real. If the aforesaid is correct, the doctrine of the will to power cannot claim to reveal what is, the fact, the most fundamental fact but is "only" one interpretation, presumably the best interpretation, among many. Nietzsche regards this apparent objection as a confirmation of his proposition (aph. 22 end).

[8]   We can now turn to the two aphorisms in *Beyond Good and Evil* I–II that can be said to be devoted to religion (36–37). Aphorism 36 presents the reasoning in support of the doctrine of the will to power. Nietzsche had spoken of the will to power before, but only in the way of bald assertion, not to say dogmatically. Now he sets forth with what is at the same time the most

intransigent intellectual probity and the most bewitching playfulness his reasons, i.e. the problematic, tentative, tempting, hypothetical character of his proposition. It could seem that he does not know more of the will to power as the fundamental reality than what he says here. Almost immediately before, in the central aphorism of the second chapter (34), he had drawn our attention to the fundamental distinction between the world which is of any concern to us and the world in itself, or between the world of appearance or fiction (the interpretations) and the true world (the text). What he seems to aim at is the abolition of that fundamental distinction the world as will to power is both the world of any concern to us and the world in itself. Precisely if all views of the world are interpretations, i.e. acts of the will to power, the doctrine of the will to power is at the same time an interpretation and the most fundamental fact, for, in contradistinction to all other interpretations, it is the necessary and sufficient condition of the possibility of any "categories."

[9]   After having tempted some of his readers (cf. aph. 30) with the doctrine of the will to power Nietzsche makes them raise the question as to whether that doctrine does not assert, to speak popularly, that God is refuted but the devil is not. He replies "On the contrary! On the contary, my friends! And, to the devil, what forces you to speak popularly?" The doctrine of the will to power—the whole doctrine of *Beyond Good and Evil*—is in a manner a vindication of God. (Cf. aph. 150 and 295, as well as *Genealogy of Morals*, Preface Nr. 7.)—

[10]   The third chapter is entitled "Das religiöse Wesen"; it is not entitled "Das Wesen der Religion," one of the reasons for this being that the essence of religion, that which is common to all religions, is not or should not be of any concern to us. The chapter considers religion with a view to the human soul and its boundaries, to the whole history of the soul hitherto and its yet inexhausted possibilities: Nietzsche does not deal with unknown possibilities, although or because he deals with religion hitherto and the religion of the future. Aphorisms 46–52 are devoted to religion hitherto and 53–57 to the religion of the future. The rest of the chapter (aph. 58–62) transmits Nietzsche's appraisal of religion as a whole. In the section on religion hitherto he speaks first of Christianity (46–48), then of the Greeks (49), then again of Christianity (50–51) and finally of the Old Testament (52). "The religiosity of the old Greeks" and above all certain parts of "the Jewish 'Old Testament' " supply him with the standards by which he judges of Christianity; nowhere in the chapter does he speak of Christianity with the respect, the admiration, the veneration with which he speaks of the two pre-Christian phenomena. The aphorisms on the Old Greeks and on the Old Testament are obviously meant to interrupt the aphorisms devoted to Christianity; the two interrupting aphorisms are put at some distance from one another in order to imitate the distance or rather opposition between

what one may call Athens and Jerusalem. The aphorism on the Old Testament is immediately preceded by an aphorism devoted to the saint: there are no saints, no holy men in the Old Testament; the peculiarity of Old Testament theology in contradistinction especially to Greek theology is the conception, the creation of the holy God (cf. *Dawn of Morning* aph. 68). For Nietzsche "the great style" of (certain parts of) the Old Testament shows forth the greatness, not of God, but of what man once was: the holy God no less than the holy man are creatures of the human will to power.

[11]   Nietzsche's vindication of God is then atheistic, at least for the time being: the aphorism following that on the Old Testament begins with the question 'Why atheism today?' There was a time when theism was possible or necessary. But in the meantime "God died" (*Thus Spoke Zarathustra*, Zarathustra's Prologue Nr. 3). This does not merely mean that men have ceased to believe in God, for men's unbelief does not destroy God's life or being. It does mean, however, that even while God lived he never was what the believers in him thought him to be, namely, deathless. Theism as it understood itself was therefore always wrong. Yet for a time it was true, i.e. powerful, life-giving. In speaking of how or why it lost its power, Nietzsche speaks here less of the reasons that swayed him than of the reasons advanced by some of his contemporaries, presumably his most competent contemporaries. Not a few of his better readers will justifiably think that those reasons verge on the frivolous. In particular it is not quite clear whether those reasons are directed against natural (rational) or revealed theology. Nevertheless the most powerful anti-theistic argument which Nietzsche sketches is directed against the possibility of a clear and unambiguous revelation, i.e. of God's "speaking" to man (cf. *Dawn of Morning* aph. 91 and 95). Despite the decay of European theism Nietzsche has the impression that the religious instinct—"religiosity" as distinguished from "religion"—is growing powerfully at present or that atheism is only a transitional phase. Could atheism belong to the free mind as Nietzsche conceives of it while a certain kind of non-atheism belongs to the philosopher of the future who will again worship the god Dionysos or will again be, as an Epicurean might say, a *dionysokolax* (cf. aph. 7)? This ambiguity is essential to Nietzsche's thought; without it his doctrine would lose its character of an experiment or a temptation.

[12]   Nietzsche provisionally illustrates his suggestion of an atheistic or, if you wish, non-theistic religiosity by the alleged fact that the whole modern philosophy was anti-Christian but not anti-religious—that it could seem to point to something reminding of the Vedanta philosophy. But he does not anticipate, he surely does not wish, that the religion of the future will be something like the Vedanta philosophy. He anticipates a more Western, a sterner, more terrible and more invigorating possibility: the sacrificing from cruelty, i.e. from the will to power turning against itself, of God which prepares the worshipping of the stone, stupidity, heaviness (gravity), fate,

the Nothing. He anticipates in other words that the better among the contemporary atheists will come to know what they are doing—"the stone" may remind us of Anaxagoras' debunking of the sun—, that they will come to realize that there is something infinitely more terrible, depressing and degrading in the offing than the *foeda religio* or *l'infâme:* the possibility, nay, the fact that human life is utterly meaningless and lacking support, that it lasts only for a minute which is preceded and followed by an infinite time during which the human race was not and will not be. (Cf. the beginning of "On truth and lie in an extra-moral sense.") These religious atheists, this new breed of atheists cannot be deceptively and deceivingly appeased as people like Engels by the prospect of a most glorious future, of the realm of freedom, which will indeed be terminated by the annihilation of the human race and therewith of all meaning but which will last for a very long time—for a millennium or more—, for fortunately we find ourselves still on "the ascending branch of human history" (F. Engels, *Ludwig Feuerbach und der Ausgang der deutschen klassischen Philosophie*): the realm of freedom, destined to perish, necessarily contains within itself the seeds of its annihilation and will therefore, while it lasts, abound in "contradictions" as much as any earlier age.

[13]   Nietzsche does not mean to sacrifice God for the sake of the Nothing, for while recognizing the deadly truth that God died he aims at transforming it into a life-inspiring one or rather to discover in the depth of the deadly truth its opposite. Sacrificing God for the sake of the Nothing would be an extreme form of world-denial or of pessimism. But Nietzsche, prompted by "some enigmatic desire," has tried for a long time to penetrate pessimism to its depth and in particular to free it from the delusion of morality which in a way contradicts its world-denying tendency. He thus has grasped a more world-denying way of thinking than that of any previous pessimist. Yet a man who has taken this road has perhaps without intending to do this opened his eyes to the opposite ideal—to the ideal belonging to the religion of the future. It goes without saying that what in some other men was "perhaps" the case was a fact in Nietzsche's thought and life. The adoration of the Nothing proves to be the indispensable transition from every kind of world-denial to the most unbounded Yes: the eternal Yes-saying to everything that was and is. By saying Yes to everything that was and is Nietzsche may seem to reveal himself as radically antirevolutionary or conservative beyond the wildest wishes of all other conservatives, who all say No to some of the things that were or are. Remembering Nietzsche's strictures against "ideals" and "idealists" we are reminded of Goethe's words to Eckermann (November 24, 1824) according to which "everything idea-like(*jedes Ideelle*) is serviceable for revolutionary purposes." Be this as it may, "And this," Nietzsche concludes his suggestion regarding eternal repetition of what was and is, "would not be *circulus vitiosus deus?*" As this concluding

ambiguous question again shows, his atheism is not unambiguous, for he had doubts whether there can be a world, any world whose center is not God (aph. 150). The conclusion of the present aphorism reminds us, through its form, of the theological aphorism occurring in the first two chapters (37) where Nietzsche brings out the fact that in a manner the doctrine of the will to power is a vindication of God, if a decidedly non-theistic vindication of God.

[14]   But now we are confronted with the fact that the vindication of God is only the inversion of the sacrificing of God to stupidity, to the Nothing, or at any rate presupposes that sacrificing. What is it that suddenly, if after a long preparation, divinizes the Nothing? Is it the willing of eternity which gives to the world, or restores to it, its worth which the world-denying ways of thinking had denied it? Is it the willing of eternity that makes atheism religious? Is beloved eternity divine merely because it is beloved? If we were to say that it must be in itself lovable, in order to deserve to be loved, would we not become guilty of a relapse into Platonism, into the teaching of "the good in itself"? But can we avoid such a relapse altogether? For the eternal to which Nietzsche says Yes, is not the stone, the stupidity, the Nothing which even if eternal or sempiternal cannot arouse an enthusiastic, life-inspiring Yes. The transformation of the world-denying way of thinking into the opposite ideal is connected with the realization or divination that the stone, the stupidity or the Nothing to which God is being sacrificed, is in its "intelligible character" the will to power (cf. aph. 36).

[15]   There is an important ingredient, not to say the nerve, of Nietzsche's "theology" of which I have not spoken and shall not speak since I have no access to it. It has been worthily treated by Karl Reinhardt in his essay "Nietzsche's Klage der Ariadne" (*Vermächtnis der Antike*, Göttingen 1960, 310–333; see also a remark of Reinhardt at the end of his eulogy of Walter F. Otto, *ib.* 379).—

[16]   It is possible but not likely that the "Sayings and Interludes" of which the fourth chapter consists, possesses no order, that there is no rhyme or reason to their selection and sequence. I must leave matters at a few observations which are perhaps helpful to some of us.

[17]   The opening aphorism draws our attention to the paramountcy of being-oneself, of being for oneself, of "preserving" oneself (cf. aph. 41). Accordingly knowledge cannot be, or cannot be good, for its own sake; it is justifiable only as self-knowledge: being oneself means being honest with oneself, going the way to one's own ideal. This seems to have atheistic implications. There occur in the chapter nine references to God; only one of them points to Nietzsche's own theology (150). There occurs only a single reference to nature (126). Instead we are confronted by nine aphorisms devoted to woman and man. Surely the knower whom Nietzsche has in mind has not, like Kant, the starred heaven above himself. As a consequence he

has a high morality, a morality beyond good and evil and in particular beyond puritanism and asceticism. Precisely because he is concerned with the freedom of his mind, he must imprison his heart (87, 107). Freedom of one's mind is not possible without a dash of stupidity (9). Self-knowledge is not only very difficult but impossible to achieve; man could not live with perfect self-knowledge (80–81, 231, 249).—

[18]   The fifth chapter—the central chapter—is the only one whose heading ("Toward the natural history of morality") refers to nature. Could nature be the theme of this chapter or even of the whole second part of the book?

[19]   Nature—to say nothing of "naturalists," "physics" and "physiology"— had been mentioned more than once in the first four chapters. Let us cast a glance at the most important or striking of those mentions. In discussing and rejecting the Stoic imperative "to live according to nature" Nietzsche makes a distinction between nature and life (9; cf. 49), just as on another occasion he makes a distinction between nature and "us" (human beings) (22). The opposite of life is death which is or may be no less natural than life. The opposite of the natural is the unnatural: the artificial, the domesticated, the misbegotten (62), the anti-natural (21, 51, 55); i.e., the unnatural may very well be alive.

[20]   In the introductory aphorism (186) Nietzsche speaks of the desideratum of a natural history of morality in a manner which reminds us of what he had said in the introductory aphorism of the chapter on religion (45). But in the earlier case he led us to suspect that the true science of religion, i.e. the empirical psychology of religion, is for all practical purposes impossible, for the psychologist would have to be familiar with the religious experience of the most profound *homines religiosi* and at the same time to be able to look down, from above, on these experiences. Yet when stating the case for an empirical study, a description, of the various moralities Nietzsche states at the same time the case against the possibility of a philosophic ethics, a science of morals which teaches the only true morality. It would seem that he makes higher demands on the student of religion than on the student of morality. This is perhaps the reason why he did not entitle the third chapter "The natural history of religion": Hume had written an essay entitled "The Natural History of Religion."

[21]   The philosophers' science of morals claimed to have discovered the foundation of morals either in nature or in reason. Apart from all other defects of that pretended science it rests on the gratuitous assumption that morality must or can be natural (according to nature) or rational. Yet every morality is based on some tryanny against nature as well as against reason. Nietzsche directs his criticism especially against the anarchists who oppose every subjection to arbitrary laws: everything of value, every freedom arises from a compulsion of long duration that was exerted by arbitrary, unreasonable laws; it was that compulsion that has educated the mind to freedom. Over against the ruinous permissiveness of anarchism Nietzsche asserts that

precisely long lasting obedience to unnatural and unreasonable *nomoi* is "the moral imperative of nature." *Physis* calls for *nomoi* while preserving the distinction, nay, opposition of *physis* and *nomos*. Throughout this aphorism (188) Nietzsche speaks of nature only in quotation marks except in one case, in the final mention of nature; nature, and not only nature as the anarchists understand it, has become a problem for Nietzsche and yet he cannot do without nature.

[22]   As for rationalist morality, it consists primarily in the identification of the good with the useful and pleasant and hence in the calculation of consequences; it is utilitarian. Its classic is the plebian Socrates. How the patrician Plato—"the most beautiful growth of antiquity" (Preface), whose strength and power was the greatest which hitherto a philosopher had at his disposal—could take over the Socratic teaching is a riddle; the Platonic Socrates is a monstrosity. Nietzsche intends then to overcome Plato not only by substituting his truth for Plato's but also by surpassing him in strength or power. Among other things "Plato is boring" (*Twilight of the Gods*, 'What I owe to the Ancients' nr. 2), while Nietzsche surely is never boring. Both Socrates and Plato are guided by, or follow, not only reason but instinct as well; the instinct is more fundamental than reason. By explicitly taking the side of instinct against reason Nietzsche tacitly agrees with Rousseau (cf. *Natural Right and History* 262 n.). Instinct is, to say the least, akin to nature— to that which one may expel with a hayfork but will nevertheless always come back (cf. aph. 264; cf. the italicized heading of aph. 83, the first of the four italicized headings in chapter four). We are entitled to surmise that the fundamental instinct is the will to power and not, say, the urge toward self-preservation (cf. aph. 13). What we ventured to call Nietzsche's religiosity, is also an instinct (aph. 53): "The religious, that is to say god-forming instinct" (*Will to Power* nr. 1038). As a consequence of the irrationality of the moral judgement, of the decisive presence of the irrational in the moral judgement, there cannot be any universally valid moral rules: different moralities fit, belong to, different types of human beings.

[23]   When Nietzsche speaks again of nature, supplying the term again with quotation marks (aph. 197), he demands that one cease to regard as morbid (as defectively natural) the predatory beings which are dangerous, intemperate, passionate, "tropical": it was precisely the defective nature of almost all moralists—not reason and not nature simply—, namely, their timidity which induced them to conceive of the dangerous brutes and men as morbid. These moralists did not originate the morality stemming from timidity; that morality is the morality of the human herd, i.e. of the large majority of men. The utmost one could say is that the moral philosophers (and theologians) tried to protect the individual against the dangers with which he is threatened, not by other men, but by his own passions.

[24]   Nietzsche speaks of the herd-instinct of obedience which is now almost universally innate and transmitted by inheritance. It goes without saying

that originally, in pre-historic times, that instinct was acquired (cf. *Genealogy of Morals* II). While it was very powerful throughout history, it has become simply predominant in contemporary Europe where it destroys at least the good conscience of those who command and are independent and where it successfully claims to be the only true morality. More precisely, in its earlier, healthy form it implied already that the sole standard of goodness is utility for the herd, i.e. for the common good; independence, superiority, inequality were esteemed to the extent to which they were thought to be subservient to the common good and indispensable for it, and not for their own sake. The common good was understood as the good of a particular society or tribe; it demanded therefore hostility to the tribe's external and internal enemies and in particular to the criminals. When the herd morality draws its ultimate consequences as it does in contemporary Europe, it takes the side of the very criminals and becomes afraid of inflicting punishment; it is satisfied with making the criminals harmless; by abolishing the only remaining ground of fear, the morality of timidity would reach its completion and thus make itself superfluous (cf. aph. 73). Timidity and the abolition of fear are justified by the identification of goodness with indiscriminate compassion.

[25]   Prior to the victory of the democratic movement to which, as Nietzsche understands it, also the anarchists and socialists belong, moralities other and higher than the herd morality were at least known. He mentions with high praise Napoleon and, above all, Alcibiades and Caesar. He could not have shown his freedom from the herd morality more tellingly than by mentioning in one breath Caesar and Alcibiades. Caesar could be said to have performed a great, historic function for Rome and to have dedicated himself to that function—to have been, as it were, a functionary of Roman history, but for Alcibiades Athens was no more than the pedestal, exchangeable if need be with Sparta or Persia, for his own glory or greatness. Nietzsche opposes men of such a nature to men of the opposite nature (aph. 199–200). In the rest of the chapter he speaks no longer of nature. Instead he expresses the view that man must be counted literally among the brutes (aph. 202). He appeals from the victorious herd morality of contemporary Europe to the superior morality of leaders (*Führer*). The leaders who can counteract the degradation of man which has led to the autonomy of the herd, can however not be merely men born to rule like Napoleon, Alcibiades and Caesar. They must be philosophers, new philosophers, a new kind of philosophers and commanders, the philosophers of the future. Mere Caesars, however great, will not suffice, for the new philosophers must teach man the future of man as his will, as dependent on a human will in order to put an end to the gruesome rule of nonsense and chance which was hitherto regarded as "history": the true history—as distinguished from the mere pre-history, to use a Marxian distinction—requires the subjugation of chance, of nature

(*Genealogy* II. n. 2) by men of the highest spirituality, of the greatest reason. The subjugation of nature depends then decisively on men who possess a certain nature. Philosophy, we have heard, is the most spiritual will to power (aph. 9): the philosophers of the future must possess that will to a degree which was not even dreamed of by the philosophy of the past; they must possess that will in its absolute form. The new philosophers are or act, we are tempted to say, to the highest degree according to nature. They are or act also to the highest degree according to reason, for they put an end to the rule of unreason, and the high—the high independent spirituality, the will to stand alone, the great reason (aph. 201)—is evidently preferable to the low. The turn from the autonomy of the herd to the rule of the philosophers of the future is akin to the transformation of the worshipping of the nothing into the unbounded Yes to everything that was and is; that transformation would then also be evidently reasonable.

[26]   But what becomes then of the irrationality of the moral judgement, i.e. of every moral judgement (aph. 191)? Or does it cease to be rational merely because one must be strong, healthy and well-born in order to agree to it or even to understand it? Yet can one say that Nietzsche's praise of cruelty, as distinguished from Plato's praise of gentleness, is rational? Or is that praise of cruelty only the indispensable and therefore reasonable corrective to the irrational glorification of compassion (cf. *Genealogy*, preface, nr. 5 end)? Furthermore, is not Nietzsche's critique of Plato and of Socrates a grave exaggeration, not to say a caricature? It suffices to remember the difference between the *Protagoras* and the *Gorgias* in order to see that Socrates was not a utilitarian in Nietzsche's sense (cf. aph. 190). As Nietzsche says in the same chapter (202), Socrates did not think that he knew what good and evil is. In other words, "virtue is knowledge" is a riddle rather than a solution. Socrates' enigmatic saying is based on awareness of the fact that sometimes "a scientific head is placed on the body of an ape, a subtle exceptional understanding on a vulgar soul" (aph. 26); it implies awareness of the complexity of the relation between *Wissen* and *Gewissen*, to use a favorite distinction of Nietzsche which in this form is indeed alien to Socrates. To considerations such as these one is compelled to retort that for Nietzsche there cannot be a natural or rational morality because he denies that there is a nature of man: the denial of any cardinal difference between man and brute is a truth, if a deadly truth; hence there cannot be natural ends of man as man: all values are human creations.

[27]   While Nietzsche's turn from the autonomous herd to the new philosophers is in perfect agreement with his doctrine of the will to power, it seems to be irreconcilable with his doctrine of eternal return: how indeed can the demand for something absolutely new, this intransigent farewell to the whole past, to all "history" be reconciled with the unbounded Yes to everything that was and is? Toward the end of the present chapter Nietzsche

gives a hint regarding the connection between the demand for wholly new philosophers and eternal return; the philosophers of the future, he says, must be able to endure the weight of the responsibility for the future of man. He had originally published his suggestion regarding eternal return under the heading "*Das grösste Schwergewicht*" (*Gay Science* aph. 341).

[28]   From the desideration of the new philosophers Nietzsche is naturally led to passing judgement on the contemporary philosophers, a sorry lot, who are not philosophers in a serious and proper sense but professors of philosophy, philosophic laborers or, as they came to call themselves after Nietzsche's death, men who "do philosophy." They are in the best case, i.e. only in rare cases, scholars or scientists, i.e. competent and honest specialists who of right ought to be subservient to philosophy or handmaidens to philosophy. The chapter devoted to this kind of man is entitled "*Wir Gelehrten*"; it is the only one in whose title the first person of the personal pronoun is used: Nietzsche wishes to emphasize the fact that apart from being a precursor of the philosophers of the future, he belongs to the scholars and not, for instance, to the poets or the *homines religiosi*. The emancipation of the scholars or scientists from philosophy is according to him only a part of the democratic movement, i.e. of the emancipation of the low from subordination to the high. The things which we have observed in the 20th century regarding the sciences of man confirm Nietzsche's diagnosis.

[29]   The plebeian character of the contemporary scholar or scientist is due to the fact that he has no reverence for himself and this in its turn is due to his lack of self, to his self-forgetting, the necessary consequence or cause of his objectivity; hence he is no longer "nature" or "natural"; he can only be "genuine" or "authentic." Originally, one can say with some exaggeration, the natural and the genuine were the same (cf. Plato, *Laws* 642c 8–d 1, 777d 5–6; Rousseau, *Du Contrat Social* I. 9 end and II. 7, third paragraph); Nietzsche prepares decisively the replacement of the natural by the authentic. That he does this and why he does this will perhaps become clear from the following consideration. He is concerned more immediately with the classical scholars and historians than with the natural scientists (cf. aph. 209). Historical study had come to be closer to philosophy and therefore also a greater danger to it than natural science. This in turn was a consequence of what one may call the historicization of philosophy, the alleged realization that truth is a function of time (historical epoch) or that every philosophy belongs to a definite time and place (country). History takes the place of nature as a consequence of the fact that the natural—e.g. the natural gifts which enable a man to become a philosopher—is no longer understood as given but as the acquisition of former generations (aph. 213; cf. *Dawn of Morning* aph. 540). Historicism is the child of the peculiarly modern tendency to understand everything in terms of its genesis, of its human produc-

tion: nature furnishes only the almost worthless materials as in themselves (Locke, *Two Treatises of Government* II sect. 43).

[30]   The philosopher, as distinguished from the scholar or scientist, is the complementary man in whom not only man but the rest of existence is justified (cf. aph. 207); he is the peak which does not permit and still less demand to be overcome. This characterization applies, however, strictly speaking only to the philosophers of the future compared with whom men of the rank of Kant and Hegel are only philosophic laborers, for the philosopher in the precise sense creates values. Nietzsche raises the question whether there ever were such philosophers (aph. 211 end). He seems to have answered that question in the affirmative by what he had said near the beginning of the sixth chapter on Heraclitus, Plato and Empedocles. Or does it remain true that we must overcome also the Greeks (*The Gay Science* aph. 125, 340)? The philosopher as philosopher belongs to the future and was therefore at all times in contradiction to his Today; the philosophers were always the bad conscience of their time. They belonged then to their time, not indeed, as Hegel thought, by being the sons of their times (*Vorlesungen über die Geschichte der Philosophie, Einleitung*, ed. Hoffmeister, 149) but by being their step-sons (*Schopenhauer als Erzieher* nr. 3). As belonging to their time and their place or country if only as their step-sons, the precursors of the philosophers of the future are concerned not only with the excellence of man in general but with the preservation of Europe which is threatened by Russia and which therefore must become a united Europe (aph. 208): the philosophers of the future must become the invisible spiritual rulers of a united Europe without ever becoming its servants.

[31]   In the seventh chapter Nietzsche turns to "our virtues." Yet the "we" whose virtues he discusses there, are not "we scholars" but "we Europeans of the time after tomorrow, we firstlings of the 20th century" (aph. 214), "we free minds" (aph. 227), i.e. the precursors of the philosophers of the future. The discussion of the virtues and vices of the scholars must be supplemented by a discussion of the virtues and vices of free minds. The virtues of the free minds had been discussed in the second chapter but their vices which are inseparable from their virtues, must also be laid bare. "Our" morality is characterized by a fundamental ambiguity; it is inspired by Christianity and by anti-Christianity. One can say that "our" morality constitutes a progress beyond the morality of the preceding generations but this change is no ground for pride; such pride would be incompatible with "our" increased delicacy in moral matters. Nietzsche is willing to grant that a high spirituality (intellectuality) is the ultimate product of moral qualities, that it is the synthesis of all those states which one ascribes to men who are "only moral,"that it consists in the spiritualization of justice and of that kind of severity which knows that it is commissioned to maintain in the world the order of rank, even among the things and not only among men. Being the

complementary man in whom the rest of existence is justified (aph. 207), standing on the summit, nay, being the summit, the philosopher has a cosmic responsibility. But "our virtues" are not the virtues of the philosopher of the future. The concession which Nietzsche makes to the men who are "only moral" does not prevent him from treating both the reigning moral teachings (altruism, the identification of goodness with compassion, utilitarianism) as well as their critique by moralists as trivial, not to say with contempt; the superior morality which flows from that critique or which is its presupposition does not belong to "our virtues." The reigning moralities are unaware of the problematic character of morality as such and this is due to their insufficient awareness of the variety of moralities (cf. aph. 186), to these moralists' lack of historical sense. The historical sense is "our" virtue, even "our great virtue." It is a novel phenomenon, not older than the 19th century. It is an ambiguous phenomenon. Its root is a lack of self-sufficiency of plebian Europe, or it expresses the self-criticism of modernity, its longing fo something different, for something past or alien. As a consequence, "measure is foreign to us; we are titillated by the infinite and unmeasured"; hence we are half-barbarians. It would seem that this defect, the reverse side of our great virtue, points to a way of thinking and living that transcends historicism, to a peak higher than all earlier peaks. The discussion of the historical sense (aph. 223–24) is surrounded by a discussion of compassion (aph.222 and 225): the historical sense mediates in a manner between the plebian morality which boasts of its compassion with those who have been neglected by nature (aph. 219) and which is bent on the abolition of all suffering, and the opposite morality which goes together with awareness of the great things man owes to suffering (aph. 225). The next aphorism (226) is the only one in the chapter with an italicized heading ("We immoralists"): we immoralists are "men of duty"; "our" immoralism is our virtue. "Our virtue which alone is left to us" is probity, intellectual probity; it is, one may say, the positive or reverse side of our immoralism. Probity includes and completes "our great virtue of the historical sense." Yet probity is an end rather than a beginning; it points to the past rather than to the future; it is not the virtue characteristic of the philosophers of the future; it must be supported, modified, fortified by "our most delicate, most disguised, most spiritual will to power" which is directed toward the future. Surely our probity must not be permitted to become the ground or object of our pride, for this would lead us back to moralism (and to theism).

[32]   For a better understanding of "our virtue" it is helpful to contrast it with the most powerful antagonist, the morality preached up by the English utilitarians which accepts indeed egoism as the basis of morality but contends that egoism rightly understood leads to the espousal of the general welfare. That utilitarianism is disgusting, boring and naive. While it recog-

nizes the fundamental character of egoism, it does not realize the fact that egoism is will to power and hence includes cruelty which, as cruelty directed toward oneself, is effective in intellectual probity, in "the intellectual conscience."

[33]   To recognize the crucial importance of cruelty is indispensable if "the terrible basic text *homo natura*," "that eternal basic text" is again to be seen, if man is to be "re-translated into nature." That re-translation is altogether a task for the future: "there never was yet a natural humanity" (*Will to Power* nr. 120). Man must be "made natural" (*vernatürlicht*) together "with the pure, newly found, newly redeemed nature" (*The Gay Science* aph. 109). For a man is the not yet fixed, not yet established beast (aph. 62): man becomes natural by acquiring his final, fixed character. For the nature of a being is its end, its completed state, its peak (Aristotle, *Politics* 1252b 32–34). "I too speak of 'return to nature,' although it is properly not a going back but an ascent—up into the high, free, even terrible nature and naturalness . . ." (*Twilight of the Idols*, 'Skirmishes of an untimely man' nr. 48). Man reaches his peak through and in the philosopher of the future as the truly complementary man in whom not only man but the rest of existence is justified (aph. 207). He is the first man who consciously creates values on the basis of the understanding of the will to power as the fundamental phenomenon. His action constitutes the highest form of the most spiritual will to power and therewith the highest form of the will to power. By this action he puts an end to the rule of non-sense and chance (aph. 203). As the act of the highest form of man's will to power the *Vernatürlichung* of man is at the same time the peak of the anthropomorphization of the non-human (cf. *Will to Power* nr. 614), for the most spiritual will to power consists in prescribing to nature what or how it ought to be (aph. 9). It is in this way that Nietzsche abolishes the difference between the world of appearance or fiction (the interpretations) and the true world (the text). (Cf. Marx 'Nationalökonomie und Philosophie', *Die Frühschriften*, ed. Landshut, pp. 235, 237, 273.)

[34]   It is however the history of man hitherto, i.e. the rule of non-sense and chance, which is the necessary condition for the subjugation of non-sense and chance. That is to say, the *Vernatürlichung* of man presupposes and brings to its conclusion the whole historical process—a completion which is by no means necessary but requires a new, free creative act. Still, in this way history can be said to be integrated into nature. Be this as it may, man cannot say Yes to the philosophers of the future without saying Yes to the past. Yet there is a great difference between this Yes and the unbounded Yes to everything that was and is, i.e. the affirmation of eternal return.

[35]   Instead of explaining why it is necessary to affirm the eternal return, Nietzsche indicates that the highest achievement, as all earlier high achievements, is in the last analysis not the work of reason but of nature; in the last

analysis all thought depends on something unteachable "deep down," on a fundamental stupidity; the nature of the individual, the individual nature, not evident and universally valid insights, it seems, is the ground of all worthwhile understanding or knowledge (aph. 231; cf. aph. 8). There is an order of rank of the natures; at the summit of the hierarchy is the complementary man. His supremacy is shown by the fact that he solves the highest, the most difficult problem. As we have observed, for Nietzsche nature has become a problem and yet he cannot do without nature. Nature, we may say, has become a problem owing to the fact that man is conquering nature and there are no assignable limits to that conquest. As a consequence, people have come to think of abolishing suffering and inequality. Yet suffering and inequality are the prerequisites of human greatness (aph. 239 and 257). Hitherto suffering and inequality have been taken for granted, as "given," as imposed on man. Henceforth, they must be willed. That is to say, the gruesome rule of non-sense and chance, nature, the fact that almost all men are fragments, cripples and gruesome accidents, the whole present and past is itself a fragment, a riddle, a gruesome accident unless it is willed as a bridge to the future (cf. *Zarathustra*, 'Of Redemption'). While paving the way for the complementary man, one must at the same time say unbounded Yes to the fragments and cripples. Nature, the eternity of nature, owes its being to a postulation, to an act of the will to power on the part of the highest nature.

[36]   At the end of the seventh chapter Nietzsche discusses "woman and man" (cf. aph. 237). The apparently clumsy transition to that subject—a transition in which he questions the truth of what he is about to say by claiming that it expresses merely his "fundamental stupidity deep down"—is not merely a flattery, a gesture of courtesy to the friends of woman's emancipation. It indicates that he is about to continue the theme of nature, i.e. the natural hierarchy, in full awareness of the problem of nature.

[37]   The philosophers of the future may belong to a united Europe but Europe is still *l'Europe des nations et des patries*. Germany more than any other part of non-Russian Europe has more of a prospect of a future than, say, France or England (aph. 240, 251, 255; cf. Heine ed. Elster IV 510). One could find that Nietzsche stresses in his chapter on peoples and fatherlands more the defects of contemporary Germany than her virtues: it is not so difficult to free one's heart from a victorious fatherland as from a beaten one (aph. 41). The target of his critique here is not German philosophy but German music, i.e. Richard Wagner. More precisely, European nobility reveals itself as the work and invention of France, whereas European commonness, the plebianism of the modern ideas, is the work and invention of England (aph. 253).

[38]   Nietzsche thus prepares the last chapter which he entitled "*Was ist vornehm?*" "Vornehm" differs from "noble" because it is inseparable from

extraction, origin, birth (*Dawn of Morning*, aph. 199; Goethe *Wilhelm Meister's Lehrjahre* [*Sämtliche Werke*, Tempel-Klassiker, II 87–88] and *Dichtung und Wahrheit*, Vol. 2, *ed. cit.* 44–45). Being the last chapter of a prelude to a philosophy of the future, it shows the (a) philosophy of the future as reflected in the medium of conduct, of life; thus reflected the philosophy of the future reveals itself as the philosophy of the future. The virtues of the philosopher of the future differ from the Platonic virtues: Nietzsche replaces temperance and justice by compassion and solitude (aph. 284). This is one illustration among many of what he means by characterizing nature by its "Vornehmheit" (aph. 188). Die vornehme Natur ersetzt die göttliche Natur.

Works Cited

Works by Friedrich Nietzsche

The Antichrist. In *The Portable Nietzsche.* Translated by Walter Kaufmann, 568–656. New York: Vintage, 1954.

Assorted Opinions and Maxims. In *Human, All Too Human.* Translated by R. J. Hollingdale, 209–99. Cambridge: Cambridge University Press, 1968.

Beyond Good and Evil: Prelude to a Philosophy of the Future. Translated by Walter Kaufmann. New York: Vintage, 1967.

The Case of Wagner. In *The Birth of Tragedy and the Case of Wagner.* Translated by Walter Kaufmann, 153–92. New York: Vintage, 1967.

Daybreak, Thoughts on the Prejudices of Morality. Translated by R. J. Hollingdale. Cambridge: Cambridge University Press, 1982.

Ecce Homo. In *On the Genealogy of Morals and Ecce Homo.* Translated by Walter Kaufmann, 215–335. New York: Vintage, 1969.

The Gay Science. Translated by Walter Kaufmann. New York: Vintage, 1967.

Human, All Too Human: A Book for Free Spirits. Translated by R. J. Hollingdale, 1–205. Cambridge: Cambridge University Press, 1968.

Kritische Gesamtausgabe: Werke. Edited by Giorgio Colli and Mazzino Montinari. Berlin: de Gruyter, 1967–.

On the Genealogy of Morals. In *On the Genealogy of Morals and Ecce Homo.* Translated by Walter Kaufmann, 13–163. New York: Vintage, 1969.

On the Uses and Disadvantages of History for Life. In *Untimely Medita-tions*. Translated by R. J. Hollingdale, 57–123. Cambridge: Cambridge University Press, 1983.

"On Truth and Lie in an Extra-moral Sense." In *The Portable Nietzsche*. Translated by Walter Kaufmann, 42–47. New York: Vintage, 1954.

Richard Wagner in Bayreuth. In *Untimely Meditations*. Translated by R. J. Hollingdale, 195–254. Cambridge: Cambridge University Press, 1983.

Thus Spoke Zarathustra. In *The Portable Nietzsche*. Translated by Walter Kaufmann, 112–439. New York: Vintage, 1954.

Twilight of the Idols. In *The Portable Nietzsche*. Translated by Walter Kaufmann, 463–563. New York: Vintage, 1954.

The Wanderer and His Shadow. In *Human, All Too Human*. Translated by R. J. Hollingdale, 301–95. Cambridge: Cambridge University Press, 1968.

The Will to Power. Translated by Walter Kaufmann and R. J. Hollingdale. New York: Vintage, 1968.

Works by Leo Strauss

The Argument and the Action of Plato's Laws. Chicago: University of Chi-cago Press, 1975.

The City and Man. Chicago: Rand McNally, 1964.

"Correspondence of Karl Löwith and Leo Strauss," trans. George Elliott Tucker. *Independent Journal of Philosophy/Unabhängige Zeitschrift für Philosophie* 5/6 (1988): 177–92.

De la tyrannie. Paris: Librairie Gallimard, 1954.

"Farabi's Plato." In *Louis Ginsberg Jubilee Volume*, 357–92. New York: American Academy of Jewish Research, 1945.

(with Jacob Klein). "A Giving of Accounts." *The College* (St. John's College, Annapolis, Md.) 22 (1970): 1–5.

History of Political Philosophy, 3d ed. Edited by Leo Strauss and Joseph Cropsey. Chicago: University of Chicago Press, 1987.

"How to Begin to Study *The Guide of the Perplexed*." In *The Guide of the Perplexed*, by Moses Maimonides. Translated by Shlomo Pines, xi–lvi. Chicago: University of Chicago Press, 1963.

Liberalism Ancient and Modern. New York: Basic Books, 1968.

"The Mutual Influence of Theology and Philosophy." *Independent Jour-nal of Philosophy/Unabhängige Zeitschrift für Philosophie* 3 (1979): 111–18.

Natural Right and History. Chicago: University of Chicago Press, 1953.

"Note on the Plan of Nietzsche's Beyond Good and Evil." *Interpretation* 3 (1973): 97–113. Reprinted in his *Studies in Platonic Political Philosophy,* pp. 174–91.

"On the Interpretation of Genesis." *L'Homme: Revue française d'anthropologie* 21 (1981): 5–36.

On Tyranny: An Interpretation of Xenophon's Hiero, revised and expanded ed. Edited by Victor Gourevitch and Michael S. Roth. New York: Free Press, 1991.

Persecution and the Art of Writing. Glencoe, Ill.: The Free Press of Glencoe, 1952.

Philosophie und Gesetz: Beiträge zum Verständnis Maimunis und seiner Vorläufer. Berlin: Schocken, 1935.

Philosophy and Law: Essays toward the Understanding of Maimonides and His Predecessors. Translated by Fred Baumann. Philadelphia: Jewish Publication Society, 1987.

The Political Philosophy of Hobbes: Its Basis and Its Genesis. Translated by Elsa M. Sinclair. Chicago: University of Chicago Press, 1952. Original publication, Oxford: Clarendon, 1936.

"Progress or Return? The Contemporary Crisis in Western Civilization." In *An Introduction to Political Philosophy: Ten Essays by Leo Strauss.* Edited with an introduction by Hilail Gildin, 249–310. Detroit: Wayne State University Press, 1989.

The Rebirth of Classical Political Rationalism: An Introduction to the Thought of Leo Strauss. Selected and introduced by Thomas L. Pangle. Chicago: University of Chicago Press, 1989.

Socrates and Aristophanes. Chicago: University of Chicago Press, 1989.

Spinoza's Critique of Religion. Translated by E. M. Sinclair. New York: Schocken, 1965.

"The Spirit of Sparta or the Taste of Xenophon." *Social Research* 6 (1939): 502–36.

Studies in Platonic Political Philosophy. With an introduction by Thomas L. Pangle. Chicago: University of Chicago Press, 1983.

Thoughts on Machiavelli. Chicago: University of Chicago Press, 1958.

What Is Political Philosophy? and Other Studies. Glencoe, Ill.: The Free Press of Glencoe, 1959.

Xenophon's Socrates. Ithaca: Cornell University Press, 1972.

Xenophon's Socratic Disourse: An Interpretation of the "Oeconomicus." Ithaca: Cornell University Press, 1970.

Works by Other Authors

Adler, Eve. "Leo Strauss's *Philosophie und Gesetz.*" In *Leo Strauss's Thought*, edited by Alan Udoff, 183–226.

Ahrensdorf, Peter J. "The Question of Historical Context and the Study of Plato." *Polity* 27 (1994): 113–35.

Alfarabi. *Alfarabi's Philosophy of Plato and Aristotle.* Translated with an introduction by Muhsin Mahdi, rev. ed. Ithaca: Cornell University Press, 1969.

Bacon, Francis. *Works.* Edited by J. Spedding, R. L. Ellis, and D. D. Heath. 14 vols. 1847–74. Reprint, New York: Garrett Press, 1968.

Brague, Rémi. "Leo Strauss and Maimonides." In *Leo Strauss's Thought*, edited by Alan Udoff, 93–114.

Bruell, Christopher. "Strauss on Xenophon's Socrates." *Political Science Reviewer* 14 (1984): 263–318.

Calasso, Roberto. *The Ruin of Kasch.* Translated by William Weaver and Stephen Sartarelli. Cambridge: Harvard University Press, Belknap Press, 1994.

Cantor, Paul A. "Leo Strauss and Contemporary Hermeneutics." In *Leo Strauss's Thought*, edited by Alan Udoff, 267–314.

Christian, William. *George Grant: A Biography.* Toronto: University of Toronto Press, 1993.

Cicero. *Tusculan Disputations.* Loeb Classical Library. 1927.

———. *Brutus.* Loeb Classical Library, 1939.

Clay, Diskin. "On a Forgotten Kind of Reading." In *Leo Strauss's Thought*, edited by Alan Udoff, 253–66.

Descartes, René. *Discourse on Method.* Translated by Donald A. Cress. Indianapolis: Hackett, 1980.

Diogenes Laertius. *Lives of the Philosophers.* Translated and edited by A. Robert Caponigri. Chicago: Henry Regnery, 1969.

Drury, Shadia. *The Political Ideas of Leo Strauss.* New York: St. Martin's, 1988.

Emberley, Peter, and Barry Cooper, translators and editors. *Faith and Political Philosophy: The Correspondence between Leo Strauss and Eric Voegelin, 1934–1964.* University Park: Pennsylvania State University Press, 1993.

Gadamer, Hans Georg. "Das Drama Zarathustras." *Nietzsche Studien* 15 (1985): 1–15.

Gourevitch, Victor. "Philosophy and Politics." *Review of Metaphysics* 22 (1968): 58–84, 281–328.

Grant, George. *Technology and Justice.* Notre Dame: Notre Dame University Press, 1986.

———. "Tyranny and Wisdom." In his *Technology and Empire: Perspectives on North America.* Toronto: House of Anansi, 1969.

Green, Kenneth Hart. *Jew and Philosopher: The Return to Maimonides in the Jewish Thought of Leo Strauss.* Albany: State University of New York Press, 1993.

Grotius, Hugo. *The Rights of War and Peace.* Translated by A. C. Campbell. New York: M. Walter Dunne, 1901.

Harvey, Warren Zev. "The Return of Maimonideanism." *Jewish Social Studies* 42 (1980): 249–68.

Kant, Immanuel. *Critique of Practical Reason.* Translated by L. W. Beck. New York: The Liberal Arts Press, 1956.

Lampert, Laurence. *Nietzsche's Teaching: An Interpretation of Thus Spoke Zarathustra.* New Haven: Yale University Press, 1986.

———. *Nietzsche and Modern Times: A Study of Bacon, Descartes, and Nietzsche.* New Haven: Yale University Press, 1993.

Longinus. *On the Sublime.* Translated with a commentary by James A. Arieti and John M. Crossett. Toronto: Edwin Mellen, 1985.

Lowenthal, David. "Comment on Colmo." *Interpretation: A Journal of Political Philosophy* 18 (1990): 161–62.

——— "Leo Strauss's *Studies in Platonic Political Philosophy.*" *Interpretation: A Journal of Political Philosophy* 13 (1985): 297–320.

Machiavelli, Niccolò. *The Prince.* Translated by Harvey C. Mansfield, Jr. Chicago: University of Chicago Press, 1985.

Mansfield, Harvey C., Jr. *Machiavelli's New Modes and Orders: A Study of the Discourses on Livy.* Ithaca: Cornell University Press, 1979.

Masters, Roger D. "Evolutionary Biology and Natural Right, Leo Strauss: Natural Science and Political Philosophy." In *The Crisis of Liberal Democracy: A Straussian Perspective.* Edited by Kenneth L. Deutsch and Walter Sofer, 48–66. Albany: State University of New York Press, 1987.

McGowan, Margaret. *Montaigne's Deceits: The Art of Persuasion in the Essais.* London: University of London Press, 1974.

Momigliano, Arnaldo. *On Pagans, Jews, and Christians.* Hanover, N. H.: Wesleyan University Press, 1987.

Montaigne, Michel de. *The Complete Essays of Montaigne.* Translated by Donald M. Frame. Stanford: Stanford University Press, 1958.

Newman, John Henry, Cardinal. *Apologia pro vita sua.* Edited by A. Dwight Culler. Boston: Houghton Mifflin, 1956.

Orwin, Clifford. "Leo Strauss, Moralist or Machiavellian." *The Vital Nexus* 1 (1990) 105–13.

Plato. *Euthyphro.* Loeb Classical Library. 1914.

———. *Hippias Minor.* Translated by James Leake. In *The Roots of Political Philosophy: Ten Forgotten Socratic Dialogues.* Edited by Thomas L. Pangle, 281–99. Ithaca: Cornell University Press, 1987.

———. *Laws.* Translated by Thomas L. Pangle. New York: Basic Books, 1979.

———. *Phaedrus.* Loeb Classical Library. 1914.

———. *Republic.* Translated by Allan Bloom. New York: Basic Books, 1968.

———. *Sophist.* In *The Being of the Beautiful: Plato's "Theaetetus," "Sophist," and "Statesman."* Translated by Seth Benardete. Chicago: University of Chicago Press, 1984.

———. *Symposium.* Loeb Classical Library. 1925.

———. *Theaetetus.* In *The Being of the Beautiful: Plato's "Theaetetus," "Sophist," and "Statesman."* Translated by Seth Benardete. Chicago: University of Chicago Press, 1984.

Plutarch. *Nicias.* In *Plutarch's Lives,* vol. 3. Loeb Classical Library. 1916.

———. *Table Talk.* In *Plutarch's Moralia,* vol. 8. Loeb Classical Library. 1969.

Redondi, Pietro. *Galileo: Heretic.* Translated by Raymond Rosenthal. Princeton: Princeton University Press, 1987.

Rosen, Stanley. *Hermeneutics as Politics.* New York: Oxford University Press, 1987.

———. "Leo Strauss and the Quarrel between the Ancients and the Moderns." In *Leo Strauss's Thought,* edited by Alan Udoff, 155–68.

———. "Politics or Transcendence?" In *Faith and Political Philosophy,* edited by Peter Emberley and Barry Cooper, 261–66.

———. *The Question of Being: A Reversal of Heidegger.* New Haven: Yale University Press, 1993.

Rousseau, Jean-Jacques. *The First and Second Discourses.* Edited by Roger D. Masters, translated by Roger D. Masters and Judith R. Masters. New York: St. Martin's, 1964.

Schaefer, David Lewis. "Shadia Drury's Critique of Leo Strauss." *The Political Science Reviewer* 32 (1994): 80–127.

Sokolowski, Robert. *The God of Faith and Reason: Foundations of Christian Theology.* Notre Dame: Notre Dame University Press, 1982.

Toland, John. *Clidophorus.* In his *Tetradymus.* London, 1720.

Udoff, Alan. "On Leo Strauss: An Introductory Account." In *Leo Strauss's Thought,* edited by Alan Udoff, 1–29.

Udoff, Alan, ed. *Leo Strauss's Thought: Toward a Critical Engagement.* Boulder and London: Lynne Rienner, 1991.

Wilhelmsen, Frederick D. *Christianity and Political Philosophy.* Athens: University of Georgia Press, 1978.

Index to Strauss's "Note on the Plan of Nietzsche's *Beyond Good and Evil*"

Citations are to paragraph numbers

Citations are to paragraph numbers

Citations are to paragraph numbers

General Index